This edition, issued in 1961, is for members of The Companion Book Club, 8 Long Acre, London, W.C.99, from which address particulars of membership may be obtained. The book is issued by arrangement with the original publishers, William Heinemann Ltd.

D0358697

*Also by*

# C. E. LUCAS PHILLIPS

★

CROMWELL'S CAPTAINS
THE SMALL GARDEN
COCKLESHELL HEROES
ESCAPE OF THE "AMETHYST"
THE GREATEST RAID OF ALL
THE VISION SPLENDID
*The Future of the Central African Federation*

F  R  A  N  C  E

Bilbao    •Biarritz
        Hendaye
    San Sebastian
•Vitoria    Pamplona•                Toulouse
                                            •Perpignan
        •Huesca
•Soria                              •Gerona
        Zaragoza    Lérida
                                    Barcelona

dalajara        Tortosa•
    •Teruel
        Castellón
    Segorbe
        Valencia
    El Perelló
•Albacete
                                    B A L E A R I C  Is.
        Alicante

•Murcia

    Cartagena
meria

*Alan Bowdery 1960.*

# THE SPANISH PIMPERNEL

*"A blessed companion is a book"*—JERROLD

# THE SPANISH PIMPERNEL

*

C. E. LUCAS PHILLIPS

THE COMPANION BOOK CLUB
LONDON

© C. E. Lucas Phillips, 1960

*Made and printed in Great Britain*
*for The Companion Book Club (Odhams Press Ltd.)*
*by Odhams (Watford) Limited*
*Watford, Herts.*
S.461.W.R.

# CONTENTS

7

# ILLUSTRATIONS

## MAPS

# AUTHOR'S NOTICE

THIS book is a chronicle of the exploits of Captain E. C. Lance, D.S.O., during the Spanish Civil War of 1936-9. Based, for the greater part, on information and contemporary records supplied by him and by other participants in those events, it is as reliable as I have been able to make it under the clouds that obscure much of that dark and bloody conflict. Fear still prevents many from speaking openly, bias many from speaking impartially and the fallibility of memory others from speaking with certainty on points of minor detail. Authentic official records are sparse and difficult of access. For any small inaccuracies that may have crept in I therefore ask the indulgence of those who may have been concerned in these affairs and whom I have been unable to reach.

The names of some persons are indicated either by an initial letter, or by single inverted commas. This has been done sometimes because the identities, especially of a few of the escapists, are uncertain, sometimes to spare pain or embarrassment, and in yet other instances to avoid the sharp knives of malice or revenge that might even now await the participants in these events. For more obvious reasons, certain of the British diplomatic and consular officers also are intentionally made anonymous.

For convenience of narration, some of the minor events have been placed a little out of their actual chronological sequence.

Among the several people who have so kindly assisted me in assembling these facts, I am specially grateful to Mr E. G. de Caux, the distinguished correspondent of *The Times* in Madrid during the Civil War.

C. E. LUCAS PHILLIPS

CHAPTER ONE

# IN THE EMBASSY BAR

ON a hot summer morning in 1936 a cheerful company of men and women gathered together before luncheon in the Embassy Bar in Madrid. It was a small, modern, smart little place in the Paseo de la Castellana, not at all typically Spanish and frequented by a lively, cosmopolitan crowd.

As they came in severally from the Castellana, where the pavements and the buildings quivered in the overpowering noonday heat, the visitors relaxed in the cool shade, greeted one another cheerfully in English or Spanish and called for drinks. For the most part they drank extremely dry sherry or iced pomegranate juice with soda. With these they also ordered *camarones*, the shrimps which in Spain are continually nibbled to ward off the morning hunger. To these *habitués*, who were mainly British, Americans and Spaniards of the smarter set, life pursued an equable and agreeable tenor, not seriously disturbed by the tremblings of the earthquake which was not very far beneath their feet.

Among those who came in from the withering heat were Captain Edwin Christopher Lance, British civil engineer, and his wife Inger Mary, better known as Jinks, or sometimes Jingles. They had just come from matins at the British Embassy church nearby. Both were slight, fair, vivacious, gregarious, and on this morning they were in high spirits. To them, as to their friends, the dense and sombre crowd in the Castellana, through which they had forced their way, was a commonplace in the fevered existence of Spain. As they entered the bar, they saw a group of people clustered before a window, glasses in hand, and among them they recognized the tall and handsome Eric Glaisher and the rugged, vivacious little Bill Hall, both of the London and South-American Bank. One of them called out:

"Come and watch the fun!"

Joining them, the Lances looked with animated amusement

upon the scene that was staged in the broad, tree-lined Castellana outside. There in the harsh sunshine they saw a great mob in shirt sleeves, some of them armed, swaying and shouting with excitement, waving their fists in the air as they faced a large platform draped with many flags. Mounted Civil Guards, impressively smart in their grey uniforms and glossy, black, tricorn hats, stood on guard on either side, and on the platform itself, in sombre incongruity, there sat a party of men clad in black. Lance could not help laughing as he said to Jinks:

"Just like black beetles!"

One of these figures, fat and white-faced, rose to his feet as they watched and, doffing his hat to disclose a bald pate, "began to wag his baldness up and down" and to harangue the crowd with the rattle and volley of his urgent Castilian.

Inside the Embassy Bar one of the Spaniards said:

"Good heavens! It's Azaña!"

Others had recognized him, too, and in the group of spectators in which Lance and his wife found themselves there was a quickening of interest. This could be no ordinary or casual meeting, for Manuel Azaña was President of Republican Spain, no less. There also, the spectators noticed, was Largo Caballero, extremist leader of the Spanish Socialist Party.

The group of foreigners watched with added interest, but still with an amused detachment, for Spanish politics, a thorny dialectic jungle in which some twenty-four different parties and groups contended with increasing confusion amid an entanglement of their own creation, were no concern of theirs. With the rarest possible exceptions, the British and other foreigners took no sides in Spanish politics, which they looked upon either with complete indifference or with some element of cynical amusement.

Accordingly, even Azaña's presence would not for long have held the attention of the spectators in the Embassy Bar, especially as they could hear nothing of what he said. They were about to turn away when a troop of cavalry appeared right ahead, leading a procession of some sort. What now? Were the Anarchists or the Communists about to hot up the so-called Socialists? Or was it some right-wing outfit?

Whoever the new arrivals were, they brought sensation with them. As the head of the procession came abreast of the cluster of "black beetles", someone hurled a hand-bomb on to the platform. As one man, those on the platform went flat on their faces.

They waited for several seconds. Then, as no second attack came and no one seemed to be hurt, they rose to their feet as the smoke cleared away and looked apprehensively around as pandemonium erupted and spasms of indiscriminate musketry crackled and flickered over the disordered scene. The meeting began to disrupt.

To the spectators in the Embassy Bar, one might have supposed that the violent act would have caused consternation. That, in the twentieth century, men should throw bombs among a crowd in the capital of a western European state must, one would think, have appeared an outrage upon society. But no such feelings occurred to Lance and his friends. Indeed, they merely burst into laughter at the comicality of the prostrated politicians and the spectacle of mass funk that it represented. For such episodes had become commonplaces of life in Spain, to such an extent that any sense of moral outrage, or even of surprise, had long atrophied. However, on this occasion the disorder and the shooting were near enough to be alarming to those in the Embassy Bar. As the senseless rifle-fire proliferated and the bullets ricocheted and whined, Lance said to his wife:

"Better get away from all this glass, Jinks. Pop yourself in a corner while I get some suitable drinks."

As everyone withdrew from the windows Lance went up to the bar and ordered:

"A cognac and soda for the señora, please, and, for me, I think the most appropriate thing to steady the nerves would be one of your iced vodkas."

Outside, the crowd swirled and roared in the broad avenue under the dusty acacias. Lance and his wife were marooned for more than an hour, and then, against everyone's advice, they escaped, using the back door of the bar. They had not gone ten yards down the street before, from a recessed doorway, a rifle-shot rang out at Jinks's ear. She was unhurt, but Lance hurried her home as quickly as possible to their flat in the Calle de

Espalter. On arrival, they found ther trusted Spanish maid, Petra, in a state of high excitement. She had been told by Antonio, the porter of the flats, she said, and by various friends that terrible times were about to begin in Spain. She had never spoken in such a manner before and the Lances were surprised.

"Señor," she said, "it is going to be worse than anything else that has happened before. We are going to be bombed and war is going to begin. Mother of God protect us!"

Lance, who enjoyed times of excitement, chaffed her gently and tried to re-assure her.

"Put a smile on your face, Petra," he said, "and let us have lunch. We're starving. It will all be over in a few days—like all the others."

So he and Jinks thought. But years afterwards, it was that moment which he fixed in his mind as the beginning of the physical and moral collapse that was to plunge Spain into a savage and bloody conflict, a conflict in which he himself was numbered for the firing squads.

# CHAPTER TWO

# BACKGROUND TO ADVENTURE

CHRISTOPHER LANCE, or "Dagger" Lance as his wife and a few other intimates usually called him, was a man of moderate stature, lean and wiry of figure, with thick, rust-brown hair and small moustache, open-hearted and vivacious in disposition. He had a strong nose set in a face of quizzical and buoyant good humour. Occasionally he wore spectacles, which, sitting astride his bold nose, served to emphasize the impression of a jovial sparrowhawk. He was deep-voiced and slow-spoken and he laughed heartily with a sparkle in his eye. His gay disposition, his warm good-nature and his frank and open manner were a quick passport to good company, but were also the mask of a resourceful, resilient and nimble mind, for he was not a man who was easily put off his purpose. Beneath his extrovert and breezy good-nature there was not only a fund of native courage but also a warm spring of compassion. He hated cruelty, was quickly moved by suffering and could never say no to any appeal for help. Indeed, the foundation of his nature was kind-heartedness. To all those Spaniards among whom he moved in the Civil War he appeared a latter day St. George and to Angus McDonnell, his chief in London, he was a born Don Quixote, an instinctive fighter for lost causes.

For the rest, Christopher Lance loved sailing, riding and tennis and was tremendously fond of a party. Because of what is to follow, we may note also that he was extremely particular about his personal cleanliness. His hands and his hair were always well cared for and even when he had to get up at two in the morning he was always freshly shaven.

Lance was at this time forty-three years old but looked a great deal younger. He was a West Countryman and the son of Prebendary E. M. Lance, of Wells Cathedral. He caught the fever for sailing in early boyhood through his friendship with the

Bristol pilots of Pill, with whom, like young Raleigh and the mariners of old, he spent many rapt and happy hours, fascinated by the glimmer of visions beyond the horizon. From his earliest days he loved adventure, seeing a challenge in every danger signal, and he was always up to some boyish exploit, "vexing the souls of the deans", but usually laughing his way out with a whole skin. He went to Lancing College and afterwards to the City and Guilds School in London, courting "the hard-grained Muses of the cube and square" to train as a civil engineer. He joined the yeomanry and at the start of the 1914 war was a trooper in King Edward's Horse.

Learning, however, that there was no immediate likelihood of his regiment's being sent to the front, he absented himself together with a friend, in light-hearted unconcern of the legal implications, and enlisted as a private soldier on a Regular engagement for five and seven years in the West Yorkshire Regiment. His ambition to get to the Western Front was quickly realized, but when, some time later, King Edward's Horse also arrived in France, he was recognized. He was arrested in the front-line trenches and court martialled for desertion and illegal enlistment, but the evidence roused a sporting brigadier-general to gusts of hearty laughter and he was let off with the loss of his lance-corporal's stripe.

Very soon afterwards he was awarded, as could be done in those days in exceptional cases, an immediate commission in the field and posted to his own county regiment, the Somerset Light Infantry. A little later, while still a subaltern, he was awarded the D.S.O. in the grim and murderous battle of Delville Wood in the Somme in 1916—an altogether exceptional distinction for a junior officer and very close to a Victoria Cross.

After the defeat of Germany, still hungry for active service, he went to Russia in March, 1919, to join a small force, which was in the nature of a "private army", operating in the frozen wastes of Karelia in support of Kerensky's abortive offensive against the Bolsheviks. Badly wounded in an engagement with the enemy, he was lucky, in the extremely primitive conditions of that wild enterprise, to get home alive and still laughing. He was laid out for eighteen months and resigned his commission in 1921. He remained ever afterwards a period piece of 1914-18, seeming casual under stress and his speech larded with "Hell's bells", "old girl", "topping" and so on.

Soon afterwards he went to South America as an assistant engineer on the construction of the Argentine Western Railway. On the tennis courts of Buenos Aires he met Inger Mary Church, the daughter of his Chief Engineer. She was half-Norwegian by birth, small, fair, blue-eyed, of a wild-rose complexion, a trifle plumper than she wanted to be and as lively and vivacious as Lance. They married in Buenos Aires in 1925, to begin a joint life of the warmest devotion and high adventure.

This was the cheerful and popular young couple who, after a short spell back in England, went off to Spain in 1926. Alfonso XIII was still on the throne and General Primo de Rivera exercised an authoritarian sway over a country at last super-ficially calm, but its deep-seated political problems still unre-solved after three hundred years of bad government. Lance's job was the survey and location of a new railway line from Santander to the Mediterranean. Here he met Primo de Rivera himself, who, in high spirits, paid a visit to Lance's camp in San Leonardo forest and threw a "terrific beano", which ended in a midnight boar hunt in which the astonished and now slightly vinous Lance was expected to attack a charging wild pig with a torch and a knife.

This was a full and happy three years for "Dagger" and Jinks, with plenty of good riding on Irish hunters and good company among Spaniards and British of all sorts, but at the end of it they went back to South America, where Lance was appointed to a road construction job in the Chilean Andes. For the first time they became involved in serious political unrest, which began by Lance, while building his road, being caught in a battle between a battleship and a coastal battery. They lost everything they had and were lucky to get away with their lives.

Then back to Spain in 1931 for their last assignment. This time Lance went to represent the British capital, headed by Colonel the Hon. Angus McDonnell, on the board of the important Madrid civil engineering firm of Gines Navarro & Sons, with head offices in the Paseo del Prado and other offices in Valencia and Alicante. His chairman was Don Gines Navarro, a "topping old boy" with a pointed beard, for whom Lance formed a great affection. They built roads, bridges, the big Soria dam, a hydro-electric plant near Granada and a Zeppelin mast at Seville. Primo de Rivera had resigned in broken health and died and, in the tur-moil that followed, King Alfonso had withdrawn with calm and dignity from his troubled throne to permit the bloodless establish-ment of the Republic. The new government, however, brought no repose or stability. Outbreaks of revolutionary strikes and anti-clerical outrages disturbed the land and when the Lances arrived churches were being burned down by the mobs all over Spain.

From these affairs the Lances stood apart. "Dagger" was very busy, travelling all over central and southern Spain and across the sea to Morocco, away for a fortnight every month. Nonethe-less, he and Jinks contrived to enjoy themselves and to learn more of the life of Spain. They settled in an upper-floor flat at 11, Calle de Espalter, just behind the famous Prado Gallery and close to the Retiro Park, and in Antonio, the porter of the flats, they found a friend who was to be a valuable ally in times of trouble.

They found Madrid a splendid city, with its broad, tree-embroidered avenues, threaded with clanging trams, noisy with the incessant clamour of horn-blasting cars, adorned with fine shops and public buildings, peppered with boot-blacks, infested with beggars displaying their sores. They found its mountain air, high on the great central plateau of Spain, benignly exhilarating for the greater part of the year, but in July and August, the heat was like the blast of a furnace, whereas in winter the sharp knives of the mountain wind, whetted by the snows that enveloped the Guardarramas to the north, swept keenly through the streets, rattling the shutters on the stuccoed houses and chasing the desiccated leaves that fell in showers at the touch of its breath in the splendid avenues.

In this great and versatile city, noisy and throbbing with colourful life, the Lances made their home, finding friends every-where and in all classes. They engaged a Spanish maid named Petra, tall, brown-haired, blue-eyed, very devout, to whom they very soon became much attached.

The Lances soon made themselves at home. They accustomed themselves to the siesta and the extremely late hours—learning to lunch at half-past two and dine at ten—. They took kindly to the *vino*, absorbed much garlic and olive oil, and watched the nightly *paseo*, in which the citizens of a country noted for its good taste in dress and deportment decorously paraded the main streets. They admired the fine carriage, the lustrous eyes, the delicately dressed hair of the Spanish women, who spoke a secret language of flowers and scented fans. They noticed quickly the Spaniards' tender affection for children—*los niños*—but it took them longer to discover, as we all too soon shall discover, that in a Spaniard tenderness can in a flash be transformed into savage cruelty.

Thus the Lances entered fully into Spanish life. Jinks could not stomach bull-fighting, having seen a horse disembowelled at her first visit, but Lance found himself obliged to go as a matter of business duty and, getting in with a circle of experts, frequented the principal rings, mainly in Seville, and soon himself became an acknowledged *aficionado*. He was a healthy and robust Philistine, working hard and playing tennis hard and enjoying life to the full. Though they lived but a few yards from the Prado, he visited the famous picture gallery only once though Jinks went more often.

Perhaps their greatest pleasure together was picnicking in the summer to escape the torrid heat of the city, taking with them a bottle of wine and the special omelettes that the Spanish call *tortillas*, sandwiched in a flat, round loaf of bread, without which no Spanish picnic is complete, though Lance himself was perfectly happy with a plain garlic sandwich. At times, following a road on which Lance was later to run headlong into Franco's army, they would motor out to the beautiful island-garden of Aranjuez, so fondly celebrated in the sparkling verse of Calderón, where they would buy plump strawberries and fat asparagus from black-eyed peasant girls. Or they would go northward to the pine-clad Guardarrama mountains, purple in the distant haze, where Lance was to have a critical front-line encounter with *La Pasionaria*. More often, however, they would drive out in the evening to the Escorial, Philip the Second's great fortress-palace thirty miles out in the rugged countryside at the foot of the Guardarramas, where there were good cafés and orchestras, and stay there half the night till yawning sent them home again.

Of the many friends that the Lances made in this busy and agreeable life there was one who, had they been able to look into the future, they would have known was tied to them by the cords of destiny. This was Miss Margery Hill, the young matron of the British-American Hospital of which Lance was a member of the committee.

Margery Hill was a very attractive woman, *petite* and dark, whose small, rather shy figure we shall see moving through all the troublous scenes that are to follow with the quiet poise and composure of her profession, to which she was completely dedicated. She was a devout and modest woman, recoiling from limelight, concerned only with her mission to bring help to any man or woman in trouble. Yet she had also a jolly disposition and a nice sense of humour. Her medical training had been at St. Thomas's Hospital in London, but she had been born in Alicante and lived most of her life in Spain, and thus spoke perfect Spanish. She had a host of friends, Spanish, British and American, for everyone was fond of her.

Her little hospital was in the Calle Montalvo, on the edge of the New University City, then in course of construction to the north-west of Madrid, and before long to be in the front line. It was in the upper parts of a large house owned by Dr. Luque, who had his own clinic on the ground floor, and there Margery Hill had a devoted assistant in Pilar Marin, a Spanish woman who had qualified at Guy's Hospital in London.

We need not pursue in detail the chaotic and confusing course of Spanish politics of those years, but if we are to understand the drama that is about to be played we must lightly paint in the scenic background. After Alfonso had made way for the establishment of a Republic, there at once arose a disappointed cry from the extremists: "We have our republic; now let us have our revolution!" The unsuppressed outbreaks of lawlessness, the innumerable strikes, the fierce quarrels between the twelve parties of the Left, the administrative chaos and the persecution of the Church brought the first Republican government to decisive defeat at the next elections. But the Right-inclined government that followed did little better. In five and a half years there were twenty-six changes of government and several local revolutions and civil wars, including a very serious one in the northern province of Asturias. After years of debate a reasonable constitution was agreed upon, but the insistence of left-wing parties on a proviso to hold it in abeyance stultified the hopeful proposal. Thus republican ideals were betrayed by the Republicans themselves, a betrayal to which the Civil War was directly attributable. Spain was rotting with constitutional disease and showing herself totally unsuited to the western pattern of a parliamentary democracy.

Out of the turmoil the issues began to define themselves more sharply. In January 1936 the twelve parties of the Left joined hands in the "Popular Front" under the leadership of Manuel Azaña and in the next month's elections came back to the Cortes with a majority. Before we get caught up in the hell that was immediately let loose, we must make a brief acquaintance with some of these parties of the Left, of whom we shall see so much and among whom Lance and Margery Hill were to come and go in such extraordinary circumstances.

In the strangely assorted political medley of the Left, the local home-rule parties of the Catalans and the Basques, who joined the Popular Front merely for their own separatist ends, and various moderate elements, such as the Republican Union, rubbed shoulders with some totally different allies, who were all imbued to some extent with Communist doctrines, whatever might be their labels. Among these we find the Socialist Party (so-called) and several highly explosive trade unions, each maintaining its own private army of gunmen often openly at war with one another, of which the most extreme was the National Labour Confederation (CNT), a party of violence and passion, closely associated with the Anarchists.

To this volatile mixture were added some very extreme people indeed in the Syndicalist Party, the official Communist Party and the Anarchist Federation. The Syndicalists were never very strong and the Communists also were but a small party at the beginning of the trouble. Far more menacing and powerful at this stage were the Anarchists, a sanguinary collection who held life, law and property in contempt and whose object was the dissolution of the State itself and the breakdown of all organized administration, yet often, Lance found, "quite charming fellows".

"I always," he said, "got on well with blackguards and when I was in prison I liked the Anarchists much better than the Communists, although I knew all about their unspeakable villainies."

It was not long, however, before, with infiltration of the delegation from Soviet Russia, called in to the assistance of the Republican government immediately after the Civil War began, the Communists gradually grew to greater and greater influence and power until, as our story progresses, they dominated the scene. Lenin's pronouncement that the next Soviet republic must be Spain was a commonplace of Bolshevik literature and the campaign for subversion had all been carefully laid on in the Eighth Congress of the Communist International at Moscow in 1935. The chief agent of that policy, haunting the Kremlin in pursuit of it, was Alvarez del Vayo, whom Lance was to meet as Foreign Minister, while Largo Caballero was dubbed by Moscow itself as "the Spanish Lenin." Yet both were officially members of the Socialist Party, not the Communist.

We shall see less of the right-wing parties, but may note that they were of nearly as mixed a breed, including Radicals, Liberals and their own local home rule groups, as well as the red berets of the old Carlist party of Navarre and others. Of far greater significance was the newly born party that was soon to dominate the revolutionary scene—the Spanish Falange.

This was a frankly Fascist organization founded by José Antonio Primo de Rivera, son of the dictator-General. At the time when our story begins it was a very small party indeed, unrepresented in the Cortes, but, like the Communists on the other side, it was to grow rapidly in numbers and influence; yet the man who was chosen to lead the revolution of the Right— General Francisco Franco—was not a member of it.

There remained two other forces, though not parties, in Spanish politics—the Catholic Church and the Army. Of the Church we shall see little in this story, for the powerful influence that it had exerted for centuries in every sphere of Spanish life— influences beneficent in some directions but repressive in others, "serving free soup with cold dogma", as was said—had been entirely broken by the persecutions that began under the Republic and were to be renewed and multiplied in terms of blood and flames under the Popular Front.

The Army was another matter. Always very politically minded, it exercised a tremendous influence both behind the scenes and openly. It was not a very large army and, like most politically-minded armies, the standard of its military competence was not high; otherwise the Civil War would have been over far sooner than it was. Every tenth man was an officer and every hundredth officer a general. The officers were by no means a "class" corps, many senior ones, including two or three generals, having risen from humble walks of life, but they were very conscious indeed of their ability to wield political power. The inclination of the majority was towards the Right, but the left-wing politicians of the Republic very soon took care to arrest that inclination by the promotion of officers friendly to them, by dismissals and by postings to the Spanish overseas possessions in Africa and the Canaries. One officer who was thus got out of the way, or so it was supposed, was General Francisco Franco, who was sent off as G.O.C. the Canaries. Two very important corps—the artillery and the air force—were to be found mainly aligned at the critical moment on the Left, a circumstance which at the outset seriously embarrassed the insurgent forces.

Christopher Lance got to know a great many Army officers at the Savoy Hotel near his flat in Madrid and liked them. He found that they had an exceptional sense of humour and easy good manners, many spoke excellent English and several of the more patrician had been to school in England. Like the general body of Spaniards, they had a high and historic regard for Britain, epitomized in the phrase *palabra inglesa* ("the word of an Englishman"), long current among Spaniards themselves.

Such, in the simplest possible terms, was the composition in February 1936, when Lance had completed nearly five years of his second sojourn in Spain, of those elements that were so soon to boil over in the crucible of Spanish life, bringing misery and death to many thousands, horrifying Europe by the savageries that were to ensue and dividing much of the world into fierce partisanships over a quarrel which was none of theirs and which

23

many of them, applying to Spain the catch-phrases of their own domestic politics, wholly misunderstood.

The triumph of the Popular Front at the polls shot the political temperature immediately to flash-point. Those whose first duty it was to safeguard the lives and property of all subjects became intoxicated with the opportunity for revengeful excesses against those whom they hated. Thousands of political prisoners were set free to take private vengeance on whom they would. A judge was robbed and murdered by the convict he had sentenced to imprisonment. Priests, monks and nuns were slaughtered and no man or woman who escaped dared to appear in religious habit. The castanets jingled as the women, even more ferocious than the men, danced round the leaping flames of church and convent. Monasteries, convents and seminaries were seized and found to make excellent prisons. Gangs of men broke into houses to shoot down whom they would. Shops were plundered at pistol point. Bands of peasants seized land and defied the law. Cattle were wantonly slaughtered or mutilated and the crops burnt in the fields. The press was intimidated and the salute of the clenched fist was everywhere to be seen. In the residential districts, as Lance himself could observe in the silent, close-shuttered flats immediately opposite his own, supporters of the Right went to earth or shut themselves up, stealing out dressed as servants when it was necessary to buy food.

To add to the confusion, violent quarrels very soon broke out between the parties of the Left as Largo Caballero, intoxicated with his rôle of "Spanish Lenin", declared war on his fellow Socialist, Prieto, and strove to hoist himself to power on the shoulders of the "proletariat". As the tommy-gunners of the two rival leaders clashed, civil war became inevitable. Throughout Spain each of the big trades unions were openly drilling its own private army of gunmen and pistoleers, with the CNT easily ahead of all others in the supply of arms. Largo Caballero declared that "Spain must be destroyed in order to make it ours; on the day of vengeance we shall not leave a stone upon a stone." Likewise Margarita Nelken, demanding a revolution, called for "flames that will be seen throughout the planet and waves of blood that will redden the seas."

24

Obviously the supporters of the Right did not take all this lying down, and murder was answered by murder. Thus the country was in the grip of hopeless indiscipline and mob rule was deliberately encouraged by a government that made no attempt to stay the breakdown of executive authority. In four months there were 3,300 assassinations; 171 churches, 69 clubs, 10 newspaper offices and 284 other buildings were burnt; 113 general strikes and 218 partial strikes took place.

When Calvo Sotelo, the Spanish Renaissance deputy, revealed these figures to a shocked Cortes in July and declared that "this was not what we voted for in the Constitution", Casares Quiroga, the Prime Minister, told him grimly that he "would be held personally responsible for these revelations" and Dolores Ibarurri, to become famous in the world's press as *La Pasionaria*, rose with clenched fist and, with that concentrated fury which Lance himself was soon to experience, cried:

"You have made your last speech."

Two days later, in fulfilment of those words, Sotelo was murdered by Assault Guards, the government's special strong-arm shock police.

Inevitably the smouldering and outraged forces of the Right were fanned into violent combustion. The next day Madrid was seething. Who would be next?

All these electric events Lance and his friends looked upon with detached interest. The evidence of the burning churches and the prowling bands was all too evident, but Jinks and Petra were still able to go about their shopping in the markets unmolested and Lance went to and from his works, considering all this wild misrule as nothing more than a periodical ailment that must be expected to break out every now and then in Spanish political life. He warned his principals at home that a storm was brewing, but thought that it would blow itself out in the usual way. After all, had not the Prime Minister himself said: "Nothing will happen"?

So, with a Union Jack on his car, Lance went out confidently and undisturbed. There was nothing to worry about and, once the politicians and the mobs had blown off steam, everything would be quiet again.

# CHAPTER THREE

# THE PICNIC

On July 18, the inevitable storm broke. Away in Spanish Morocco the garrison of Melilla revolted. It was an apparently spontaneous and isolated episode, but was in fact the first step in a plan prepared by the Spanish Military Union and word of it was very soon being flashed to a number of expectant senior officers in garrisons throughout Spain and her overseas territories. General Franco, flying in an aircraft formerly belonging to the Duke of Windsor, chartered in England from Major Hugh Pollard and piloted by Captain Cecil Beed, left the Canary Isles at once to take charge in Morocco. Thus was begun the *movimiento nacional* of those who were to become known as "Nationalists". They rose, they declared, "not against the law, but for the law, so that law and authority should rule; not against the people, but for the safety of the people".

In their flat in Madrid the Lances heard the news of the rising next day on the government radio and the claim, repeated at intervals throughout the day with too much emphasis, that it had been immediately crushed. As the day wore on the air throbbed with rumours of an attempted military *coup de main* in Spain itself, of wholesale assassinations and of some fresh spark in the already excited atmosphere. To the Lances it appeared to be no more than another bubbling in the cauldron of Spanish politics, another attempt by someone to seize power. They, like the rest of the foreign communities in Madrid, took only a detached interest in the news. It was all "according to form".

Madrid stifled in the furnace of the July heat. In the handsome avenues the trees stood motionless in the sultry air, their leaves pale with dust. The night of that fateful Saturday was suffocating and feverish. The city drooped from insomnia. High in their flat next morning, Lance said to Jinks in his slow, deep voice:

"Too hot for church, old girl; let's go off somewhere for a picnic."

Jinks agreed gladly: "Not likely," she said, "that we shall run into any trouble, I suppose?"

"Oh lord, no," Lance replied. "Everything's perfectly quiet."

"All right; let's go to the Escorial, then."

So Petra made a *tortilla* while Jinks packed up some fruit and *vino corriente*, of which they had a particularly good supply from a friend's vineyard in Valdepeñas, while Dagger brought the car out of his garage opposite the flats. They gave Petra and the chauffeur the day off.

The sun was already very hot as they set out and they looked forward to getting into the country. There were no signs of excitement or disorder. On the contrary, everything was extraordinarily quiet and still. No other car but theirs was to be seen. Certainly that was very strange, but there seemed to be no cause for alarm.

They had gone only a few miles, however, before they had their first jolt. At Las Rosas, a few miles out of Madrid, a band of armed workmen in shirt-sleeves suddenly fanned out across the road and called upon them to halt. They were ordered out of the car and searched, Jinks by a peasant girl and Lance by a sombre fellow who was armed with an antique blunderbuss. They submitted with good humour. Lance noted with amusement the odd collection of weapons that the others were carrying, mainly antique or modern fowling pieces, and, with his usual buoyancy, found it difficult to regard the situation seriously, for the "militiamen", as these armed but entirely untrained civilians came to be known, were quite polite and made no attempt at violence or robbery. The Lances chatted with them inconsequentially and, after mutual salutations, went on their way.

"Pleasure as usual, old girl!" Lance said.

"I hope you're right, Dagger," Jinks answered, "but we seem to be about the only people in Spain who think so."

They decided to go on, but the holiday atmosphere had vanished. The secondary road that led direct to the Escorial being very rough, they kept to the main road and, stopping short of their intended objective, ate their picnic lunch in a rocky, sun-

27

roasted spot a mile or two away from the Escorial without enjoyment and in an uneasy silence, relieved only by the shrill song of the cicadas all around them. In this usually popular place not a soul was to be seen but themselves, not a movement except the sudden darting of a lizard. The walls of the great palace frowned down upon them from a distance in the blistering heat, as forbidding as the austere king who had built it.

"What on earth is up and where the devil is everybody?" Lance exclaimed.

They broke off their picnic early and started for home, never imagining that there could be any difficulty in returning to Madrid.

At the village of Villalba, twenty miles north of the city, however, they were again brought to an abrupt halt. There had been no obstruction there when they had passed through before, but now a tree lay felled across the road and several upturned carts reinforced the tell-tale barrier.

"This," said Lance, "looks like trouble."

It was. A crowd of hostile men and women bore down on the car the moment it stopped, waving weapons and red flags and seething with excitement. They were a party of Anarchists, most of the men wearing the red vests and black trousers of that party and shod with the rope-soled shoes that the Spanish call *alpargatas*. As they clustered menacingly round the car, Lance experienced for the first time the full venom of that fever known as class hatred, burning in their eyes and smouldering in their attitudes and in their speech. One of them, armed with a rusty muzzle-loading gun and wearing a belt full of ammunition, thrust his head inside the car and ordered:

"Get out!"

No courtesy this time; no mere searching or interrogation. They were immediately stripped of their money, all their personal possessions and the keys and documents of the car. They were manhandled into a nearby cottage and locked in a room with the scarcely necessary remark:

"You are prisoners."

This was by no means amusing and for an hour they were kept imprisoned. The prospect was black, but partial relief came in the unpredictable way that, until things became more deadly, gave an air of comic opera to these Spanish disturbances. One of their red-vested captors came in and, to their surprise, they saw that he was smiling. He was holding their passports in his hand.

"*Camarada,*" he said to Lance, "I am glad to see that after all you are friends of the Revolution."

Surprised, Lance asked backhandedly: "How did you find that out?"

"That was easy, *camarada*; I see from your passport," and he pointed to that passage in the passport which authorized them to visit, among other countries, Soviet Russia.

Lance was very tickled but did not disabuse him, laughing good-humouredly. He very soon divined that all the documents had been handed to this man, who was the only one in the gang who could read, and, although even he read little enough, his eye had caught the words "Union of Soviet Socialist Republics". The hope of a quick return to Madrid was very soon dashed, however.

"The revolution has begun, *camarada,* and we shall need your motor-car for the cause."

It looked, therefore, as though the Lances might have to make the cottage their home for an indefinite period, for the afternoon was already spent, and Jinks at once made a housewife's appreciation of the situation. She said to the militiaman:

"If you keep us here, we must have some food and a fire to cook it by."

"*Camarada,* you may go under escort to the village to buy food if you wish."

"How are we to buy food without money?"

"That I do not know." It did not occur to their captors to return the money of which they had robbed their captives.

Time passed by uneasily, but they were saved in the end by another unexpected event. With a great roar of engines, a dozen Assault Guards in blue uniforms swept in on motor-cycles, slowing down at the barrier. Lance waved and shouted to them from the window of the cottage and when the dilemma was explained to them they ordered the militiamen to release their captives and

29

return the car. The day was drawing to a close and the guards, it seemed, were glad of a chance of making an excuse to return to Madrid, for they formed up round the car like a President's escort and roared back into Madrid in formation with blaring horns.

These Assault Guards were a force of extremely dangerous, strong-arm police, specially recruited by the government for violent arrests and official murders, and it was they who had butchered Calvo Sotelo; but it was typical of Lance and of the technique he afterwards employed with such success, that he invited the whole escort into his flat for an impromptu party in their tiny drawing-room. There were so many of them that they had to take turns to sit on the few chairs as the night wore on and they drank jovially to the prosperity of Spain. "It was," said Lance afterwards, "a hell of a binge." As we have seen, he always got on well with the Spanish working classes, who were, as he said, "jolly nice people until they became inflamed by hatreds, when they become venomous".

He and Jinks were still persisting, however, in the belief that this new rising would not be of long duration. That lingering belief was to be shattered early next day.

With the flavour of last night's extraordinary events still fresh in their minds, they were startled from sleep at seven in the morning by the sound of a heavy bombardment near at hand. Lance, Jinks and Petra rushed out to the balcony and, to their astonishment, heard the Montaña Barracks, away to the west, under heavy fire from guns and aircraft. Their reactions were characteristic. Lance exclaimed:

"Now we *are* for it!"

The devout Petra, crossing herself, cried:

"Holy Mother, protect us!"

Jinks alone was speechless. They were to learn later that, General Fanjul having hesitated too long, the revolt of the Madrid garrison had gone off at half-cock and a murderous fight was going on within the barracks between those who supported the revolt and those who opposed it. Men and officers were shooting one another down and fighting duels from room to room. In the midst of this turmoil the government, having had time to take counter-measures, had ordered the artillery and the air force, who, as we have seen, largely adhered to them, to attack the barracks. One battery of artillery was firing into the building at point-blank. Another, sited on the high ground outside the city, was promiscuously pouring ill-aimed shells into the neighbourhood. Overhead, low-flying aircraft circled the barracks, bombing and machine-gunning. The crackle of rifle-fire added to the din as armed civilians joined in the onslaught.

The civil war was well and truly alight and Madrid became a city of terror. All over the country the government had, on the day before, given orders that the arsenals were to be opened and weapons distributed to "the masses". In Madrid men and women of the left wing parties flocked to the "House of the People", the Socialist headquarters, to collect weapons that they did not know how to use. Margery Hill saw some children in the streets handling revolvers and asking each other "Which is the thing that you press?" Armed mobs were ranging the streets and the countryside, looking for prey. In those parts of Spain that were not secured by the Nationalists that state of lawlessness for which the Anarchists clamoured was realized. Local soviets and "committees" ruled town and countryside. The *alcaldes* of ancient office were murdered and replaced by *"responsables"*. The village Stalin held independent sway and there was no law but that of the rifleman.

Such scenes were now enacted immediately beneath the eyes of the Lances in their flat in the Calle de Espalter. As the barracks battle died down after about two hours, gangs of men were racing to and fro in the street beneath, waving knives, red flags and banners acclaiming Soviet Russia, and firing their newly gained weapons at random. Wild-haired women, in open shirts, stockingless and shod with *alpargatas*, ranged beside them, more savage than the men. Seeing faces crowded at the windows of the blocks of flats opposite Lance, where, as we have seen, the occupants had long shut themselves up in a terrified hermitage, the mob opened a fierce fusillade. As by magic, every window was instantly cleared and the blinds down. Someone in the street shouted orders that all shutters were to be closed, but Lance, out on the balcony of his flat, seeing a woman opposite shot dead in the act of doing so, decided not to obey.

"Down on your tummy, Jinks," he ordered as the bullets peppered the walls and smashed the windows.

"Jinks, this is going to be no joke," Lance said a little later as the sounds of shooting spread throughout the city and as flames and smoke of burning buildings could be seen. From the roof-top of the flats opposite them, some wanton gunman was shooting directly into the little passage that led from their dining-room to the kitchen, so that Jinks and Petra were obliged to crawl along it on their stomachs.

"How long is this going on?" Jinks asked unconcernedly.

"I daresay it will get a bit worse before it gets better. Like the Asturias shindy in 1934, I should think."

"We had better stock up again, then." They were no strangers to such situations. In the Asturias rising, things had looked ugly in Madrid for about ten days. In Chile and in Buenos Aires they had also experienced dangerous civil commotion. From such experiences Jinks knew that the first thing to do was to lay in a stock of water, in case the supply should be cut. She and Petra therefore filled the bath, basins and every receptacle that would hold water. Then, as there came a lull in the commotion, the two women went out composedly with their shopping baskets into the hot streets to lay in siege provisions of food, wood, coal and charcoal. It was a terrifying expedition. They found the market littered and deserted and the gangs of men and women looting the little shops at will. At one of their usual little stores, they saw "old Gonzales" with his hands up while a young ruffian held a gun into his belly and three others were loading themselves up with stores. The women came home with practically no foodstuffs and only a few knobs of coal.

While Jinks and Petra were braving these dangerous elements, Lance had made his way to his office in the Paseo del Prado. He "breezed" in and said:

"Rough night, wasn't it?"

He was met by an uneasy silence. Hook and Sims, the other British representatives, were there, but the Navarros, father and

The man in the check jacket

The Calle de Espalter, Madrid. Car is outside Lance's block of flats

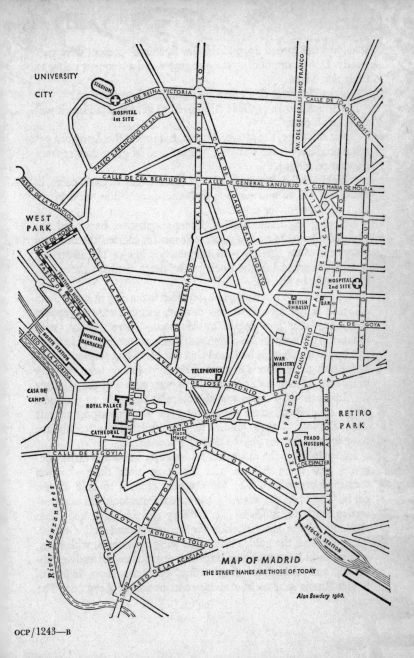

MAP OF MADRID

THE STREET NAMES ARE THOSE OF TODAY

Alan Bowdery 1960.

sons, had not turned up, and the few Spaniards present were very windy. Don Raimundo, a young engineer and a frequent visitor to their flat, asked:

"If the Navarros don't turn up again, can you carry on?"

To which Lance replied: "No need to get the wind up; it will soon be all over."

"Not this time, I'm afraid. That is, not unless the Army can get a quick victory." He was very "right" and in great danger from the armed mobs.

"We'll see," Lance replied. "If Don Gines doesn't come in tomorrow I'll go and see him at home. Meanwhile, we'd better shut up shop for the day."

Before going home himself, being inquisitive, he visited the Montaña Barracks and, unhindered, saw for himself the dreadful story, the place littered with corpses, victims of the shattering bombardment and of the duels to the death between those who had once been friends.

Similar scenes had that same day been occurring in many parts of Spain as the code word flew to units and garrisons to support the rising that had begun in Morocco. There Franco, with organized units under his command, had been completely successful, but to his chagrin he found that the Navy had refused to join in the rising, the officers in most of the ships having been savagely murdered by their own men on the express orders of the Ministry of Marine itself. Franco was therefore at first able to transport only a small force across the sea by a few hired transport aircraft until, the loss of their officers having rendered the Republican navy useless, he was able to do as he pleased.

In Spain itself the insurgent Nationalists had some quick successes and some failures and for some time their situation remained precarious. The Government seemed to hold all the cards. They had the arsenals, the communications, the administrative machine, much of the artillery and air force and other elements of the army besides the various armed police forces. They also had the gold. French left wing volunteers, with arms, poured in in large numbers under an organization already established, and volunteers from other countries soon followed. Soviet Russia sent an immediate contribution of £479,000. The beginnings of an international conflict threatened and divided all Europe.

In Madrid the Nationalist rising was completely crushed, General Fanjul and Colonel Quintana being taken and shot. The airfields of Getafe and Cuatro Vientos, together with all military establishments and stores, were in government hands. A few right wing civilians, armed with the revolvers that most of them possessed, came out in support of the revolt but were quickly overcome. From that moment the armed mobs held sway. In the unashamed words of a government official, "We armed fury and it has erupted in the streets." The gangs entered what houses they would, slaughtering and robbing. They burst into hospitals and shot patients in their beds. Madge, the English wife of Adolfo Morales, was about to begin labour when a gang of militiamen raided her father-in-law's flat and stood her up at pistol-point, so that her baby was born dead a few hours later in the British-American hospital.

Anyone known to have right wing sympathies, of whatever class, was target for the wanton bullets. Employers and managers were hunted down. Cars were seized at pistol-point, many of them only to be immediately crashed by untaught drivers. In cafés, cinemas and in the streets people were held up for forced contributions to "Red Aid". On walls and on flaunting red banners "Long Live Russia" and "Long Live the Soviet" were the only slogans and if anyone cried "Long Live Spain" he was seized upon as a "Fascist". Religious worship was officially forbidden and a crucifix in any house was a death warrant. Ten bishops and many thousands of priests, nuns, lay brothers and sisters and many other devout people were butchered for no political activity whatever.

From their flat the Lances could see six churches or convents in flames and when night fell and the roofs and towers crashed down and the flames leapt higher to the skies the aspect of terror was increased. Wherever one turned there were murderous scenes against a background of din and flames leaping high, and from the flats opposite them the Lances saw six men, including the porter, carried off for execution.

The contrast to what the Lances had been used to was heart-

35

rending, for at this time of year the Prado would be full of hurdy-gurdies, roundabouts, laughter, dancing and the jingling of castanets. The flames were coming uncomfortably close. As they watched from the balcony, Petra exclaimed:

"The devils! Mother of God, protect us!"

Even Jinks had lost her composure and said:

"Good heavens, Christopher, when will it end? Will San Jeronimo's be next?"

This was a church very near to them, where Petra went to confession, and when she heard the name she flew into an agony of anxiety, crying:

"My poor church! Mother of Jesus, protect my church! They will kill all the priests! They will kill my poor Father Pedro!"

Lance himself was sobered up, too. Their normal life, he was thinking, was finished. There could be no useful existence for them in Spain; they would have to get down to it afresh. What could they plan? How on earth was he to carry on the business? He looked out upon the city ringed with fire. These terrible things that had been hinted at—were they really going to happen?"

Reflectively he said to Jinks:

"Do you remember that dapper little Royalist at the Savoy, Colonel 'Pinilla'? Do you remember his telling me confidentially that there was going to be a show-down soon? By Jove, he was right!"

# CHAPTER FOUR

# FEAR

LANCE went down, as usual, a day or two later to the Navarro offices in the sweltering heat. The moment he entered he sensed an uneasy atmosphere and to his astonishment he found a very junior Swiss clerk, who was an Anarchist, seated at his desk.

To himself he said: "Damn the fellow! What the hell's on?" Aloud he said sharply: "What are you doing in my chair?"

With cool insolence the clerk replied:

"The workers have formed a committee and we are now in complete charge of the business. I naturally hope that I shall have your co-operation."

Lance was staggered. The damned little pen-pusher! Deciding, however, to keep his temper and not to rush the fence, he said:

"My foot! Who are the other people on this 'committee' of yours?" He had heard, of course, of the Communist notion of workers' committees who by force seized control of a business. It was happening all over Spain.

The other members of the Committee came in and were introduced to him. Of course, he knew them all and saw at a glance that they were totally unsuitable to run a technical business of this sort. Three represented the moderately Communist General Union of Workers and two the violent Anarchist National Labour Confederation—the two unions to which all the workmen of Gines Navarro & Sons belonged. He said to the Swiss:

"Get up out of my chair."

To his surprise, the fellow obeyed without a murmur, and Lance took his seat. In the interests of the firm, he was anxious not to antagonize too many of these people, for a means might yet be found of carrying on. He must feel his way. He owed his personal immunity entirely to his foreign status, but people of this kidney were quite capable of "bumping him off" in a remote spot if he stood in their way, as they plotted to do later. The "committee" now began to talk in a back-handed kind of way, telling him first that he must not interfere and then asking him about the works in hand, about which they knew nothing whatever. Thinking, "What a lot of poppycock," he said:

"It is not as easy as that. The first thing you have got to realize is that at the back of the business is finance, and you will not be able to monkey about with foreign capital. That is my business."

This was plainly something that they had not thought about and Lance went on:

"I have no intention of telling you anything about the works. I shall continue to carry on. You can go now."

They went meekly enough, but, if the political position remained as anarchic as it was, the business one was bound to get worse. Lance's chief concern was to take care of "the boodle" and at an uneasy board meeting, Gines Navarro had said that he would be obliged to leave Lance to carry on. The attitude of the office staff rapidly deteriorated. They grew slovenly in their clothes, began to affect the blue boiler-suits (or "*monos*") of the militia gangs, added bits of military equipment to it and soon swaggered in as fully armed bandits. The Swiss clerk, who very soon proved a terror to his own comrades, took the lead in these heroic attitudes and as soon as he had secured a revolver pushed its muzzle at Lance's solar plexus and demanded his signature to a cheque, drawn to himself, for £150.

Lance, determined to protect his firm's "funds", now his main concern, made suitable secret arrangements with Eric Glaisher at the bank. If business was almost at a standstill, he at once found himself deeply immersed in more critical and moving affairs in the oppressive heat. To the terror spread by the "militia" gangs there was quickly added a new fear. It soon became known that, although the Nationalist insurrection had been crushed in Madrid, the situation was very different in other parts of Spain, as Franco's tenuous forces began in the first few days to feel their way towards the capital from the south and those of General Mola, the horn-rimmed, thick-haired, able leader of the Military Union, from the north.

Clearly it was not now a matter of a sudden *coup de main*, but of a full-scale civil war, with all the barbarities that accompany internecine conflicts. The government itself was in chaos; complete changes of Cabinet took place every few hours and terrified ministers barricaded themselves in the Ministry of Marine. Every trade union and every political party of the Left was independently organizing its own militia without common purpose, without government direction, without even a general staff, although the government had at its disposal over 500 professional officers. Meanwhile, the sun glared down with unrelieved intensity, casting sharp shadows in the stifling streets and intensifying the nervous strain under which all men lived.

In this feverish situation it became clear to Lance and some of his friends that something would have to be done for the protection of the British community. The Embassy, situated in the Calle de Fernando el Santo, was at that time shut, the Ambassador, Sir Henry Chilton, and his staff having recently removed to San Sebastián, in accordance with the usual practice in the hot weather. There remained only a Consul, whose resources and personal qualities were unequal to the demands made upon him as soon as the true nature of the situation became apparent. The British community was without a leader. It was Lance who now suggested to the Consul that the Embassy should be opened and the British residents accommodated within the protection of its walls, but the harassed man replied that he could not possibly cope with so tall an order.

Lance at once said:

"Very well, I'll run the whole show if you will open up," and the Consul acquiesced with relief. It was in this relatively small way that Lance, who had been deeply touched by the anxiety and distress already evident on every hand, took the first step in that long trail of relief and rescue which was gradually to develop into an ardent and a dangerous mission.

A committee was formed and the word passed round to the British community. The response was astonishing. Instead of the estimated 350 or so British subjects in Madrid, some 600 swarmed into the Embassy as July approached its sweltering close. The Embassy was a large and handsome building standing in spacious grounds enclosed within a high wall, but, in spite of its spaciousness, it became hard pressed for accommodation.

39

Hundreds of people suddenly remembered that, on some unknown date, they had been born in a British ship or in Gibraltar. A great many could not speak a word of English and a few had even been known as actively anti-British. Nonetheless, the scene as all these came together was one of acute pathos. Bewildered old men, anxious women, children on the edge of fear, and sick of all ages were among them. Many of these unhappy women had seen their husbands shot before their eyes by the militiamen. Many more had no roots anywhere but in Spain and now faced the prospect of leaving behind them not only their tenderest memories but also all that they possessed and all the friends they ever knew. They now possessed nothing but what they stood in or could carry in their hands. Among them was a pathetic party of Irish nuns in plain clothes, who had been through an agonizing time and who had been forced by the anti-clerical outrages to abandon their conventional habits.

Lance, as he watched the crowd streaming in, said to Jinks: "Good lord! What have we let ourselves in for? This is going to be a twenty-four-hours-a-day job. We'd better doss down with the mob ourselves."

Jinks hurriedly collected a few things from the flat, leaving Petra there. Water, food, sanitation, bedding and stores of all kinds were insufficient and the extempore committee was hard pressed to handle the emergency. It was from this time that Lance began to display those qualities that were soon to raise him to a special position in the eyes of all men and women who were in adversity. It was not only his energy, his resourcefulness and his knack of dealing with Spanish officials that were of practical use, but even more to be valued was the air of confidence that he inspired among all those who looked for some leadership out of their bewilderment. To Constance, the British wife of Juan Navarro de Palencia, he was like an Elizabethan sea captain singeing hostile beards. She felt that "there was nothing he could not do" and that he seemed instinctively to know the way round all obstacles. Deeply moved by all that he saw, he set out to give heart to all who were bewildered or lost and as he went about among them with his cheerful smile and deep laugh they felt reassured and restored to hope.

Then occurred the first bombing raid that the inhabitants of Madrid had been so much dreading. It was only a small affair. Franco sent over a few aircraft which dropped some light bombs, but the anticipation of it was sufficient to cause terror to the more unstable elements in the Embassy. To Lance the cries of these women and children were more distressing than the crash of bombs.

News came from Whitehall that the Royal Navy would send HMS *Devonshire* to Valencia to take off the refugees and Lance accordingly made arrangements with the government, the railway and the police for their safe transport to the coast. He found the Republican authorities co-operative and he took special advantage of the opportunity to cultivate relations with the Security Police (*Seguridad*), especially with the Chief of the *Seguridad* personally, a good-looking, smart and highly intelligent man of middle age, whose friendship was to be invaluable in the days to come.

To his surprise, when the moment came for their escape to safety, only a handful of the refugees wanted to go; they felt safe in the Embassy and feared the journey through left-wing territory. In his perplexity, he sought out Jinks and said:

"You'll have to go, old girl."

"Go? Where?"

"Home."

"What! I wouldn't dream of going. I'm staying here with you."

"Sorry, but you'll just have to. You must set the example. If you and one or two others go, it will give confidence and the others will follow."

She hated it, but went, after paying a fond and tearful farewell to Petra at the flat, where the devoted girl had smuggled in enough food for a meal and enough fuel for a bath. When it came to the point, however, only four or five other British women accompanied Jinks on the special train on July 30, under the charge of Frank Hook, the accountant of Gines Navarro. At the station they had a terrible time at the hands of a gang of ruffians, who, seeing an old lady in the party wearing a cameo brooch and believing it to be a religious symbol, practically stripped the poor creature in public on the platform and ground the cameo underfoot.

The example of these few, however, had its effect, for, when it was known that they had got through to Valencia safely, there was a rush of applicants and five days later Lance, to his great relief, got off a train-load of about 500 in heart-rending scenes of tears and anguish.

Sorely though he missed his dear Jinks, who has by no means disappeared from our story, Lance heaved a sigh of relief at these departures. The experience had been a nightmare and there were now many other people in distress whom he was anxious to help. He was further relieved when Mr G. A. D. Ogilvie-Forbes arrived soon afterwards as Chargé d'Affaires at the Embassy, and with him Lance at once struck up a warm friendship. He was a very capable and energetic man, full of good humour, but had a strict code of diplomatic ethics and, although a Roman Catholic, and therefore likely to be unsympathetic to the Republican government, never revealed to Lance any sign of political sympathies one way or the other.

He was met on arrival by Mr E. G. de Caux, the Madrid correspondent of *The Times*, to whom he said:

"What's all this about 'indiscriminate shootings' in Madrid? Can you show me any evidence?"

De Caux replied that he would guarantee to show him convincing evidence within fifteen minutes. He drove him straight out to the New University City, close to Margery Hill's hospital, and there showed him seventy corpses. Horrified, Ogilvie-Forbes thereupon invited him to lunch next day to meet Marcel Rosenberg, the Russian Ambassador, who was exerting a powerful influence on the Republican government and even sitting at Cabinet meetings. When they met, de Caux related what he knew about these shootings, but Rosenberg's only response was to observe, with an emphatic shrug of the shoulders:

"When you have a revolution, you must expect the scum to come to the top."

De Caux found himself wondering what the shade of Lenin would have said to such a derisive remark.

Forbes appointed Lance an honorary attaché, asking him to

continue his good work on behalf of the British community and to keep him informed of what went on. Lance went back to his flat for a while, where the faithful Petra continued to look after him until it was bombed, but in the cool of the evenings he would often go round and drink good Scotch whisky in Forbes's flat in the Embassy. Under the protection of the Union Jack on their cars and wearing red, white and blue brassards, he and the remaining British residents went about with reasonable safety, for the Republicans generally respected foreigners except Germans and Italians.

Over all the city fear had now laid its chilling hand. No one with known right-wing sympathies, of whatever class, could venture into the streets without peril to his life. No one dared in public reveal his adherence to the Church. Professional men who had not declared for the Left and were engaged in the direction or management of every kind of business, together with their families, went into hiding, a little food brought to them from time to time by their devoted servants. In the chief residential streets the shutters of houses and flats were tightly closed, the occupants living shut up in the half-light provided by an electric current that grew daily weaker—without occupation, without fresh air, with very little food and almost without hope. The armed boiler-suits and shirt-sleeves, now speeding about in stolen motor-cars, their horns blaring peremptorily every few yards, continued at their work of brigandage and slaughter, without hindrance by government or police, and every morning the police death-carts were to be seen collecting their loads of corpses from the streets.

Lance's own car was taken at pistol-point from the garage and he had to depend in future on cars borrowed from the Embassy. Margery Hill, taking to the railway station an American woman whose baby had been born in her hospital a week before, found her American Embassy car halted every few yards by gangs who thrust their rifles through the windows, thirsty for the blood of "Fascists", by which name they labelled everyone who disagreed with them. Dr. Luque, the physician at the little hospital, warned in the nick of time that the gunmen were after him, fled from his ground-floor clinic to the hospital above, whither the gunmen attempted to pursue him, but were fooled on the staircase by the guards sent to protect it. Luque's clinic was then seized as a billet by the militiamen, to the great embarrassment of the hospital.

Dr. Mariano Gomez Ulla, a friend of Lance's, a surgeon of brilliance, fame and wide humanity, affectionately known among the working classes as Don Mariano, was less fortunate. He was seized by gunmen and was on the point of becoming a target for their bullets when the Republican authorities, desperately short of doctors, ordered that he should be kept prisoner and conscripted for duty in the military hospital at the Ritz Hotel.

These were minor events to show the temper of the time. Even to appear in the streets well-dressed, in collar and tie, was to risk insult in those early days. Mrs. Stowe, going out in a hat, had it snatched from her head with angry screams of "Fascist!" To go out into the streets at all after dark, when the so-called "guards" held undisputed sway, was a step that few men dared to take. The social night-life of Madrid came to an end, all the hotels and restaurants closed, except those few kept open for officials or frequented by the militia and their friends. A brash and strident Madrid took the place of the old, and the red streamers, the hammers and sickles, the portraits of Stalin, the Soviet slogans and the flood of Russian films that swept into the cinemas showed all too clearly which was the prevailing wind.

Acute shortages of every kind of commodity, due to the disruption of the normal means of supply and distribution, began further to increase the strains of life. In the windows of shops, usually so well stocked, the notice "Nothing of nothing" was soon ironically displayed. Food became scarcer and scarcer and before long there was no milk, no eggs, no butter, no meat, no fresh vegetables. Water was cut off for long periods. The American-run telephone service continued to operate with reasonable efficiency, but the electricity supplies became feebler and feebler, the trams fewer and fewer.

The callousness of Spaniards to acts of cruelty, except when they affected themselves or those dear to them, was manifested even by the gentle Petra. She came in excitedly to the sitting-room of the flat and said to Lance:

"Oh, señor! You *must* go and have a look at the corpses on that steep grass bank behind the Prado Gallery."

44

"Good heavens, Petra," replied Lance, taken aback. "I don't want to see any corpses."

"Oh, but señor, you would be most interested. There is a woman much mutilated and there is a priest propped up on the bank with a label 'I am a Fascist' round his neck." She was no more moved than if she had seen a dead mouse.

To this curious twist in Spanish nature—curious to us, at least —there seemed no answer. Quite naturally, it was otherwise when a man was threatened himself, and it was for such people that Christopher Lance and many others of the British colony, such as Margery Hill, Eric Glaisher and Bobby Papworth, devoted themselves in their mission of humanity. There was nothing political about it; simply a matter of helping men and women in adversity. They took them food and necessities, brought news of their families, or merely visited them to cheer them up, and sometimes gave them shelter in their own houses and flats. These were but small beginnings of what was to follow, but Lance soon began to take more dangerous steps.

Realizing what would be the certain fate of every right-wing Spaniard who was found to possess arms, he went round to all his friends and persuaded them to hand over their revolvers. These he greased and took out at night, at very great risk, to the Retiro Park, climbed the big spiked railings and buried them in one of the shrubberies, keeping a spade concealed in the shrubbery for that purpose. So that each man could later identify his own weapon, he pinpointed its location by counting the spikes of the park wall from the gate. Similarly he took into safe custody the jewellery of a great number of British and Spaniards, including the Duke of Alba, later Spanish Ambassador in London, being provided by Ogilvie-Forbes with an enormous safe in the British Embassy for this purpose. He never carried any arms himself.

As someone said, the Spaniards seemed to regard the British, and no doubt other foreigners also, as "bullet-proof". Lance himself, however, was by no means secure, and the first threat against him came from the workmen of his own firm, whose Committee we have already seen attempting to seize control of the business and direct it to their own ends.

The Committee did their damnedest to oust him, for he was a

serious impediment to their schemes, but, as he was a foreigner, and free from political ties, they could not have him dealt with as they would have a Spanish "Fascist". Lance, preserving his good humour and using his wits, was not to be shaken off. They tried cutting his salary by a half; no result. They stopped his salary altogether; still no result. Lance, by treaty with Glaisher at the Bank, smiled and carried on with the work that only he could do. The "Committee", angry and baffled, took a more dangerous step.

At two o'clock one night Lance was woken up by his friend the Chief of the Security Police, who came to warn him that the Committee had that evening been overheard in a café making a plot to murder him the next morning. They were to invite him to go out to the New University City, where his firm was carrying out a contract in road-surfacing of Lance's own formulation, and to ask his technical advice. The place was on the outskirts of Madrid and now, since the stoppage of building works, almost deserted. There the Committee would do away with him and dispose of his body.

Lance, on being made aware of all this, made his plans accordingly, thoroughly tickled with the whole thing and looking forward to a bit of fun. The next morning he went to the office as usual in a car borrowed from the Embassy; but another car was following at a distance bringing four Assault Guards. At the corner nearest to the office the second car stopped and concealed itself, the guards having instructions to watch for the moment of his departure for the University City and then to follow and act at their own discretion.

In his office Lance had his usual daily meeting with the Committee, with the fierce arguments that had now become almost a routine. Lance, however, was in his most cheerful mood. The meeting wore on but, to his disappointment, no mention was made of the proposed visit to the University City. He gave them every opportunity, but they would not rise to the bait of his hints.

This was maddening. Were the comrades funking it? It was raining and he knew that the road gangs would not be at work and the site would be deserted; a nice day for the job. "Well, if they are not going to make a move," he thought, "I jolly well shall." Rising to leave the room, he said light-heartedly:

46

"Comrades, I must be off now to see how that *Ciudad Universitario* job is getting on. Would anyone like to come with me?"

Silence. The aggressive looks of a moment ago slipped from their faces. They looked sheepishly down at the table.

Lance smiled his sweetest. "You, Comrade Varela, won't you come? I'd like your advice."

The *peon* addressed, who was familiar with the practical side of the job, and who was known to have been at the café meeting, said not a word.

With a still more cordial smile, Lance turned to the vicious little Swiss Anarchist chairman.

"And you, comrade? It would be convenient if you could be there to give whatever orders are necessary."

"Comrade," replied the Swiss acidly, his knuckles white with anger as he clenched his fists on the table, "we are far too busy to waste time on such unimportant matters."

Nevertheless, hoping perhaps that there might be a reception committee waiting for him at the other end, Lance went out on his inspection, alone, duly followed by the Assault Guards. Nothing happened. "A darned tame affair," thought Lance. Possibly the Committee wanted the moral and physical support of the road gangs; or possibly they had been tipped off that the Security Police had overheard their plot. But they never tried that game on again.

Shortly afterwards, as the Communists began to obtain the ascendancy over the Anarchists, the vicious little Swiss chairman mysteriously disappeared; and two years later, when Lance himself was in prison, he found him there too.

# CHAPTER FIVE

# THE DEATH PITS

MARGERY HILL, who from the first was one of the most active in giving succour to those in distress, and who already had taken into the sanctuary of her little hospital some young people whose fathers had been murdered, and others whose own lives were in danger, had some friends called Asensio. The family consisted of two girls of about nineteen and eighteen, Maria and Salud, a younger brother, Manolo; some elderly aunts and an uncle. They lived a quiet life in a beautifully appointed flat and were altogether very charming people. The girls were dark, good-looking, well-dressed and *soignées* in the manner of Spanish women. Like most others of their kind, they were prisoners in their own darkened home, unable to stir abroad for fear of death or violence.

Soon after the troubles broke out Margery Hill telephoned Lance to ask if he would call on them to cheer them up. He did so, taking some food with him, and found them in a state of great anxiety because their brother Manolo, who was only sixteen or seventeen, had been seized and thrown into prison. Lance did his best to cheer them up and then went straight off to see his friend the chief of the *Seguridad,* who gave him certain advice. Before very long, to the great delight of the Asensio family, Lance was able to inform them that he had been given a promise of Manolo's release. This was a quite exceptional achievement, for, once a man was firmly behind prison bars, it was extremely difficult to secure his release.

Late one stifling afternoon a day or two later Lance was surprised to be told by Petra that the porter of the Asensios' flats had called to see him. When they met, the *portero* said:

"Señor, the señoritas have sent me to ask if you will please go round to them as soon as possible."

Lance merely nodded and said cheerfully: "Very well, tell them I shall come without delay."

Wondering what could be the reason for such a summons, he went round almost immediately, walking through the dead streets, now littered with every kind of rubbish, past the ranks of close-shuttered, sightless houses. Reaching the Asensios' flat he found the two girls in the dim and musty drawing-room, to which daylight and fresh air had now for some weeks been denied and in which only a weak electric light shed its uncertain rays. Lance, on entering, greeted the two girls with his usual cheerfulness but found them both in a mood of great distress. Salud, the younger, spoke for them.

"Captain Lance," she said, "we are in terrible trouble and anxiety about Manolo."

"About Manolo, Salud? But they have promised to release him."

"They have not done so and we fear something dreadful may have happened."

Lance was filled with sudden misgiving. He said: "Tell me all you know."

"We know very little. Only that a person from Paracuellos del Jarama, a village about eight miles away, came to us this morning"—Salud's voice sank almost to a whisper—"and told us that he thought Manolo had been buried there last night. He saw a big grave and a lot of bodies and he thought Manolo was among them."

Lance was shocked. "I don't understand that, after they had promised to release him. What can I do to help you?"

"Will you go out to Paracuellos, Captain Lance, and find out if it is true?"

"Certainly I will go there for you, but how am I to find out if he is buried? I do not know Manolo."

"If you will ask the local people, I think they will know. You see, we have no one else to help us. We cannot ask any Spaniard to go, for fear he may get killed too. But you are British and will come to no harm."

Lance, recalling the saying that the British were supposed to be bullet-proof, was not so sure and did not at all like the assignment, but even to think of resisting such a plea was not in his nature. He felt a fearful drag at his heart as he contemplated the

49

two girls, very pale, very appealing. The elegant room, shrouded in the pale gloom from the drawn blinds and the closed shutters, took on a deeper obscurity as melancholy and dejection seemed to cloud its outlines. In that heavy moment Lance's resolve instinctively hardened. He asked the girls for a detailed description of their brother, promised them he would do all he could and took an uneasy leave.

Very early next morning, dreading what he was expecting to find, he drove out north-eastward to the village, which stood on high ground just beyond the Jarama. The sun was only just up, a milky opalescence suffusing the sky, and the air was agreeably cool. The countryside wore a mask of quietness and peace, with no barriers on the road, no armed gangs, no signs of disorder. But all was barren, colourless and broken with grey rocky outcrops and the village itself, like others of the countryside, was stark and forbidding with its harsh granite hovels, its cobbled street, its dirt and its smells.

Not a soul was to be seen. Lance drove slowly into the silent village, stopped his car close to the church and got out. There he met a wrinkled, nut-brown peasant, smelling strongly of garlic, who looked at him sombrely at first, but his initial distrust modified when he saw the Union Jack and the British brassard. Lance greeted him cheerfully and, after an initial triviality, asked him if there had been any shooting there.

Still with some caution, the peasant replied: "Not here, señor."

"Somewhere near?"

"Yes, not far."

"Do you know where they were buried?"

"Oh yes, I helped to dig the grave. I was ordered to do so by the young men, señor."

"Will you show me?"

The peasant agreed and, as the sun rose with orange light, they made their way down a cart-track away from the church, through dry dusty fields in which the chickpeas had been harvested. Round a bend in the track Lance was brought up sharply at a long, low mound. He drew in his breath sharply as the peasant said:

"There it is, señor."

As he gazed at it in consternation, several questions generated in Lance's mind. He asked:

"Were you present at the burial?"

"Yes, señor; I helped to fill in the grave."

"How deep is it?"

"Not very deep. We had to dig it in a hurry."

"Are the bodies in a single row?"

"Oh, no; they are three or four deep. Just thrown in."

Pacing the length of the mound and allowing for three bodies deep, Lance calculated that at least forty men must lie beneath that sinister barrow of freshly turned earth. He kept his angry feelings to himself, not knowing where the peasant's sympathies lay. In a matter-of-fact way, he gave the peasant a description of Manolo Asensio and asked if he had noticed a body answering to that description. The peasant nodded slowly and said that he was pretty certain of it—"a young aristocrat" of whom he had taken note because he was younger than the others and well-dressed.

Deeply shocked, Lance decided to pursue the matter further.

"Show me," he said, "where the shooting took place."

The peasant took him on a little further until they reached a road through hard, sandy soil. They turned down this a little way until they came to a long, narrow excavation along the side of the road about ten feet high, from which gravel had been dug.

"There you are, señor."

Lance pulled up short, horror-struck. Along the full 200 yards of the gravel pit, at a height of about 4 feet 6 inches there ran a channel, some 6 inches wide, deeply scored in the earth, as though some rough hand had passed down its length and, with a ragged gouge or chisel, had ripped out a running groove.

To Lance's eye the meaning of that sinister groove was at once evident. Nothing but machine-gun or automatic rifle bullets could have so eaten away that ragged channel—machine-guns fired not once, but traversed over and over again at the height of a man's breast. Clearly there had been many other shootings at this dreadful death-pit.

Sadly Dagger Lance walked back to the car and returned to Madrid. How was he to break the shocking news to the Asensio girls? Should he funk it, and tell them that he had not been able to discover anything?

Better not to prolong their agony, however. Tell them and get it over.

There was a terrible scene. The girls broke down completely. Almost equally distressed, Lance was relieved to be able to escape. The whole episode and the girls' distress made the deepest possible impression on him. The callousness of such barbarous mass-murders shook him to the heart. It was, as he said to Margery Hill afterwards, "an absolute eye-opener to me". He began to ask himself if there was a way in which he could circumvent these abominations. How could he help these unhappy people living in constant fear?

The sympathies of the British community in Madrid at large, with very few exceptions, inclined quite definitely towards the Right. Though they naturally took no part in Spanish politics, the administrative incompetence, the unchecked lawlessness and the religious persecutions of the Popular Front disposed them inevitably towards the other direction. Now the savage excesses of the armed gangs aroused humanitarian feelings that were above and apart from politics. They would have felt the same if the rôles of the Spanish parties had been reversed. Lance was of the same mind. Margery Hill said of him:

"Christopher was a very warm-hearted and compassionate man, and he always responded instantly to any call for help, without hesitation. He would jump up in the middle of the night to answer an appeal and nothing put him off. He rather liked playing with fire and the risk that he might get his fingers burnt only added to the zest."

Lance was now about to begin playing with fire.

The thing moved step by step. Lance had learnt from the peasant that the shootings took place usually at about midnight, but that the corpses were not buried at once. Determined to learn more about these events, he drove out from home next morning while it was still dark and arrived at the gravel pit as day was breaking. It was very cold and there in the gloom at the side of the road lay twenty-five corpses, one of them a middle-aged woman. They had been shot all over the body and arms but for the greater part at breast height and, after falling, wounded or dead, had been finished off, like so much cattle, by a revolver bullet fired close up to the head. Thus the heads had been blown away completely on one side or at the back. This revolver shot, he learnt later, had become general practice, not as a so-called *coup de grace*, but because at earlier shootings some victims who had fallen merely wounded had feigned death and crept away in the night after the assassination squad had gone home. It was later to become general practice also among Japanese, Chinese and some Europeans of the more brutal sort.

The gruesome spectacle filled Lance with anger. Many questions raced through his head. Why were these mass murders perpetrated clandestinely by night? Who was responsible for them? Where did the victims come from and how were they brought to the slaughter-pit? Were there any more such places of abomination? What could he, Christopher Lance, a foreigner, do about it?

Driving his car further on in the half-dark, he stopped and kept watch from a little way off. Soon after daylight he saw a truck drive up and stop at the gravel pit. Three men jumped out, let down the tailboard of the truck and threw the corpses in, like so many carcases of meat piled on top of one another. The truck then drove off and Lance followed at a cautious distance.

To his surprise, the corpses were not taken at once to a burial pit, as Manolo and his fellow victims had been, but to a building in Madrid, where they were unloaded and carried in. Seeing people go in and out without hindrance, he went in himself and discovered it to be an extempore mortuary.

Inside, the spectacle that confronted his eyes was enough to test the stomach of the most callous and cold-hearted mortal. Some eighty corpses lay on the floor, sprawling in unseemly disorder, all killed in the same way, bullet-ridden all over their bodies by untrained marksmen, their heads a mass of coagulated blood and scarcely to be recognized. Nearly all were males. The place stank unspeakably. A photographer was going round, taking exposures of each corpse, while a few men and women, in every condition of misery and dejection, were picking their way among the mutilated carcases.

53

Lance's first reaction was to recoil with horror and nausea. Quelling these instinctive emotions, he was overcome with anger and refrained only with the greatest difficulty from bursting out into violent protest at the barbaric scene. That would not help. Instead, collecting himself, he cautiously questioned a man in a boiler-suit who appeared to be attached to the place and, his British armband a shield against suspicion, was told readily enough:

"Oh, yes, comrade. These are all criminals who have been executed. We show them here for twenty-four hours, so that they may be claimed by their relatives. We must be fair, you see."

"Do you tell the relatives to come and search?"

"Oh, no; we can't do that, because we have no idea who these dead persons are. But the relatives generally know all right when to come, you know."

"Can they take away the bodies of their relatives?"

"Certainly, comrade."

"What happens if they are not claimed in twenty-four hours?"

"They are all cleared out and disposed of, to make room for the next lot."

"I see. Very interesting. What's the photographer for?"

"Oh, he's from the police. If a body is not claimed in the time, all the relative has to do is to go and inspect the photographs at the *Seguridad* headquarters. It is all very correct, you see, comrade."

"Very correct indeed," thought Lance sarcastically. He made his way out of the abominable charnel-house in savage mood.

He was going to follow this thing through as far as he could. It gave him at least one idea—that he could spare widows the agony of these ghoulish searches by undertaking them himself. That was little enough, but it was something. It was obvious from the mutilated faces, however, that, except for anyone whom he might know personally, it was essential to have a description of the clothes likely to have been worn, the shoes and the colour and quality of the hair.

He reflected, however, that to search the mortuaries would not help in those cases where the victims were buried directly after

54

shooting, as Manolo had been. In such cases, the only way to obtain information would be to visit the shooting sites themselves. A bloody and a risky business, but he would attempt it if he had to do so. Again he asked himself: why were these shootings done at night and why, also, were not all the dead taken to the mortuaries?

He continued to follow up his enquiries and soon obtained a reply to some of his questions from the Chief of Police himself. He paid a call on the Chief and asked to see the photographs of the "executions", which were, in any case, open to public inspection. There they were, in a public room, all neatly filed and numbered in several volumes, though how anyone could be expected to recognize some of those shattered and blood-obscured features he found it difficult to tell. "Passports for corpses", reflected Lance grimly. What staggered him most, however, over and above the cold-heartedness of the whole business, was to find that already, in mid-August, after only a month, the record of slaughters had reached a fearful total of more than 10,000.

He took the Chief of Police out for a more informative talk.

"Of course, we know all about these 'executions' *mi capitán*," he was told; "in fact, we provide the lorries to take away the bodies."

"Then, why are they done at night? Sounds suspicious."

"Not really. You see, these executions are not strictly authorized and the comrades who carry them out naturally want to remain anonymous and unrecognized. We could always interfere if they went too far, but actually they are doing our work for us. And, of course, it is part of our normal duties to collect any dead bodies that are found anywhere and convey them to the public mortuaries."

Lance wondered at what point the *Seguridad* would think that the self-appointed executioners had "gone too far". He made some non-committal remark and asked:

"Of course, I expect you know that sometimes the bodies are buried by the firing squads themselves?"

"Certainly."

"Why do they do that?"

"Just because sometimes the comrades think that they may

55

have been over-zealous or perhaps made some mistake in the heat of the moment."

"What you call 'going a bit too far', you mean?"

"Perhaps, but it saves us a great deal of trouble, you know. We have quite enough to do."

"So there is no record of those? No photographs?"

"No, no trace. We haven't time to go digging up dead Fascists, you know!"

That night, Lance obtained some confirmation of this curious story. The word of what he was doing had begun to be whispered round among the Nationalists like a "bush telegraph". He began to get other requests, sometimes at second-hand, sometimes directly from some agonized wife or mother. This day a woman entirely unknown to him telephoned to entreat his help. Her son had disappeared and was believed to have been seized by one of the gangs. Lance promised his help, as he invariably did, and obtained a description of her son and of how he was dressed.

Pursuing his line of information, he drove out at midnight northward along the Burgos road and, a few miles out of Madrid, turned down a sunken lane, driving slowly with his headlights full on. As he rounded a curve, the cutting became deeper and his headlights fell full upon a sinister scene that he was never to forget. Clearly revealed in the white beams of his lamps, a long line of men was ranged against the bank of the road, their faces a line of white masks facing outward to the road. They were about to be murdered. Opposite them were several armed men and on the road stood a truck.

At the approach of his car one of the armed men apparently gave an order to the unhappy victims, for they all turned round, backs to the road. At the same time one of the militiamen lifted the bonnet of the truck and several others clustered round him, obviously putting on an act that they were attending to a breakdown. Quite a clever ruse, thought Lance, but not quite clever enough.

Still with his headlights full on, he drove up slowly and stopped alongside the lorry. Stretching his hand out of the car window with fist clenched in the Communist salute, he called out:

"*Salud, camaradas,* do you want any help?"

They all eyed him speculatively, observing the Union Jack, and one of them replied:

"No, comrade, we can soon fix it."

"You bet," thought Lance grimly. He drove very slowly on, examining as closely as he could, in the light of the headlamps, the clothing of the victims whose backs were turned to him. He did not recognize the man he looked for. "Poor chaps," he thought, "I wish to God I could butt in and stop it all."

Clearly, however, intervention was quite out of the question. He could achieve nothing whatever and would merely be himself added to the number of the victims. He drove on for about half a mile, turned round, and drove back a little way with his lights off. He had scarcely stopped again before the stillness of the night was shattered by the prolonged drumming of machine-gun fire, ended by one ragged burst. Lance gripped the steering wheel, tight-lipped. A minute later came the crack-crack-crack-crack as the backs or sides of the victims' heads were blown off by revolver. He could sit still no longer, but got out of the car, pacing up and down swiftly, suffused with wrath. It was all done, he supposed, by the headlights of the truck, which he could distantly see were on.

After ten minutes or so he saw the lights of the truck move on and after a short interval he followed and stopped at the slaughter-pit. There lay the corpses—thirty-one of them—those who had been killed outright by the machine-guns lying face down, those who had been only wounded, until the revolver came along, twisted in the various piteous attitudes of death. The man whom Lance sought was not among them. He returned to Madrid for a stiff whisky and the following day told Ogilvie-Forbes all about it.

Since these shootings were now pretty common knowledge, Forbes was not wholly surprised by what Lance had to tell him, but there had been hitherto little reliable first-hand evidence. It was important that the British Government at home should have as much accurate information as possible to assist them in determining their own attitude and to deal with the charges and counter-charges being made by Conservatives and Socialists in the House of Commons, many of whom were eager to intervene on one side or the other in an affair that was none of their business.

Forbes, therefore, asked Lance to pursue the matter and obtain as much reliable information as he could on the number of these mass murders. This entirely fitted in with Lance's present purpose. More and more people, most of them entire strangers, were asking for his help in finding lost relatives. The gratitude of such people when he succeeded in finding the bodies was as touching as the searches were agonizing, although the sole satisfaction for the unhappy relative was confirmation of the death and the knowledge that the dead person was now out of misery. Though removal of the corpse from a mortuary was permitted, in no case of Lance's was the corpse ever in fact removed, for means of transport were almost unobtainable and decent disposal impossible. Since all religious observances were now illegal, burial with benefit of clergy was out of the question. All that could be done, and was always done, was for the bereaved person to seek such consolation as lay in prayer, in which Lance always silently joined.

These were very agonizing and emotional moments for Lance and placed a great strain upon both his nervous and his physical energies; for he was now out nearly every night after long and exhausting days in the torrid heat, days in which he was unceasingly occupied either in the affairs of his business or in relieving distress. No longer for him the relaxation of the siesta in the sun's fiercest hours.

The discovery of those two slaughter-pits quickly led to that of others. Of the grass bank behind the Prado Museum, Lance already knew. From Margery Hill he heard of nightly shooting a few hundred yards from the hospital and this information led him to discover a shooting-pit at an excavated bank where the Stadium had been built. Yet another was quite close in the New University, where the site used was an excavation for a building under construction. Thus there were five that Lance kept under observation, going out almost every night and visiting the mortuaries nearly every day, but, as the slaughters were going on at the rate of 2,500 a week, there must have been many more of these sites in other sectors of the city. The lorries full of corpses were always to be seen in the very early mornings, driving about quite openly, with the corpses piled high above the tail-board like slaughtered sheep.

He very soon learnt, when coming upon a massacre about to take place, not to get out of the car. On the first occasion that he did so the wretched victims were hustled back into the lorries by which they had been brought. It was important that Lance should visit the shooting sites themselves, as he could never know whether the bodies were to be brought into a mortuary or buried nearby, as being cases when the assassins had "gone a bit too far". One of the worst of these sites was the Stadium one, where the long mounds gave monstrous evidence of the deeds. For the more official evidence that Ogilvie-Forbes required, Lance was able to estimate the number of victims by measurement. For the rest, the numbers of the "passports for corpses" in the *Seguridad* office gave irrefutable evidence.

In November, when the Civil War had been on for only three and a half months, the Republican newspapers announced that the number of corpses received into the mortuaries of Madrid had reached the horrifying total of 35,000. A year later, just after Lance had disappeared from the scene, the British, American and French Governments made an agreed estimate that the total had risen to 60,000, a very large proportion of them being working-class people. The Stadium and the New University sites were two of the most notorious and at Paracuellos uncountable thousands were buried in common pits. Figures for other parts of Republican Spain were equally bad in proportion.

Nor was Franco's side blameless. Though the killings there had often the appearance at least of being officially authorized, and not perpetrated by free-ranging gangs, yet his victories were too often marred by revengeful and needless fusillades. At almost every village through which his forces passed on their way up from the south, his Civil Guards would call upon the *responsable* or *alcalde* and order: "Give us the names of ten people to be shot."

Indeed, the numbers of Spaniards who were done to death by the various methods of butchery in the war far exceeded the numbers of those killed in battle. Lázaro, the Anarchist stonemason and militia captain, who was head of the Madrid Cheka, operating in the Fine Arts Club, himself sentenced 6,000 persons to death on political grounds.

To move from the passive attitude of identifying dead bodies to the more positive one of saving the living from death was obviously but a mere step. But how much more difficult a one! To appeal to any Government official or to such law as still existed in Madrid was out of the question, since the murders had tacit approval in the "war against Fascism". It was all part of the Communist (and Fascist) pattern and programme, by means of which terror ensures subservience. Lance set out even more diligently to get on friendly terms with everyone he could among the Republicans, from high Government officials down to any militiamen he met, and particularly with the Security Police.

He wanted first of all to discover the sources of supply of this enormous quantity of machine-gun fodder and it was on another visit to the Asensios that he got the glimmer of a hint which led him finally on to the right path.

What the Asensio girls told him on this visit was that their brother Manolo had apparently been officially released from prison on the very night that he had been shot. This they had only recently heard themselves and the news set Lance busy speculating afresh. This report was certainly worth checking, for it might lead somewhere positive. Why shoot a prisoner who had just been released?

Without delay he drove out to the San Anton prison. His car was wearing the Union Flag and his brassard was on his arm. The usual boiler-suited guards were lounging at the entrance and in the hall, where a clerk was sitting at a desk.

As soon as he stepped inside, Lance sensed a hostile atmosphere. The sullen guards made no response to his usual breezy salutation. He therefore spoke somewhat briskly to the desk official, saying:

"I have come from the British Embassy, to which I am an attaché, and I should be grateful if I might have a word with the Governor. Please tell him that it is rather urgent."

After having been first asked to wait, Lance was taken, with no more words than were essential, to the Governor's office and as he entered it he saw the Governor get up from behind a desk. He beheld an athletic figure, six feet tall, with well-cut features, but of a cold, cruel and antipathetic aspect. His greasy hair went with heavy, half-open eyelids and hard and sensual mouth.

The two men having formally introduced themselves, Lance went straight to the point in a business-like way. Feigning ignorance of Manolo's death, he said:

"I have come to enquire how young Asensio is getting on. A nice boy. I always liked him and should like to see him now if I may."

"Asensio?" The Governor's manner was coldly formal. "He was released two or three weeks ago."

"Indeed! That's odd! I should have thought he would have come to see me. Do you know where he went after release?"

"No, that is no business of mine."

"When did you say he was released? Could you tell me which day?"

"One moment; I will see."

The Governor reached for a file and, as Lance expected, confirmed the fact that the date of the boy's release was the same as that of his death. He thanked the Governor and took his leave.

Musing on these strange facts on his way home, he reflected that several others of his cases had been in prison before their assassination. Why on earth had he not asked himself the significance of such a fact earlier?

In Madrid were several prisons, both permanent prisons built as such and temporary ones converted from the suppressed monasteries, convents and seminaries to house the enormous number of men and women being detained without trial. These prisoners were not common criminals but almost exclusively men and women imprisoned for political reasons of some sort. In a place where Communists were in the ascendant, Anarchists were imprisoned. Where the Anarchists held sway, they similarly locked up, or shot, the Communists. Virtually the only "criminal" acts were political ones. In Madrid, the great majority of the prisoners at that time, living in the most revolting conditions, were known or supposed sympathizers of the right wing, of all classes, and directors, managers and humbler people labelled as "stooges of capitalism".

Pressing this line of thought, Lance sought again his friend the Chief of Police, and from him he learnt the horrifying fact that whenever the Government, or the police themselves, or a trade union, wanted to be rid of one of the prisoners, but did not like to accept responsibility for official execution without trial, they would order his "release". The releases were always made at night and as soon as the unfortunate man left the prison doors he was pounced upon by the waiting militiamen, who had also been deliberately informed, and carried off to the death truck waiting at a rendezvous. Very often these "releases" were made at the demand of the militiamen themselves. Not all the prison staffs, by any means, were accomplices of the murderous militiamen. Indeed, warders from the Model Prison, at great risk to themselves, sent a secret delegation to the British Embassy reporting that illegal seizures of prisoners were taking place after nightfall, which they were powerless to prevent owing to collusion between the murderous gangs and the military guards at the prison gates.

All this information immediately gave Lance an idea. He felt tremendously elated and went off to see Margery Hill at her hospital, as he often did. He was grinning broadly as he made his way upstairs, past the loitering militiamen on the ground floor, and she said:

"You are very cheerful today, Christopher."

"I've got an idea, in which I want your help."

She waited for him to talk on.

"It's about these prison releases. How can we find out when a chap is going to be let out?"

She thought a moment. "Why do you want to know?"

"Because if I could get in before these thugs get their hands on them, I believe I could get them away."

"It sounds a wonderful idea, but fearfully risky."

"I think I can get away with it. Anyhow, I'm going to have a shot, provided we can find out when any release is due."

"Well, I suppose the *Seguridad* would know, but we could hardly ask them, you know."

"I'm not so sure. Look here, Margery, you know that little

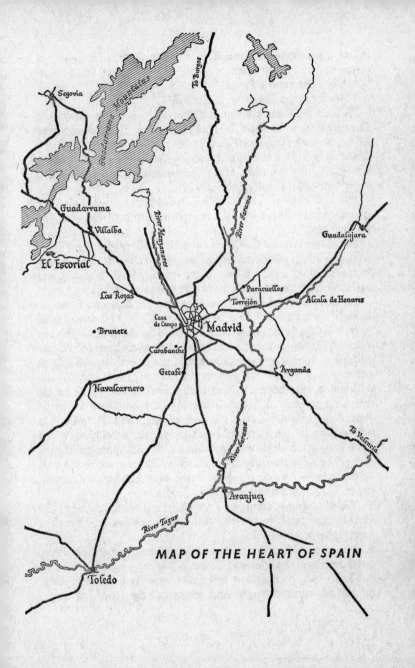

MAP OF THE HEART OF SPAIN

fellow at the *Seguridad* who often comes up here to have a cup of coffee and a cigarette with you—the smart, cheerful little fellow who looks like Sancho Panza?"

"You mean the one they call Carlos?"

"That's the chap. He thinks the world of you, you know, and I'm sure he is to be trusted. He often gives me the odd wink, and I'll bet he knows quite well what you're up to."

Margery smiled at this reference to the refugees to whom she was giving shelter, right under the noses of the militiamen. "I expect they all do, really," she said.

"Well, I think he is on our side and doesn't approve of all these horrors. He is the lad for us. Let's get him up here and then you put it to him."

So it was arranged. Carlos, a dark, well set-up, intelligent fellow, with a round and happy face, joined them a day or two later. He could not have been more helpful. Yes, he said, it was perfectly true that he often knew the names of people who were about to be released, and if there was anyone in whom Lance or Miss Hill were interested he was quite willing to let them know.

A few days later, while Madrid stifled in the heat of the last week of August, Lance had his first news of an intended release and made a cursory reconnaissance of the prison. It was a large convent, commandeered and converted to prison use. A few militiamen were hanging about at the door. Having made up his mind, he went back a little later, in a car borrowed from the Embassy, and left it outside the door of the prison. He walked in with a cheerful air, wearing his armband, and found himself in a large hall, in which there was a counter. Several more militiamen and police were standing about casually. He went up to the man at the counter, making a great show of a bundle of Embassy papers that he had brought with him, and said:

"Good morning, comrade, I am Captain Lance, attaché at the British Embassy. I've come to take 'Rodriguez' away. There has been an order for his release."

The man at the counter was perfectly civil, but did not know anything about the release.

"Then be a good fellow and make enquiries; I'm certain his release has come through. And please tell the Governor that I

64

Pepe Jurado

Lance's flat in the Embassy annexe after the bombing

should like a word with him if he can spare a few minutes."

While he waited, Lance wandered about the hall, chatting inconsequentially to the guards in his slow, deep voice. He wanted to make himself prominent so that he should be known again, deliberately behaving with breezy cheerfulness and quite unlike a Spaniard. The Governor appeared quite soon—a tubby, black-haired man who was very civil.

"That is quite right, *mi capitán*," he said to Lance, "I have had an order for the release of Rodriguez, but have not yet informed the staff. I will give orders for him to be sent for at once."

There followed a long wait of half an hour or more. Lance was feeling very much on edge, wondering if he could pull the thing off, but he put on his most cheerful air and took advantage of the delay to fraternize further with the comrades, talking "right off the point", away from the war, trying to make them laugh—seldom an easy achievement with the average Spaniard under such conditions. After a time there appeared in the background a figure with a brown paper parcel under his arm, white-faced and visibly trembling with fear. Lance said to one of the guards:

"Is that Rodriguez?"

They replied affirmatively and Lance called out:

"Come along, Rodriguez!"

After a parting salutation to the guards, he walked boldly out of the door, followed by the shrinking Rodriguez, who clearly thought that he was going to his death. As soon as they were outside Lance said:

"You are quite safe. Get in the car quickly."

The astonished fellow almost fell into his seat, dazed, uncomprehending and incredulous. As they moved off, Lance said:

"I am from the British Embassy. I am going to take you to safety. Tell me quickly the address of a friend who will be willing to shelter you. *Not* your own home."

Looking at him, wide-eyed, Rodriguez said after a long pause:

"It is not true; it is a trap."

"Pull yourself together, man; hurry up and tell me where to take you. Look at my flag!"

Not until they got to the address that he at last gave did Rodriguez believe his extraordinary good fortune. He was a perfectly blameless bank clerk with a wife and three children somewhere, starving and in despair. He had not seen the sun, which now beat down on him so fiercely, for more than a month. Lance took the opportunity of gaining what information he could about existence inside the prison and learnt that everyone there knew only too well what was meant by "release" and that in the atmosphere of fear in which they all lived, "release" was the one word they feared most.

Lance returned highly elated and later told the news to Margery. "Thank God he is free; that's one life saved," he said. Ogilvie-Forbes, that same night in his flat over a dram of whisky, said:

"Take care you don't get that big nose of yours into trouble."

Lance grinned. "If I do, I shall know you are there to bail me out."

"I couldn't bail you out, my dear fellow, if you got bumped off. Have another dram."

Within the next ten days or so Lance secured the release of four or five more men from the same prison. On each occasion, in order that the custodians should treat his applications as a matter of course, he used the simple opening formula: "Good morning, comrade, I have come for so-and-so." He released another man from another prison, and yet another from the evil place where Manolo Asensio had been imprisoned. He never returned any of those he rescued to their own homes, but always to some place of hiding where the man was not likely to be sought. He felt quietly satisfied that he was now actually saving lives. He was acting perfectly legitimately for men officially released. But he was now to take a more dangerous step.

This time he was asked to rescue a prisoner for whom no release had been authorized. The request came from Señor Escolano, a director of Marconi's, who was greatly concerned for the life of one of his technical men, the Syndicalists having decided to demand his release for the benefit of the firing squads. Lance was completely taken aback. It was a damned dangerous thing to ask of a man. Was Escolano a secret left-winger, trying to trap him? But he hesitated for only a fraction of a second; he never could, and never did, say no to any appeal.

66

It was useless, however, to attempt to get an official release and Lance therefore resolved upon the extremely risky step of getting Señor C out by bluff.

Employing his usual tactics he walked in to the prison, gave a cheerful greeting to the guards, who now knew him well, went up to the custodian of the counter and said:

"*Salud, camarada.* I've come for another 'body'. It's Señor C this time. Will you get hold of him and I'll take him off. Don't be long, as I'm in a bit of a hurry."

They complied without a murmur, taking it as a matter of course and not even referring it to the Governor. Out came Señor C while Lance was joking with the guards. Lance hurried him away as quickly as he could to the hiding place arranged, feeling very ill at ease, and he never went back to that prison again. Later, when he had elaborated his more daring escape plans, he got Señor C clean away out of the country.

One step followed another. These rescues from prison, Lance realized, must have a limited scope, for obviously the militiamen would not indefinitely allow themselves to be robbed of their prey. Better than getting people out of jail, therefore, was to save them from getting in. He found what could be done when the wife of one of his own workmen came to him in tears to say that her husband had been arrested. Without a moment's delay, he went straight off to the *comisaria*, where people were interrogated before being actually put in jail, and tackled the officials with persuasive forcefulness. What was the charge? What had the man done? What was the evidence? There must have been some mistake and the man ought to be released pending further enquiry. Triumphantly he took his man away, free.

The news of what he could do spread like wildfire. More and more wives and mothers, of all classes, came or telephoned for his help. Appeals soon became a daily occurrence, but he never said: "I'll come later," and always responded instantly—in the middle of the night, in the middle of a meal, dropping anything else on which he might be engaged, however desperately tired he might be. When, in the middle of a conference on hospital affairs with Margery Hill and Eric Glaisher, a boy came running in to say that their home was being raided, Lance instantly got up to go, saying to the others: "You can't leave these things; a moment's delay may be fatal."

The *comisaria* of Bella Vista came to know him well and over and over again he got his man away. He soon learnt not to take him home, for the police simply came again the next day and rearrested the man. When he had exhausted his own resources, he took his refugees to one or other of the foreign embassies, most of which, of whatever political colour, were prepared to give shelter to anyone threatened by the barbarities of that murderous régime.

# CHAPTER SIX

# IN THE BAG

AUGUST passed and September had nearly run its course. The end of summer brought a kinder climate but no kindness in the savagery of the civil conflict. Largo Caballero had become Republican Prime Minister, vigorously prodded by the Russians, and Franco was about to be proclaimed Generalissimo and "Head of State" of the Nationalist forces, in preference to Mola. The war began to take a definite shape, with typical Spanish lethargy, neither side anxious to fight during the sacred hours of luncheon and siesta. The Nationalist forces were still extremely small and the various independent Republican forces still disunited, untrained, going their own ways and imperceptive of the difference between a war and the ways of guerilla banditry so long traditional in Spain. In Madrid, the populace had little idea of the military situation, for the Government press and radio services were more concerned with propaganda than with fact.

But the tension increased. The savage shootings continued. A tighter grip was taken by the *Seguridad* and the Secret Military Intelligence, the dreaded S.I.M., moulded on the Russian Ogpu and known even among Republican Spaniards as the Gestapo. Food became still scarcer, lentils, dried beans, bread and oranges becoming before long almost the only diet obtainable. The Nationalists stepped up their bombing attacks and in one of these Lance's flat was so severely damaged, while Petra was in it, by a bomb that demolished the block of flats opposite, that it became uninhabitable. At Ogilvie-Forbes invitation, Lance moved into a flat in the British Embassy, regretfully saying goodbye to the faithful Petra. He found at the Embassy a valuable new friend and adherent in fierce old Dolores, of the caretaker staff, who, however terrifying she might be to other people, became entirely devoted to Lance. So also did Miguel, the doorkeeper, who, in those dangerous days, developed a shrewd technique in the lightning opening and closing of the doors.

His scope for useful work for Gines Navarro and Sons, though they had large contracts with the Government, became less and less as the control of labour degenerated further. Lance, however, had still the responsibilities which his conscience imposed upon him. He therefore made frequent visits to the works that were supposed to be in progress, if only to ensure that the firm's gear and equipment were not jeopardized, either by falling into the hands of the advancing Nationalists or by irresponsible action on the part of some village Soviet.

It was not long before these trips suggested themselves to him as a means of looking for escape routes for those people who were living in fear or distress. He knew from the very outset that any such projects were confronted with many difficulties.

To enable himself to move about freely, Lance therefore took calculated steps to arm himself with a very impressive pass. Issued by the Public Works Department (*Obras Publicas*), it was stamped also by the Embassy and Consulate, by at least six workmen's syndicates and by the War Office, where he found the basement full of Russian General Staff officers under General Goriev, who had arrived in September and had begun at once unobtrusively to dominate Republic military councils. Very few of the innumerable sentries to be found everywhere could read and Lance knew full well that the really impressive thing was to have numerous rubber stamps and plenty of red ink endorsements.

Armed with this, he set out on a series of visits to different parts of the country to the North and the West of Madrid, swanning about the countryside in grey flannels and sports shirt, his flag on the car's bonnet, making each trip a picnic, and sometimes driving along until he found himself being shot at by the Nationalists, for the Republicans never seemed to know where their enemy was until he reached the outposts. To get away from the strained and morbid air of Madrid was in itself a relief and he found the militiamen at the front much better company than those at the back—an experience common to all wars. He got on well with such men—usually simple, friendly and likeable people in their normal relations. On these trips he was often accompanied by Bobby Papworth, whom he found a cheerful and stout-hearted companion.

His problem, of course, was to find a secure way through the Nationalist lines, but no one knew where the Nationalist lines were, as the Government's announcements on the progress of military events were so disingenuous and chiefly concerned just then in whipping up hate over the Nationalist shootings at Badajos. All that was known of the military situation, broadly speaking, was that Franco was slowly creeping up over the parched fields and the dust-clouded roads from the south by way of Cadiz, Seville and Merida, thence turning inwards up the Tagus valley towards Talavera on the way to Madrid, and that Mola, coming from the North and East, was threatening the mountain gates of the Guardarramas.

In fact, Franco, with a tiny force of only 6,200 troops and a few irregulars, occupied Talavera, scene of Wellington's great victory, on September 3. Then, after spending 19 days in covering the 23 miles to Maqueda, only 46 miles from Madrid, he made a tactical mistake, allowing himself to be diverted for sentimental reasons south-eastward to Toledo. The diversion was to provide him with an occasion to meet Christopher Lance, but to lose him Madrid.

Toledo, city of ancient kings, of El Greco and of swordsmiths, rising in tawny and dramatic splendour from the enclosing brown arms of the Tagus, was at that time the scene of one of the most spectacular episodes of the war. Here a mixed thousand of soldiers, cadets of the Military Academy, Civil Guards and civilians, declaring for the Nationalist uprising, had shut themselves up in the Alcázar, the antique fort that overlooked the Tagus, under the command of Colonel Moscardó. The Republicans, who held the town all about, had seized his seventeen-year-old son and, in the traditional fashion of banditry, had sent Moscardó an ultimatum that unless he surrendered the fort his son would be shot. They even put the boy himself on the telephone to speak to his father, but with calm deliberation Moscardó replied: "My dear son, I order you to die like a hero, calling out: 'Long live Spain and Christ the King!' "

Invested at close quarters, bombed, shelled and mined, suffering severe deprivations, the garrison had been holding out for over two months when, towards the end of September, Lance, knowing nothing whatever of the military situation, visited Toledo. He was combining a half-hearted inspection of some work near by with a rather more genuine reconnaissance for an escape route and, to be quite candid, with a still more genuine searching for adventure for its own sake. He was driving a large Ford and Bobby Papworth was with him.

A mile or so outside the town they were halted at a barricade and a sentry of the Republican forces, having been duly satisfied with their impressive pass, warned them that if they proceeded beyond the next bend they would come under fire from the "Fascists" in the Alcázar along a stretch of the road for a distance of 600 yards.

This was an eye-opener to Lance.

"*Caramba!*" he said characteristically, "I had no idea there was any war on here."

This was a nuisance. To avoid the direct road would mean a long detour.

"What d'you think?" he asked Papworth.

Papworth grinned. "Have a go."

Lance slipped into gear and was quickly in top, accelerating to the limit. The road was abominable, scored with deep pot-holes. The big car shot up to seventy-five miles an hour, but it was with the utmost difficulty that Lance held it to the road. Papworth, thrown violently about, was clinging to the dashboard. A cloud of brown dust billowed up astern. Beyond the bend other spurts of dust were soon kicked up ahead and abeam of them as the rifles and machine-guns of the Alcázar opened fire. At that speed they were a terribly difficult target, but as they crashed into an extra deep pot-hole there was a metallic crack as a front spring broke. The car began to swerve and bounce even more violently as Lance struggled to control it. He reduced speed and somehow kept control for a further 200 yards, but at that point the car swung out of his hands, its nose in the ditch and a few inches from a telegraph pole.

There was no missing the target now. The bullets whistled about them, hitting the car repeatedly. They leapt out and threw themselves into the ditch. There they remained for some five or six hours till it was dark, when they found the car miraculously unhurt in any vital part. They drove back the forty-three miles to Madrid at walking pace, arriving in the early hours of the next morning.

This was one of the earliest of several such trips of exploration that Lance carried out, usually in company with some friend. He had another narrow escape, though of a different nature, up in the Guardarrama Mountains. He was again accompanied by Papworth and had been provided also with two Assault Guards as escort by the local sector commander of the Republican troops on account of the dangerous situation there. These escorts the Republicans were always very prompt and willing to provide, even when Lance did not want them.

On this occasion the two Englishmen and their escort, driving by hairpin bends through the balsam-scented pine woods, arrived at the little mountain town of Guardarrama itself, with its charming group of bourgeois hotels and houses set in magnificently austere country. Lance intended to visit a road-repair site half-way up the mountain beyond the town, where he thought there was also a likely escape route. He found, however, that the black and commanding heights were all occupied by Mola's Nationalists and that the Republicans' advance posts were just beyond the town. His site was therefore in No-Man's-Land. A little desultory crackling of rifle-fire was going on among the wounded pines, reverberating to and fro in the rocky clefts and gullies of the mountains.

In conversation with an officer in command of some armoured cars, he expressed his disappointment at not being able to get where he wanted and got the surprising reply:

"Why can't you? Are you afraid? I will lend you one of my armoured cars to get there. All you have to do is to get a pass." There was always some pass required!

Lance, wondering what other army in the world would have allowed a civil engineer to go pottering about beyond the front line, thanked him for his kindness and asked: "Where do I go to get a pass?"

The officer pointed to a small ruined building ahead and replied: "That villa there. You will find the commandant there and when he has given you a pass my armoured car will take you on. There will be no trouble."

Forgetting for once the over-optimism of the Spanish, Lance and Papworth went forward and in the "villa" found two people poring over a map. One of these was a grey-haired, spectacled, gentle old man who, they were astonished to be told, was the "commandant". The other figure, even more surprisingly, was a woman—a formidable, middle-aged woman, broad and stout, with a strong, determined face, dressed, Lance thought, like the cook of a good family, and looking anything but *simpática*.

Lance addressed himself to the commandant and found him a most agreeable old fellow. The woman went on studying the map. The commandant began to write out the pass when suddenly the table was shaken by an angry thump. Lance turned to find the formidable woman glaring up at him with a look of fury and loathing such as he had never seen before. She shrieked:

"Not a step further! They are spies!"

She snatched the paper from the commandant's hands as he was writing and tore it to pieces. The poor old commandant looked scared out of his wits as she continued to shriek:

"Spies! Spies! Get out, or I will have you shot!"

There was no gainsaying this fury. The two Englishmen, feeling very small, went back to the town and told the armoured car officer what had happened. He looked a little crestfallen and said:

"I am sorry. Do you know who that was?"

"No idea."

"That was *La Pasionaria*."

Dolores Ibarruri, famous in the world's headlines as *La Pasionaria*, was at once one of the most feared and most loved personalities of revolutionary Spain. A founder of the Communist Party, and now a member of the Cortes, she wielded an extraordinary influence and was known everywhere for her passionate hates and loves and her fiery speeches. While Lance and Papworth were waiting in Guardarrama she, having left the villa, passed them in the street, her eyes piercing them again with loathing and fury. A moment later she turned to speak to her bodyguard of militiamen and instantly her eyes became soft and full of kindness, her face radiant with smiles. It was easy to see, Lance thought, why she was so loved by all these rough militiamen. But he thought also that those frenzied shrieks of hers must have been very like her shrieks at Calvo Sotelo in the Cortes only a few months ago and considered himself lucky to have escaped that politician's violent fate.

The twenty-fifth of October was a beautiful Spanish autumn day. There had been some rain of late and the sun in its course had declined to a genial warmth. It was a Sunday. Beyond the harsh and stony plateau, Christopher Lance reflected as he looked over the roof-tops from his room in the Embassy, there must now be some pleasant verdant spots. He wondered also where the "front" might be and what was going on there. It would be fun, and it might be useful, to go and find out. Navarros had a repair contract near Navalcarnero on the Talavera road, to the south-west; it would be a good thing to make sure that his plant was safe and to see if there was an escape route that way, for so far he had had no luck in that matter, the war being much too fluid.

Afterwards, he thought, it would be an agreeable change from the rigours of Madrid to turn off to the left and go on for a picnic tea in the garden pleasaunce of Aranjuez. However, it wouldn't be much fun to go alone, so he rang up two or three friends to go with him, but they all hummed and hawed. "Too risky, old boy." Then he called Bill Hall, the rugged-faced deputy manager of the London and South America Bank. He also demurred at first.

"Bit chancy, Christopher?"

"Not a bit of it, Bill. There's darned little serious scrapping going on, from what I can make out, and if we go out after lunch they'll all be fast asleep. Come along now. I'll borrow an Embassy car."

He was delighted when Hall agreed, for Hall, small-statured, strong-jawed, big-nosed, spectacled, was a splendid companion, always laughing. They had lunch at a small restaurant kept by a cheerful little proprietor who, being a member of the Madrid Control Committee, was still able to give them "a bit of a meal". He was also a very staunch Roman Catholic, however, and later on, when they were both in prison together, Lance had the unhappy experience of seeing him shot before his prison window.

Luncheon over, with the Union Jack on the car and wearing sports shirts and grey flannels, the two Englishmen drove out

75

light-heartedly on the Talavera road and so through Naval-carnero, eighteen miles out. All was peaceful. It was the siesta hour and not a living soul was to be seen except a drowsy boy on a drooping donkey.

A little beyond Navalcarnero, however, they were stopped by a militia detachment that was strolling casually about the road on top of a crest. Lance gave the usual salutation, produced his pass and asked:

"Where is the front line?"

Having seen no other troops about at all, he was surprised when the leader of the detachment answered:

"This is the front line, comrade."

"*Caramba!* We had no idea it was so near Madrid."

"We had to retire about thirteen kilometres last night, com-rade."

"Well, the place I want to get to is still about a mile ahead—a place where there is a road-gang hut and some stone-crushing plant."

"Very well, comrade, but you must go on foot; I will send two good comrades to go with you as escorts."

They left the car and set out in the serene quiet of the after-noon. Lance remarked:

"Not a very bloody war here, so far."

"Darned sight bloodier in Madrid," Hall replied.

All the same, the two Englishmen edged discreetly to the side of the road, close to the ditch, while the two militiamen strolled along the middle of the road, without the slightest care for cover. Lance and Hall were astonished that these armed civilian bands, of whom they had seen so much in Madrid, could be sent to the "front" without the slightest vestige of military training or discipline.

After walking thus for a quarter of an hour in the warm autumn sunshine, they topped a slight rise, beyond which Lance knew he would see his roadside hut. There it was, indeed, but also, parked beside it, was one of Franco's tanks, which Lance recognized as an Italian "whippet".

The two militia innocents, right on the skyline and in the middle of the road, stood and gazed at it, till a burst from the tank's machine-gun cracked the peaceful surface of the day and the bullets whistled past their ears.

The marksmanship was bad and it was with mingled amusement and apprehension that Lance found that the two militiamen, with typical Spanish optimism, expected to be able to dash forward, together with the Englishmen, capture the tank and drive victoriously through to Salamanca. He threw cold water on this notion and, as they scuttled back under the defilade of the hill, Lance and Hall had a good laugh.

"That looks like the end of a contract for you, Christopher," Hall said, "and the end of a perfect day for us both."

"Not a bit of it. I'm not going to be done out of my tea. Let us maintain the offensive and beetle on to Aranjuez, as planned."

Regaining Navalcarnero and reversing the car, he turned right down the secondary road that led south-eastward, crossed the Toledo road, where there was another militia detachment, and gained the Aranjuez road, on which they turned to the right. Here some militiamen of about platoon strength were digging a trench at the side of the road in a leisurely way. Only nine miles to go.

They had not gone very far down the Aranjuez road before, on some high ground ahead, a small party of militia was seen running hard towards them, sweating and in a state of panic. Lance said to Hall:

"What on earth is worrying these chaps? There's not a sign of war anywhere."

As they met, he pulled up to question them, but they spoke asking Lance if he had "seen anyone on the road?"

"Scarcely a soul, *camaradas*."

"No *Facistas*?"

Laughing, Lance tried to reassure them and was about to ask them where the front line was when they took to their heels again and fled.

"The poor blighters," Hall said, "haven't a clue; and I don't think we have many. What do we do now, Christopher?"

"Beetle on," Lance replied.

They drove on for another two or three miles, enjoying the

sunshine and the quiet. On their right hand the road was lined with trees, diminishing in perspective over the brow of a slight plateau ahead. As the car rose to the plateau, Hall said:

"Look, Christopher! On the left!"

There on the skyline was a patrol of cavalry. Lance slowed down and remarked:

"They look fine. First Government Regulars I've seen."

"Have a squint on the starboard bow, then—there's a tank!"

It was on some raised ground above the road and Lance exclaimed:

"We *are* doing well. Never knew the Government had any tanks. Some real soldiers at last, Bill."

"They certainly look pretty snappy to me."

Lance, as a one-time cavalryman, was watching with approbation a drill-book movement as, obviously in obedience to a word of command, the cavalry dismounted and, leaving a horse-holder for every four horses, doubled to the ditch at the side of the road and took up positions under cover.

"Damned good!" he exclaimed.

The words were scarcely out of his mouth before a volley from the hidden carbines spouted from the ditch a hundred and fifty yards ahead. The chassis of the car was hit.

"By God! They're Franco's party!" exclaimed Lance. He jammed on the brakes.

Hall said: "What the hell do we do now?"

"Sit tight, and wait. Damned awkward."

Ahead they saw a Spanish officer stand up and make some signal.

"What the devil does he mean?" Lance asked, but Hall had no idea either.

Lance then noticed that there was an aircraft overhead and it occurred to him, instinctively recalling his old training, that perhaps the officer was ordering them to move the car under cover of the line of trees on the side of the road, the aircraft being supposedly a Republican one. He therefore engaged gear and moved the car to that direction, but was immediately fired on again, without being hit.

"Damned bad shooting," he said to Hall as he stopped the car again. The officer again made signals and it was Lance's turn to ask: "What do we do next?"

Hall replied: "I think what we've got to do is to hop out and hold our hands up, old boy."

He nipped out on the left, in the middle of the road. Lance got out on his own side and fell straight into the ditch on top of two dead militiamen. As he recovered himself, Hall shouted:

"Wave your handkerchief or something."

Lance replied: "Hell's bells, I don't like this white flag business." But he pulled his handkerchief out of his cuff and waved it overhead, saying as he did so:

"Dammit, I feel an awful ass."

Three officers were coming towards them, very smartly dressed in khaki, riding boots and Sam Browne, very like British cavalry officers. As they drew near they obviously noticed the Union Jack on the car, for one of them, who was a captain, said in perfect English:

"I take it from your flag that you are British. What on earth are you doing here?" They were smiling broadly at something.

Lance answered: "Actually we are from Madrid and we are on our way to have a nice little tea in Aranjuez. I hope you are not going to spoil the party."

They roared with laughter. Lance asked:

"Can I take my hands down now?"

He did so and to his embarrassment saw that the handkerchief that he had been waving was a red bandana. So that was what they had been laughing at.

"Damn," he said, "I thought it was a white one."

"Very incriminating, you know," said the Spanish captain, still laughing cheerfully. "But tell me—what on earth are you doing in Madrid? Pretty ghastly there, isn't it?"

"I'm in Madrid because my job is there and I am an honorary attaché at the British Embassy."

The Spanish officer turned to ask Hall who and what he was and then questioned them both about conditions in Madrid. Was it true that they were starving? Was there much damage? Two of the three spoke very good English.

They were entirely friendly and breezy, but Lance soon got tired of this and said:

"Look here, time is getting on. If you will excuse us, we must get back to Madrid. You have properly messed up our party."

"Oh, no," replied the captain, "we can't let you do that, I'm afraid. You'll have to come along with us now. Besides, if you go back now the Reds will shoot you up for a certainty. You'll find things much better on our side—plenty to eat and drink and plenty of everything."

This totally unexpected outcome the Englishmen heard with dismay. Hall said: "This is infernally awkward. I've simply got to get back. I've got the keys of the bank at home and no one can get in without me."

Nothing would move them. The Spanish captain got into Lance's car, saying: "Come along, we are going to regimental headquarters." Thus, with Lance at the wheel and their captor as passenger, the Englishmen drove themselves off into captivity—and with the Union Jack still flying at the bonnet. Lance could not refrain from saying with some exasperation:

"This is a damned rum go."

To which the Spaniard replied: "Oh, I don't know. It's becoming quite a habit. You are the second lot today."

"Good heavens! Who were the others?"

"A bunch of journalists—American and British. At the very spot where we got you. In fact, the corpses you fell on were their escorts."

Exasperated though they were, they couldn't help liking this Spaniard, and when they got to headquarters, which were in a farmhouse, they found themselves among a gathering of the same kind—a cheerful lot who nearly all spoke English and who welcomed them more as guests than as captives, refreshing them with some excellent wine. They all thought that they would be in Madrid in a couple of days and Lance could not help reflecting that, if they really got a move on, there was nothing to stop them driving straight into the city in less than one hour.

The Englishmen were then sent off to a higher headquarters in Toledo and provided with an officer escort. He was the young Duke of Monte Allegre, rather small and dark, very smart in his person, a gay and cheerful companion who spoke good English and was a *caballero* to his finger tips. The three of them set off after dark that evening, without lights and so close to the front that they could see the occasional flash of rifle or machine-gun. Lance was still driving and his car still wearing the Union Jack. The whole situation was slightly preposterous; here they were driving about in their own car, being hospitably treated, yet virtually prisoners in "enemy country", caught up in a war which was no concern of theirs. At Toledo the two Britons were interviewed light-heartedly by a little grey-haired Colonel, who was full of life and humour and highly amused by the situation.

"How very English of you!" he said. "Calmly driving out for a picnic in the middle of someone else's war! Tea indeed! Horrible stuff! Quite mad of you, you know."

He chuckled and went on:

"Really I don't know what to do with you, gentlemen. It is all most unusual and unofficial. Not allowed for in the regulations at all. I shall have to telephone General Varela."

He did so, with Lance and Hall standing beside his desk. Having explained the situation, he turned to look up at the Englishmen with a wicked twinkle in his eye, and went on:

"What shall I do with them, General? Shall I have them shot—or shall I invite them to dinner? . . . Very well, Sir."

He put down the telephone and said with mock solemnity to the captives:

"The General says that you are to dine *first*."

In the course of informal conversation, Lance mentioned his recent experience at Toledo and the little Colonel sent for an officer who had been in the besieged garrison of the Alcázar. It was the first time that the Englishmen had heard anything about that dramatic event and Lance in his turn then told the officer of his own escapade at Toledo. The Spaniard was astonished.

"*Caramba!*" he exclaimed. "Was that really you? It was I who gave the order to fire on you. We all thought you were safely dead!"

The conversation over, the little Colonel told the Duke to take the two Englishmen out to dinner at a little restaurant where he knew they would get good food. Now very hungry, Lance and

Hall were much relieved but, after their war-time experience in Madrid, did not expect to get much in the way of food and were not more hopeful when the Duke took them into a dark, squalid little café. Off its sordid main room, however, was a smaller one with four of five tables covered with spotless linen, the air embalmed with the savours of fine food and garlic. They were served with food of a sort unobtainable in Madrid for three months, including fresh trout and casserole of chicken, washed down with good Rioja and served by a handsome, raven-haired *dueña*.

The situation was an extraordinary one. Hall, in buoyant good humour, was pulling the Duke's leg.

"Look here, Duke," he asked, "what the devil are we? Prisoners? Do you treat all your prisoners like this?"

Monte Allegre smiled and shrugged. "I just obey orders," he said. "Let us say that you are guests we don't want to lose."

The same night Lance, Hall and the Duke drove on to Talavera, where General Varela's headquarters were, but, not arriving until two a.m. put up for the night at a café, where Hall lost the toss for the two mattresses and was obliged to lie on the insanitary floor.

It was Lance who with typical and impish resourcefulness found a way out of Hall's problem with the keys of the Bank. The next morning, Monte Allegre not feeling well, he offered to go out and get him some medicine, promising not to escape. Having first got the medicine he slipped into the post office accompanied by Hall, and simply sent off a telegram to Angus McDonnell in London, telling him what had happened and asking him to inform the London head office of the bank where the keys were to be found, so that the bank could in turn telegraph its Madrid branch. Lance was about to write another telegram to Jinks when the Duke walked in to the post office. He flushed with anger on seeing them, but soon recovered his natural good temper.

Next morning they were taken to the Hotel Española to see General Varela himself, another of the Nationalist Generals who had risen from the ranks, having been a Sergeant of Marines and twice awarded the Spanish equivalent of the Victoria Cross. They found him a well-built, friendly man, who, like everyone else so far, treated the matter as a joke and was most amused at the story of their capture, but told them that General Franco personally wanted to see them at Salamanca.

This was a tremendous and impressive surprise, and as they left the General's office in high good humour, Hall remarked: "We seem to be jolly important people over here!"

To which Lance replied: "I should feel a darned sight more important if I could have a shave and a bath." They were then taken off to a gathering of Spanish officers, exciting great interest, and there they met the British and American journalists who had been "bagged" just before them.[1] Then, treading again in Wellington's footsteps, and creating something of a sensation wherever their flagged car was seen, they drove on to the ancient city of Salamanca, the autumn sun displaying at its best the tawny and gold splendour of its antique buildings. The city was being lavishly decorated in the red and yellow colours of the Nationalists in preparation for victory celebrations on the fall of Madrid.

Their introduction to the lustrous old city, however, was far from propitious, for they were dossed down in a small room in an unsavoury lodging-house, the Duke naturally bagging the only bed as of right and leaving Lance and Hall, still wearing only flannel trousers and sports shirts, blanketless upon the floor. Bill Hall, squirming on the harsh boards for an hour, cried out:

"How I wish I had been born a duke!"

Monte Allegre stirred in the bed and answered: "You don't want my mattress, do you? You're not cold?"

"Oh, no, Duke. We can keep ourselves warm by scratching, and by tomorrow we shall be as ripe as cheese. How nice that will be for your generals when we meet them!"

Unwashed, unshaven, tousled, the Englishmen were nonetheless hospitably received next morning by the officers of the headquarters mess, who, their curiosity about these sensational captives satisfied, talked to them about the beauty of the English gardens and countryside, the peculiarities of the pubs, and the "beastliness" of the draught beer. They were taken to see the

[1] Dennis Weaver of the *News Chronicle*, James Minifie of the *New York Herald-Tribune* and Henry Gorrell of the United Press.

ceremonial mounting of the guard and were tremendously impressed by the contrast between the smartness and discipline of the Nationalist troops in their khaki uniforms, so similar to those of the British Army, and the unshaven slovenliness of the militiamen of Madrid. No less glaring was the contrast between the dirt, disorder and scarcity of Republican Spain and the contentment, normality and relative plenty on the Nationalist side.

"But what struck us most," Lance said afterwards to Ogilvie-Forbes, "was the happy faces, the absence of tension, the cheery priests and the welcome sound of the church bells once more."

Their stay in Salamanca, however, had a very disagreeable ending. They were taken, separately, to be interrogated by Antonio Bolin, formerly noted for his right-wing articles in the Madrid press. He was a tall, good-looking man, but otherwise a very unpleasant person indeed and had evidently made up his mind in advance that the two Englishmen were Republican spies. Sneering, sarcastic and contemptuous, he gave them both a vicious cross-examination and set out to ridicule them and to pump them on Republican military dispositions.

"You call yourself a military attaché," he said to Lance, "and you do not even know the military dispositions in Madrid."

Lance, who was a very simple person and no dealer in the commerce of words, protested in vain and was very soon tied up in verbal knots. He left the venomous atmosphere of the room feeling that the whole case was lost and he said to Bill Hall afterwards:

"Quite the most unpleasant creature I've ever met."

Hall replied even more emphatically.

A little later Monte Allegre came into their squalid room with a broad smile and said:

"Well, gentlemen, you are to be received by the Generalissimo tonight!"

Hall roared with laughter and said:

"Good heavens! Received by the Generalissimo in these togs! That *will* be jolly."

The Duke grimaced but said: "We ought to be able to fix you up; I'll see what I can do."

He was as good as his word and shortly afterwards took them

round to an hotel, where they met Sir Percival Phillips, the war correspondent, who generously came to their aid and fitted them both out completely from top to toe.

It was therefore with their "morale" very much higher that they went to the reception at eight o'clock that night to meet Franco and waited a while in the brilliantly lit hall of the hotel with a crowd of Spanish officers, watching Señora Franco arrive, who looked exceptionally elegant. Lance found himself feeling buoyant and confident, glad to be clean again, away from their sordid lodgings and anticipating an enjoyable evening.

The reception, however, did not follow the expected pattern. They entered a large room which appeared to be a mess and sat down at a table with officers of high rank, Lance being particularly delighted at finding himself next to the legendary veteran, General Millan Astray, a much scarred warrior with one arm and one eye who, together with Franco, had organized the famous *Tercio*, or Foreign Legion, several years before. Lance found him a fascinating companion, but wondered what was the purpose of this entertainment, for they had not yet been presented to Franco: were the Spaniards, he wondered, trying to fill them up? If so, both he and Hall could take that all right.

He was soon undeceived. Somewhere about ten o'clock, as Lance chatted, the Generalissimo appeared at their table and the two Englishmen, rising, were presented to him. It was a highly disagreeable experience. They beheld a small, dark man, severe and aloof, and the conversation was short, cold and formal. Quite clearly Franco had been falsely advised by the objectionable Bolin, for he said, very meaningfully:

"You are in a dangerous position here and you know the penalty for the kind of business you are on. However, I shall give you a chance. I shall instruct your escort to take you to Burgos, where you will see Señor Merry del Val, who will give you certain instructions."

After the very friendly entertainment that they had just enjoyed, the two Englishmen were so amazed, so taken aback at this obvious accusation of espionage, that they could not think of a word to say in the short pause that followed. Franco went on:

"If you will give the *palabra inglesa* that you will carry out the instructions you receive, you will be given your freedom."

He then walked away, leaving Lance and Hall very much in the air. The atmosphere had suddenly become taut and stiff. The wine turned sour in their mouths and the hospitality false and hollow. Dammit, it was Franco's own friends whom they had been helping these three months and to be now called spies was an affront and a thorn in the breast.

The Duke escorted them back to their sordid and insanitary quarters and left them feeling very let down and resentful particularly about Bolin, whom they guessed at once had put Franco against them. Lance's anxious thoughts as he squirmed on the hard boards, went to all those unhappy people in Madrid who were looking to him for help and who would surely be wondering why he no longer came to see them. What would *they* say if they knew Franco had called them spies? Recollection of the shootings surged over him like a nightmare and he was filled with anguish as he imagined the word going round in all those shuttered houses of fear, "Even the British are letting us down now; there can be no more hope." What did Franco mean? Was Merry del Val going to exact a promise from them that they would return to England? He hoped not, because, although he longed to see his dear Jinks again, his heart was now entirely devoted to the rescue of men and women from terror, imprisonment and death. At all costs, he *must* get back to Madrid. Thus it was a sleepless and a miserable night that he spent on the hard floor of his hovel.

The next morning, still wearing Phillips's clothes, they motored on with Monte Allegre to Burgos, the Nationalists' governmental headquarters, where they met Don Pablo Merry del Val, son of the former Spanish Ambassador in London. He was not unfriendly to the two Englishmen but after a preliminary talk he made them an astonishing proposition. He handed to Lance a list of some twenty persons and said:

"Those are some important friends of ours who are in hiding in Madrid. The Generalissimo requires that you should give the word of an Englishman that you will return to Madrid and do everything you can to get them out."

Lance, once more taken aback by the totally unexpected, raised his eyebrows. He raised them even more when he glanced at the names on the list. He was a good deal shocked at Merry del Val's proposition and said to him with some emphasis:

"The Generalissimo seems to have made up his mind that we are spies, but you must yourself know perfectly well that we are not. I am sorry that he should have been induced to think so. It is quite preposterous."

"Well, we will not discuss that. Will you agree?"

Lance, turning the list over in his hands, thought hard. He regarded the allegation with the utmost distaste and disliked agreeing to a condition which seemed to imply an admission of guilt; but at the same time it precisely suited the compulsion that he felt to return to stricken Madrid to do what he could to save life. But what about Bill Hall? He turned to him with a questioning look. Hall smiled and winked.

"You realize, of course," said Lance to Merry del Val, "that you are asking us to do something extremely dangerous?"

"Possibly; but that is what the Generalissimo requires."

Another pause, while Lance thought hard, keeping his eyes on Hall for any further sign. Then he said:

"All right, we are prepared to have a shot at it; but we can't promise any more than to do our best, and only for the reason that this is exactly the work I am trying to do in Madrid already. *Not* spying, señor, but helping to save your friends from the firing squad. You might tell the Generalissimo that."

Merry del Val answered coldly:

"Very well; I shall accept your word and I shall instruct Monte Allegre to escort you both to the French frontier. You can make your way back to Madrid from France."

As they came away, Hall said:

"By God, Christopher! That was a bit hot."

"It certainly surprised me. But better than being shot."

"How the hell are we going to smuggle Francoists out of Madrid?"

"Matter of fact, I've been doing a bit of thinking over that already. Look here, this is much more my pigeon than yours. You're far too busy to go the whole hog. Where you really can help is to see that the cash is forthcoming for all the cheques; because this business is going to cost a packet."

"I'll do that all right, and anything else necessary. But the first thing to do is to get rid of that darned list. Can't possibly be found with that thing on us in Madrid."

"No fear. I'll have to memorize it and then we'll burn the thing."

That afternoon they drove on to the fashionable holiday resort of San Sebastián, and, in contrast to the miserable quarters they had been given before, were lodged at one of the best hotels. The Duke, in his best humour, was very easygoing. They dined and wined excellently at his expense and strolled out alone together on the sea-front, where they were arrested by the police but returned to join a gay party late into the night.

Next morning, October 30, they drove through Irun, shattered by Franco's bombs, to the French frontier and here at last said good-bye to Monte Allegre, who had been to them more a host than a guard, paying for all their meals and lodging, for they were penniless. They thanked him for looking after them on what Hall described as "this Cook's tour" and he replied with a smile:

"It's been a most enjoyable trip. Good luck to you both."

Nevertheless, although Lance retrieved his Union Flag, the Duke pinched the Embassy car.

In France, still in Phillips's clothes, they made for Hendaye, where Sir Henry Chilton was carrying out as best he could his duties of Ambassador by "remote control". When he had heard their extraordinary story, he said:

"For heaven's sake get out and go home."

"I'm afraid I can't do that, sir," Lance answered, "you see, I have given the *palabra inglesa*."

He wrote to Jinks:

*I must get back to save the business—and there are several people there waiting for me and trusting me to save their lives. Otherwise I should go straight home, as I have had enough.*

# CHAPTER SEVEN

# TOUCH AND GO

THEY were back in Republican Spain within twenty-four hours, travelling by train to Toulouse and thence by air to Alicante. There the Civil Governor, Don Francisco Valdes Casas, who was yet another friend of Lance's, promised them a car to take them to Madrid, but the sparks of trouble were still flying upward and, instead of a car, two detectives arrived at their hotel. Once more they were arrested and once more on a suspicion of espionage. First one side, then the other. Both Republicans and Nationalists suffered from spy-fever. They were detained for two days before, Forbes having taken the appropriate steps, a message to release them came from the Minister for Foreign Affairs, the Moscow-trained Alvarez del Vayo. Instead of going by car, they flew by what was actually the last civilian aircraft to reach the capital, passing over the very spot where they had been captured ten days before.

Hall and Lance were both the sort of people who could enjoy a good laugh against themselves. Notwithstanding the awkwardness of their predicament, they had rather enjoyed their stay in Nationalist Spain, on which the only serious blot had been the objectionable Bolin and what followed from his baseless representations to Franco. They had been well treated by people of civil manners and they had been impressed by all that they had seen on the Nationalist side of the fence. Yet Lance at least was glad to get back to dirty, hungry, fear-ridden Madrid, for this was where his friends were and this was where he could be of service to people sorely in need of human sympathy and help.

But he was worried by the promise that he had given to Merry del Val. The hazards came home to him now with new emphasis, but his conscience warned him that, if he shied, he would be guilty of having evaded Franco's firing squad under false pretences. He said to Margery when he told her the story:

"Is a man bound by a promise given under duress?"

"Of course not, Christopher. Think of Jinks. There's plenty of good work you can do here without poking your fingers into the fire."

"I'm not so sure," he said, "I'm not so sure."

He got back quickly into his working rig of flannel trousers and open-necked shirt. One of his first acts on returning to Madrid was to pay a call, accompanied by Forbes, on Alvarez del Vayo to thank him for securing his release and to apologize for giving him so much trouble. The natural act of courtesy served to make yet another important contact in high places which was to prove valuable when he got into a tight corner later on. Alvarez del Vayo was vastly amused at the story of their capture and even more at Lance's tale of the preparations in Salamanca to celebrate the fall of Madrid.

Nevertheless, Lance found that the immediate fall of the capital was daily expected by a great many people, both by those who longed for the victorious advent of the red and yellow standard and by those who feared it. Lance himself, having seen how little there was in the way of Franco's forces, having seen the confidence of the Nationalist side, and having noted the contrast between the two armies, nevertheless only half-expected to find the city already taken. It was over a week since he and Hall had been captured scarcely twenty miles or so away, but the over-confidence that he saw in the Spanish character and their disinclination to "get a move on" caused him to feel no surprise at finding that the situation was much the same as when he had left.

The only change was a higher state of tension in the city. Franco, instead of concentrating on cutting the south-eastward communications with Valencia and thus sealing the fate of the capital, had crept a little nearer on the western hand and was daily expected to attack. Those who hoped for his victory were preparing to rejoice, those who were not partisan and whose chief longing was for peace (the unregarded majority in most civil wars) looked forward to relief from the privations and the strains from which they had been suffering. On the other hand, Lance saw very clearly that numbers of left-wing waverers, who might have welcomed a bloodless deliverance by Franco, were stiffened in their resistance by the news of the indiscriminate shooting by the Nationalist Civil Guards and the fear that the same fate might befall them too.

On November 6, the Republican cabinet, having plastered the city walls with exhortations to "Fight on", quitted it themselves, transferring the seat of government to Valencia and leaving the safety of Madrid to a Junta of Defence headed by the popular General Miaja, the "bald-headed eagle", but the moving force of which was the international Communist general known by the alias of Emil Kleber.

Thus it was to a Madrid throbbing with a new excitement that Lance returned and he now met there a picturesque and exhilarating character who was to enliven no little the drab scene of the capital. This was Miss Fernanda Jacobson, who came in charge of one of those admirable Scottish Ambulance Units that so often hasten wherever there is a war, disturbance or distress. Miss Jacobson was a little, middle-aged, sandy-haired woman, who, to the astonishment not only of the Spanish, but also even of the British community, presented herself to the world in a man's kilt, tartan hose, bare knees and a glengarry. She spoke bad Spanish with a broad Scots accent. She was a cheerful and a very forceful character and to her team of Scottish men ambulance-drivers was very much the commanding officer. She was very "Left" and her Unit had, in fact, been sent to serve the Republican armies, under whose orders she came. She got on very well with the militiamen, had no interest in saving people from the firing squads, somewhat disapproved of the work that Lance and Margery Hill got up to later on, but nonetheless was on very good terms with them and always ready to help the British community and any humanitarian cause.

It was about now also, on the eve of the attack on Madrid, that General Mola, commanding the Nationalist forces pressing down from the north, gave utterance to a phrase that was to spread round the globe and to become before long a commonplace in all the world's languages. The Nationalists, he said, were converging on Madrid in four columns, but they had also a "fifth column" eagerly waiting in Madrid. Lance, knowing his Madrid, observed grimly to Hall:

91

"This means trouble."

For the innocents within the capital there could have been no more unhappy announcement. The Junta of Defence revived and intensified its measures to rout out these "fifth columnists", by which malignant term they for the first time denounced all those within the gates whom they hated, feared or suspected. For a few days the tommy-guns cracked with augmented venom at the slaughter-pits, the revolvers blazed with heightened frequency within the raided houses, the common graves scored fresh scars in the riven soil, the prison doors clanged without cease and the radio trumpeted with new threats and exhortations. Lance, dodging from tree to tree on his way home, barely escaped the wanton fusillades.

Almost at once, within a few days of Lance's return, the battle was on. All to the westward, beyond the winding banks of the Manzanares, the air was filled with explosive sound as the artillery and the aircraft on both sides engaged and with the throb of the machine-guns as the infantry clashed. Eagerly the boiler-suits poured out to fight their fellow-countrymen and the Moorish regulars of Franco's colonial forces. Very soon the shells were falling in the western streets of Madrid itself and the unwithered leaves in the avenues fell shattered before their time. The Nationalists pressed forward to the old royal park known as the Casa de Campo and to the north-west they crossed the Manzanares and penetrated the half-finished buildings of the New University City.

It was a moment of high crisis, when it seemed that only one more effort was needed by Franco's small force to win the capital. And it was at this moment that the little British-American hospital in the Calle Montalvo became in grave danger. As the rival forces clashed only a few hundred yards beyond it, the hospital came under actual shell fire. Margery Hill's staff, carrying on under the most exacting conditions, with lights forbidden and many shortages, were daily in danger as they ran the gauntlet of Franco's fire to get supplies. They hung on, expecting that Franco's advance would be continued and normality return.

The situation became critical, however, when a Republican battery of field guns was sited very close to the hospital and began a duel with the distant Nationalist battery, whose line of fire almost directly enfiladed the street in which the hospital stood. The immediate rescue of the hospital was imperative.

When news of the crisis reached Lance, he acted immediately, taking charge of the operation himself. Accompanied by Papworth, he raced to the scene, with Miss Jacobson and her Scottish Ambulances following. Miss Jacobson was apprehensive that her ambulances might be blown to bits, but Lance, remembering the old drill in these affairs, halted them all under cover a little way off with orders to come up one at a time when he summoned them. Then he and Papworth went forward in the car. The Republican guns barked just behind them and the Nationalist shells crashed about. It was, thought Lance, quite like old days.

He found Margery Hill, who had been warned by telephone to have everything ready for a quick getaway, entirely composed and collected. He greeted her with his usual cheerfulness, but stopped abruptly when he went upstairs and saw the score or so of Spanish refugees to whom she was giving sanctuary. Thinking of the platoon of Republican troops quartered in the ground floor, he said:

"Quick, Margery, wrap them up in bandages."

She broke into a smile. "Oh, of course."

"Got any crutches? Any walking sticks?"

"Just a few."

"Dish them out then."

Quietly and quickly everything was arranged and Lance called forward the ambulances one at a time in brief lulls of the artillery duel, while the militiamen watched from the ground-floor windows. In less than half an hour all the patients, the staff, refugees, the bedding and the more important stores were got away safely. Margery, Lance and Papworth left last in the car with the blast of the guns in their ears.

They moved straight into a flat in a palatial house that Eric Glaisher, the energetic treasurer of the hospital committee, had secured at short notice in the Calle Velasquez at the corner of the Calle de Ayala. This flat, which possessed 19 bedrooms and 5 bathrooms, had belonged to the playwright Pedro Muñoz Seca, who had displeased the working classes by poking fun at them on the stage and whom they had accordingly murdered at the same shooting-pit where young Asensio had met his fate. He had been Glaisher's friend.

As they began to settle in to their new home, with the battle still raging to the west, Lance, admiring the calm and efficiency of the hospital staff and the *panache* of Miss Jacobson, summed up the little exploit by remarking to Papworth:

"Really, all we needed to complete the picture, you know, was a braw Hieland piper!"

Only an hour or so after they had settled, a squad of the most villainous militiamen they had yet seen broke in and said:

"You must clear out at once. We are taking possession." Seeing Margery, they added menacingly: "You are Muñoz Seca's girl. We shall want you."

There was a very tense scene, with everyone's life hanging on the pressure of a trigger, until at last, by Lance's firmness and tact, the boiler-suits were persuaded to go away. But again a detachment of troops was quartered on the ground floor, very much on the *qui vive* as the sounds of the battle throbbed and echoed among the expectant houses.

The little battle of the hospital, however, marked virtually the limit of Franco's advance. His attempt on the capital had been made too late and with too slender a force. His leisurely approach had enabled the Republican Government, in the nick of time, to bring up the First International Brigade, that foreign legion of volunteers who, with little knowledge of the real issues, had rushed in from many countries to fight for what they believed to be the cause of freedom and democracy. Tumultuous cheers and characteristic shouts of *Viva Rusia* and *Viva el Soviet* greeted their impressive march through the tensed and excited city. A week later the Second International Brigade arrived. With this and other assistance the advance of the red and yellow standard was halted—and halted for more than two years. The Casa de Campo, its delightful grounds scarred with trenches, the West Park and the unfinished buildings of the New University became the more or less settled front-line areas, now boiling up into bloody disputations, now stagnating in surly silence.

Thenceforward Lance and his friends lived in a city of war, with the front line on its western and southern fringes, not indeed "besieged", as the propagandist language of the time represented, but becoming daily more and more hard-pressed for the necessities of life. Franco's guns dug in beyond the Casa de Campo, behind the crest of the Carabancheles southward on the Toledo road and on Garabitas Hill on the high road to Coruña. Parts of the city came frequently under shell fire, somewhat indiscriminately at first, but soon restricted mainly to the western district of Rosales and the Royal Palace, and occasionally in the central districts so well-known to all—the Puerta del Sol, the Plaza Mayor and the Telefonica in the Gran Via.

To this shelling the Republican batteries replied actively, mainly from the advantageous high ground north of the city. The small remaining British community lived between two fires, at first somewhat disrupted in their daily activities but soon accustoming themselves to all these noises of a war which they were in but not of.

Franco declared that he would exempt from attack by bomb or shell an area of the city which included the British and other embassies, advising the inhabitants to remove into it, and this promise he kept, but the *Madrileños*, unfrightened and fatalistic, took small advantage of it.

Lance was worried about his undertaking to Merry del Val, under duress though it had been, but for the time being he could do nothing about it. His hands were more than full with relief work of immediate urgency. Appeals for help of all kinds came to him by day and by night. Instinctively, automatically and immediately he answered them, forcing himself to visit the gruesome mortuaries and shooting grounds, hurrying to homes that were being raided or to the *comisaria* to release people from arrest, taking food, clothing, soap, medicines and other necessities to those in hiding, comforting the distressed or merely bringing his cheerful smile to the lonely and anxious. Jinks was now regularly sending him a parcel of food, tobacco, soap and so on every week from London, but virtually all of it he gave away.

Armed with his pass, he resumed also his occasional visits to the front. The heightened tempo of operations, however, made this increasingly difficult, and he had no wish to be bagged again by Franco's forces, though he only narrowly escaped when, on another visit to the Guardarramas, he was pinned down by an unexpected machine-gun which opened fire at short range as he turned a corner. The simple truth was that he loved danger and his propensity for "sticking his big nose into trouble" seemed incurable.

For these purposes he took pains to cultivate relations with all sorts of officials, police and militiamen. With all these he got on uncommonly well. They liked his frank and open manner and his cheerful and confident laugh and, as a foreign neutral, he was outside those considerations of politics and of personal hatred which alone normally cloud the charm of the Spanish character. But he knew only too well how malignant a change there would be if, by some ill chance, he were to fall foul of them.

His resourcefulness in dealing with the situation brought smiles to everyone when they heard how he had solved the problems of Commander Ivan B. Franks, a breezy retired naval officer who, with the concurrence of the Republican government, had been sent out by the new Air Raid Precautions branch of the Home Office to study the effects of aerial bombing. Willing enough at first to co-operate in "this humanitarian work", the Madrid Junta of Defence for some reason quickly cooled off and Franks soon found himself at a loss. One of his tasks was to measure bomb-craters, which innocent act the Junta had forbidden him to do and had ordered the militia sentries who were placed at all bomb-craters to prevent him.

Lance, when told about this predicament, said to Franks:

"What nonsense! Come along, I'll show you how to measure the darned thing; it's quite easy."

Off they went to the nearest crater, which was in the middle of a street, and strolled up to its lip, the sentry eyeing them carefully. Lance took out a packet of cigarettes, lit one slowly and contemplatively, knowing that the tobacco-starved sentry was watching with envious desire. Lance then threw the packet casually down into the crater.

The surprised sentry looked down and saw that the packet was a nearly full one. He laid down his rifle, clambered into the crater, collected the packet and stood up.

"Well," said Lance to Franks, "do you agree that he is about five feet ten and that his head is about two feet below road level? Is that near enough for you? Now for the diameter."

As the sentry climbed up again, Lance stalked casually round the perimeter of the crater, counting his steps. Coming back to Franks, he said: "That's the circumference; just apply the schoolboy's formula for your diameter."

Together they did this over and over again. Splinter-marks on walls they stared at apparently aimlessly but in fact they memorized them and drew diagrams as soon as possible afterwards. It was expensive in cigarettes, but, as Franks said: "Working with you is about three times as fast and efficient as trailing round with that chattering liaison officer."

Even the liaison officer provided by the Junta, however, came in useful. His name was Captain José Maria Gallan Sancho and he claimed to have been educated at what he suspiciously called "King's College, Oxford". His usefulness was suggested by Captain E. C. Richards, the shrewd Assistant Military Attaché, for when Franks was forbidden also to take photographs of bomb effects, Gallan Sancho was coaxed into taking them for him.

By such little incidents was the grim life of Madrid occasionally lightened as the guns barked and the shells cracked not very far away; as it was also by Ogilvie-Forbes himself, when to overcome his revulsion at the horrors to be seen daily in the streets, which, he said to Lance and Franks, "are properly getting me down", he took to playing the bagpipes in the evening, to the open-mouthed astonishment of all Spaniards within hearing. Life was further alleviated by the generosity of a British wine merchant, who, when evacuated from Madrid, left a consignment of liquor for use in the Embassy. Tobacco and cigarettes, which for months had been unobtainable in the city, together with bully beef, tinned salmon, precious tinned milk and other supplies, were landed for the British community by the Royal Navy at Alicante or Valencia and brought up by Embassy lorry. Thus was the daily fare of lentils, dried beans, oranges and bread somewhat alleviated, but most of the extra food was given away to starving Spaniards.

Under the more straitened and dangerous conditions in the city there were now a good many more British subjects, or those who claimed to be such, who were anxious to get away. After the evacuations by train in the last week of July there had been a steady trickle of further applicants. Their names had been noted and they had been told to return to their homes and wait. As their numbers had mounted, Lance, again taking the initiative in these matters, had suggested to Forbes that, there being no more trains, they should be evacuated by road convoys. Forbes heartily approved and asked Lance to take charge of the operation. Christopher eagerly agreed. One thing Forbes insisted upon, however —everyone *must* have proper papers. It was in this manner that Lance took a further step forward on that path which was to lead him on to those dangerous fields where his special mission lay.

He threw himself into his new task with his customary alacrity and enthusiasm. There was a tremendous amount to be done— passes, permissions to leave Madrid, facilities from the police, the War Office, the Foreign Office, the evacuees themselves to be documented and collected. Not all by any means were right-wing sympathisers, as a party from the Scottish Ambulance showed when they sang the "Red Flag" on board a British warship while their companion travellers were undergoing a bitter ordeal ashore. Nor (as we may significantly note for the future) were all legally British; there were British wives of Spaniards, Spanish servants of Britons and others who had some special as-sociations. The Consul made lists of these for the Republican authorities and asked if there was any objection to their leaving the country. The rest of the preparations fell largely on Lance's shoulders. He had an extraordinary way with Spanish officials. They were co-operative, and the military junta provided two army lorries and drivers, but they imposed some stringent re-strictions: in particular, that no jewellery was to be taken by the evacuees and only a stated minimum of money. Lance therefore collected all their jewels and surplus money, adding them to the store of paper parcels he already had in the big Embassy safe.

Finally, as there were going to be a lot of women and children in these convoys, he recruited the colourful Fernanda Jacobson as an ally and she promised to bring along one of her ambulances.

Margery Hill also gave Lance her valuable aid, lending him the hospital's big, black Chevrolet and her remarkable chauffeur, José ("Pepe") Lopez Jurado. It was the beginning of a memorable association, carried on into the more dangerous days to come. Pepe Jurado was altogether an exceptional fellow, with a shrewd intelligence, a devoted loyalty and a very stout heart. An ardent royalist and formerly a chauffeur in the service of the royal family, he had all the good breeding of the old-fashioned servant. In a fashion that has almost vanished, he never addressed Margery or Lance in the second person, but in the third. Swarthy and slight, he was the pattern of good manners and the soul of discretion, but when some joke was made to him or when he was encouraged to relax his formality he would break into an infectious smile and his eyes sparkle with good humour.

Thus prepared, Lance began his convoys, making for palm-fringed Alicante on the Mediterranean, where Forbes made arrangements for them to be taken off in British warships when available. The direct road to Alicante having been cut by Franco on that September day when Lance and Hall were captured, the convoys were obliged to start out by way of the road to Valencia and thence through Albacete.

Leaving the Embassy in the bitter cold of two in the morning, when Franco's guns habitually sent a brisk scattering of shells into the city, the evacuees, crowded into the comfortless lorries, had an exhausting journey. Lurching into the pot-holes with which all the roads were pitted, they traversed innumerable dirty little villages blotted with the charred shells of churches, passed fallow fields which seemed to be in motion as the cloud-shadows raced across them before the merciless north wind, beside green-grey olive groves, ghost-like in the dawn, through naked vineyards laid out in rigid ranks—scenes in which the war seemed remote enough until they came suddenly upon one of the innumerable posts where the boiler-suited guards brandished their weapons and demanded passes. Lance, however, as we have seen, was very well up in that particular, and he had again equipped himself with a document that would impress any sentry. Few of them could read it, often scrutinizing it upside down, but the rubber stamps and the red ink were all.

Lance, knowing that these men loved holding people up in the exercise of their small authority but knowing also that most of them, beneath their unshaven exterior, were decent and friendly until their passions or suspicions were aroused, paid studied attention to these guards. First noting carefully where they were all located, he took pains to be on good terms with them. Whenever stopped, he got out of the car, held a lighthearted conversation with them and offered them cigarettes, quick passports to the hearts of nearly all. Had they been to the front recently? What was it like there? Wasn't the road dreadful? There would be some nice repair jobs for Gines Navarro's when the war was over! They would part with a *Salud* or with one of the numerous popular catch phrases of the Republican side, such as *Viva la Republica, Viva la Rusia*, "Death to the Fascists," or the more significant *No pasarán*, imitated from the heroic "They shall not pass" of the French at the defence of Verdun.

He gave no bribes, other than a few cigarettes, making this a fixed rule from the outset and adhering to it till the end and he did nothing to offend Republican laws. From the beginning, however, he made it a deliberate policy to make himself conspicuous and easily remembered. His un-Spanish breeziness and his deep-throated laugh were no doubt enough, but he also made himself conspicuous in dress, wearing on these occasions a jacket with a very bold check and the prominent tie of the Lancing Old Boys in chocolate, pink and grey.

He was always glad to leave behind the cutting winter winds that swept the central plateau and come to the more genial air and the luminous sky of Alicante. It was a favourite old haunt of his and here he had spent many happy days with Jinks and here, in the end, he was to be undone. From the smooth arc of the Mediterranean shore, the town climbed steeply up the slopes of the amphitheatre of parched and whitened hills that embraced it, roasting for most of the year in a fierce heat, dominated by the high hill of Santa Barbara, crowned with its ancient fort, and throwing out seaward the long, clasping arms of its jetties, where

Lance on more than one occasion was to be within an inch of tragedy.

Most memorable of Alicante's features, however, embroidering the esplanade that fringed the sea's curving lip, was the spendid double avenue of palm-trees that swept round the entire front, making dark green tunnels to give cool shade by day, but, in times of peace, transformed each night into brilliant walks of coloured lights, in which the *Alicantinos* paraded in the dignified ceremony of the evening *paseo*.

Landward of the long avenues stretched the buildings on the sea-front, where Gines Navarro had their offices and where stood Lance's favourite hotel, the Victoria. Over all this scene there hung a sky of such intense luminosity, at its keenest in June and in winter, that it seemed to be of a profounder blue than anywhere else in the Mediterranean.

Now, however, only the colours and the scenery remained the same. No longer did the bright lights illumine the palms for the evening *paseo*. Laughter had ceased and town and harbour were in the grip of the Anarchists. They had just murdered José Antonio Primo de Rivera, son of the old dictator and founder of the Falange, whose name is today publicly commemorated all over Spain. An Anarchist committee ruled the docks and through the sharp scrutiny of these extremists Lance had to manœuvre his charges before they were allowed to embark. They did not recognise as sufficient any pass or permit granted by any officer of the central state and, in the typical Anarchist manner, constituted themselves as the ultimate authority to grant permission to leave the country. They were a particularly bitter and flinty-hearted lot, with whom even Lance found it trying to deal and with whom he was never on as good terms as he was with others of their kind.

There was a terrible time when young Juan Navarro de Palencia and his English wife Constance came face to face with this fierce committee. Their flat in Madrid had been ransacked by the gangs and all their clothes stolen. Thus Navarro was clad in an old black dress coat with velvet collar, belonging to his father, very smart and conspicuous and looking very "Fascist". He had been obliged to make the journey from Madrid lying on a stretcher in the ambulance, to avoid observation, especially the "avid eyes of the militiamen" who clustered round them at Albacete. For no other reason than his dress, he was arrested immediately he arrived on the quay and put through a vicious questioning.

All the other evacuees, including the red-flag Scottish Ambulance party, passed through, boarded the launches from the British warship lying outside and were taken to safety. The Navarros and Lance were left alone, surrounded by a hostile audience as the scowling committee pressed their questions.

Constance, trembling with apprehension, turned very white and began to scream. Lance, gripping her wrist, said reassuringly: "Keep quiet, Constance; don't intervene yet." He then left her side mysteriously.

Standing a little way off, Constance and some friends with her could plainly hear what was going on at the interrogation. The local militia were then short of ammunition and accordingly, instead of shooting their victims, they were tying stones round their necks and throwing them off the quay. Constance now clearly heard them threaten her husband with the same fate and she saw him "turn green." She herself felt turned to stone, cold and rooted to the ground. Then she heard one of the committee say:

"All right, chuck him in."

Two others seized him by the arms, but at that precise moment Lance reappeared. This time there was no cajolery about his manner. He called out forcibly:

"Take your hands off that man at once. He is under the protection of the British Embassy and if he comes to any harm you shall answer for it."

The surprised committee stopped in their tracks, taken aback, for, as Constance Navarro said, Lance could give the law most convincingly when it was necessary. While the committee stood uncertain, a policeman, whose friendship Lance had cultivated, arrived and began to talk to the committee. It was to create this diversion that Lance had gone off so suddenly and he now quite calmly stepped forward, took Navarro by the arm and said "Come along." He led him and the distraught Constance straight to the

British naval launch that was waiting patiently for them at the landing steps and said to the fresh-faced young officer in command:

"A near thing, old boy; get 'em away quick."

After the tensions that these convoys imposed, how heart-warming it was at the end of the journey to behold the trim, grey shape of the British warship riding in the bay and to experience the exhilaration with which the vision of the White Ensign always suffused him! There under her sway dwelt sanity, cleanliness, trust and efficiency.

Lance could not help reflecting wistfully how easy it would have been for him to sail away in those ships of hope, back to Jinks, to a green country and a quiet fireside, but, although on more than one occasion he actually went on board, he knew that he would hate himself if he turned his back on all those who were looking to him for help in the grim streets of Madrid.

It was on these convoys, from which he returned with supplies of tinned foods, medical stores, soap and tobacco provided by the Royal Navy for the British community, that he built up a foundation of experiences on which he was to base his future activities. Very observant and attentive to detail, he stored up all that he learnt on the tablets of his memory. He kept contact with Don Francisco Valdes Casas, the Civil Governor of Alicante, as well as with Mr. H. C. Brooks, the British Vice-Consul there, a man very much admired by British and Spanish alike. Not least, he reached a close understanding with "Ernesto," the porter of the Victoria Hotel, where he always stayed as of yore.

Everywhere he took pains to make himself conspicuous, and soon he became known among the Spaniards as "the gentleman of the check jacket" (*el señor de la chaqueta cuadrada*), a breezy, extrovert *inglés* who was always cracking jokes. One could not suspect any mischievous intent in this "mad Englishman," who merely chatted light-heartedly when a tommy-gun was thrust through his car window or pointed at his belly.

Dim ideas began to form in Lance's mind. As the war situation had tightened up so much that he had been unable to find a safe escape route by land, what about the sea? Here was a way out of

Spain, not reserved only to foreigners and not denied to Spaniards who did not arouse suspicion or hatred, for whom a permit to leave Madrid could be obtained and whom he was able, by cajolery or bluff, to pass through the piercing scrutiny of the Anarchists who ruled the port. He kept his thoughts to himself, however, knowing that they were leading him to dangerous ground, and he moved slowly, for of all the things he had learned, the one that weighed most heavily upon him was the realization that the lives of those whom he escorted depended upon him.

At the turn of the year Ogilvie-Forbes removed the Embassy to the new seat of government at Valencia, where premises had been secured in the Calle Colón, and he asked Lance to go there with him. Lance declined, however, for he could not tear himself away from the work to which he was now dedicated nor bear the thought of leaving his friends in the lurch.

The Madrid Embassy being therefore closed, except for a caretaker staff, Lance, at Forbes's invitation, moved out to a flat on the top floor of an adjacent house which had been taken as an annexe. The house belonged to the old Marquesa de Argueso, who lived in some state in the basement and whom he found to be excellent and amusing company—an aristocrat of the old school, spirited, voluble, having a grand sense of humour and complete disdain for the "Reds." Lance called her his "Duchess" and she accepted the chivalric promotion with lively humour. Disregarding Lance's entreaties, she would sit on the balcony in her brightest finery and jewels in full view of the boiler-suits. Here both she and Lance were waited upon with impressive efficiency by Hilario, a tall and handsome butler from the Embassy staff, who was to be Lance's last "customer" on a night of high adventure.

Lance's stay there, however, was short. Almost every day people were coming to him for help of some kind. One of these was Mrs. Angela Norris, the Spanish wife of a Briton, who called on him at his flat on the top floor of the annexe on the bitter evening of January 8, begging him to get her Spanish servant away to safety.

Under the dim electric light Lance was sitting in an armchair, just beside the sideboard, and Mrs. Norris sat opposite him. There was a lone aircraft flying near and very low overhead. Nobody was shooting at it, so supposedly it was a Republican one.

In the middle of their conversation two bombs burst down the street and a second later a third crashed through the roof immediately above their heads. The room was wrecked, plunged in darkness and filled with swirling dust and smoke. Lance was knocked out by a blow from a falling beam and when he had recovered himself he heard cries from Angela Norris. By the illumination from an incendiary now flooding through the hole in the roof, he groped his way round a hole in the shattered floor and saw her lying trapped under timber and debris, bleeding from the head and covered in dust.

They were rescued by the Scottish Ambulance and taken to the British-American hospital to have their wounds dressed. They were not serious, but the next day Lance developed 'flu and Margery insisted that, now homeless, he should live permanently at her hospital and he did so, occupying a small, sparsely furnished private room, until the end. Subsequent investigations showed that the aircraft was almost certainly a Republican one, sent up to drop a few bombs on the Embassy neutral zone, with the intent of creating an "international incident" unfavourable to Franco. The bomb that destroyed Lance's flat had in fact gone clean through the Union Jack painted large on the roof.

By the end of January yet another list of applicants for evacuation had been built up at the consulate. Lance, paying a visit there to see the list, opened his eyes at some of the names. The *palabra* that he had given to Merry del Val was worrying his conscience, duress or no duress, but so far he had had no chance to do anything about it.

By now most of the embassies in Madrid, including those of countries that ardently supported the Republicans, such as Mexico, were carrying on a regular traffic in refugees, on a basis which, it was said, was highly profitable to some of the diplomatic representatives left in charge.

This traffic they were said to carry on by the simple process of bribery, for a great many of the officials of all grades, especially those who were not indoctrinated fanatics, were highly corrupt, the Anarchists being usually a notable exception. This traffic was pretty common knowledge and the truth was that the Republican authorities, quarrelling fiercely among themselves and their unions often openly in arms against each other, did not bother themselves very much about the flight of Spaniards from Spain unless they were persons whose blood they were after. But the temper of the local "committee" was a different matter and where the way had not been paved or when the documentation was not unquestionable there was always acute danger. For the Republican guards and police had no compassion and anyone who took liberties was liable to be shot out of hand or thrown into an unspeakable prison, without reference to any superior authority.

The British, in the matter of bribery, however, had a good name and Lance, as we have seen, set his face against it from the beginning, simply because he was a man of high principles who considered bribery to be an evil thing. Moreover, he had no money to dispense in ways of corruption, for the idea of taking fees from those whom he befriended was totally repugnant to him. It was never said of him, as it was of others, that he was lining his pockets.

As a result, he was tremendously respected and trusted by all Spaniards among whom he moved and who had already begun to look upon him as a man who could achieve anything. He had not "lost" a single man or woman from his convoys to the militia and had not failed in any single mission to which he had been called.

He was brought hard to thinking on these things one critical day late in January. He had been given the use of a room in the offices of the Commercial Attaché, detached from the Embassy itself, and here, feeling very tight-lipped and rebellious after another morning of tragedy and horror, he began to make his plans for his next, and last, convoy.

First he telephoned Forbes in Valencia, who gave his approval for the convoy and promised to let him know when the next British warship would be available. Next he spoke to the Consul to secure his co-operation and to have all those on his list warned. Then, filling his pipe with navy tobacco, he sat drumming his fingers on the desk but pulled himself up when he realized how ominously it sounded like the thudding of the guns which, even at that moment, were shelling Franco's outposts in the scarred skeletons of the New University buildings.

The capture of Madrid by the Nationalists, he reflected, looked as far away as ever. There seemed to be no prospect of succour for all those to whom the Republican régime meant hardship, danger and bereavement. He thought of them now without fuel in this bitter weather, without adequate food, without soap, without fresh air in their shuttered houses, without medical aid, short of clothing, short of everything. The British element who might still want to get away had been getting smaller and smaller. Wasn't it high time, therefore, that the gateway to freedom was opened more widely? Not, certainly, to anyone who was genuinely an active "enemy of the Republic," but to those perfectly innocent persons who were jeopardized merely by their class, their religion or other associations. Not Franco's pals. Not yet. Not in any exodus that was under British protection. That would be against his conscience. For these he would have to be personally responsible.

Like other members of the committee and Margery Hill herself, he was also concerned at the number of refugees who had taken sanctuary in the hospital. It was now as full as could be. Living daily with them, as he now was, he saw clearly the need to thin them out. Thus there was a double purpose to fulfil.

Knocking out his pipe, he walked round there, deep in thought, oblivious to the litter that strewed the streets and to the freezing wind that whistled round the corner. After their meagre meal of lentils and oranges, he went into Margery's office, which looked out over the leafless acacias of the Calle de Velasquez on to a derelict garage beyond, and began to talk to her of what was in his mind. In his slow, measured speech he said:

"We really must do something about clearing out some of these pals of yours."

She looked at him sharply, not sure what he meant.

"There's nothing I'd like better, if there's a safe place."

"Well," he said speculatively, sounding her out, "what about getting them out on the next convoy?"

She was taken by surprise but answered eagerly:

"That would be splendid! But wouldn't it be fearfully risky?"

"A little, of course; but not seriously if the thing is handled the right way. D'you think they'll be prepared to take the risk?"

"I'm sure most of them would be only too glad to, especially if they know you are going to take them out. They've tremendous faith in you."

"All right, then," he said. "Will you pick out the people you want to send first and put it to them, terribly tactfully?" He knew that she would be the soul of discretion, and went on: "There are a few of my own people I want to get out too. But I shall want your help, Margery."

"Of course. What can I do?"

"Well, I know how awfully good you are at handling these officials and these tough guys on the road. Do you think you could tear yourself away for two or three days and come with me?"

She jumped at the suggestion, saying: "I'd love to. You know I'll do anything to help. Besides, it will give me a chance to get some more medical supplies from the Navy."

Lance was delighted and broke into his wide smile. "That's wonderful!" he said. "You'll be a tower of strength."

"There may," she said, already thinking of whom she would take first, "be one or two invalids and perhaps babies. D'you think you could persuade Miss Jacobson to lend us one of her ambulances?"

"I'm sure she would. What's more, I bet she'll come herself."

After a few days, word came from Forbes that a ship would be available at Alicante on February 6 and Lance accordingly made arrangements for the convoy to leave Madrid at about three in the morning on that day. The Government, as before, lent three military lorries. But as the day approached Lance felt his anxiety rising. He felt very responsible for this convoy, both because he did not want to let Forbes down by any serious diplomatic "incident", but more particularly because he knew that so many lives would depend upon him and he wondered how some of them could hope to show any satisfactory documents.

At first there were only some thirty names on the list, but as word went round more and more people asked to be taken. Lance put down one or two of the "safer" of his own circle, warning them, however, that they must produce some acceptable papers. He watched the list grow with feelings of amusement not unmixed with some anxiety. Eric Glaisher startled him with a very "dangerous" name. As we have seen, Glaisher had been the friend of the murdered playwright Pedro Muñoz Seca, whose flat the hospital was occupying, and he now asked Lance to take Muñoz Seca's daughter. Lance whistled. "Damned risky, Eric," he said, but it was not in him to refuse. Another very dangerous applicant was Fernandez Shaw, the architect of the original hospital, who was known to be "wanted" by the gunmen.

The lists were finally closed with seventy-two names. Many of them, particularly those on the Consul's list of applicants, were quite unknown to Lance and only twelve of them were known to have British passports. Nearly all had Spanish names. All were advised to report at the Embassy not later than eight p.m. on the fifth and Lance personally collected from their hidings all those who could not safely come outdoors alone. Though he wore a buoyant air to give them all confidence, he was inwardly very anxious, especially when someone plucked his sleeve as the people were coming in to the Embassy and said:

"Good gracious! Do you know who *that* is?"

They were nearly all, he noted, very frightened people, though most of them appeared to shed their fear when they were safely within the Embassy walls. They were a silent crowd, talking little together, save for some few who greeted old acquaintances with surprise. There were many women and several children, including three or four babies in arms. How relieved he felt that he had got Margery Hill and Fernanda Jacobson with him! When they were all assembled, he addressed them, telling them to hand in all their jewellery and any money in excess of the sum allowed by the Government, for safe keeping in the Embassy. He also warned them of the risks that were run by everyone who had no adequate papers and told them that they could go home if they liked.

They then all filed before him to hand in their valuables and show their papers. Lance's face grew longer and longer. Many of the people had no papers at all, including several on the Consul's list, and the best that most of them could produce were such scanty things as membership cards of the British Chamber of Commerce or of the British-American Club. The fact was that, in their extremity, these people were equipped only with a trustfulness that somehow Captain Lance would find a way. He took a chance on them, however, knowing how much he could hope to get away with by a little boldness.

Yet he was perturbed and late in the evening he went to see the Consul, showing the names of those on the Consulate list who had no papers. None of those, the Consul said, could be allowed to go. They had a few disagreeable words together, for Lance was not on very good terms with the Consul, who said, in a manner that had infuriated Lance more than once before: "I can do nothing."

Feeling angry and troubled, Lance returned to the Embassy, went into Forbes's old room and sat down to think and pray. What was the right thing to do? Obey the letter of the regulations or save life? The ever-present picture of the murder-pits was sufficient to decide him.

No, he could not let down these poor, frightened people who had put their trust in him. He had not the heart to tell them to go home. It was humanly impossible. It was not even difficult for him to come to that decision, for it was the only one.

He went down again and told Margery Hill and Miss Jacobson all about it and asked them their opinion, without disclosing his own. What did they think he should do? Send them all home? Margery was emphatic.

"Good heavens!" she exclaimed. "That's unthinkable."

"Would it be unfair to these people? Ought we to allow them to run the risk?"

"It would be even more than unfair to send the poor creatures home now; it would be inhuman. You know quite well what that would mean."

Miss Jacobson added:

"You gave them the chance to back out and they've accepted the risk. Besides, you've seen us through before and I'm sure you'll do it again."

Much relieved, Lance said: "Well, I knew you'd think that way, but I just wanted to be sure."

Thus supported in his decision, Lance went ahead. They all lay down for a few hours' rest on the mattresses that still lay in the Embassy. At two a.m. Lance rose, washed and shaved as was his wont and summoned his flock. They moved off in the very cold early hours of that February night. As on the previous occasions, Pepe was driving the car in which Lance and Margery rode and they had one of the sick fugitives with them also. Three more invalids rode in the rear vehicle with Fernanda Jacobson, driven by one of her Scottish drivers. The other sixty-eight evacuees, including the babies and children, rode in three Republican lorries, very crowded and uncomfortable.

Thanks to his check coat and his colourful tie, which he wore as usual, Lance was immediately recognized everywhere by the sentries and controls. At each of the thirty-two posts he got out of the car, greeted the sentries breezily and chatted about anything but his business. The majority of the sentries never even asked him any questions and they parted with a *Salud,* raised fists and *No pasarán.* Other posts, as he knew, were less easygoing and at these, before they themselves had a chance of asking for his safe-conduct, which he had not got for this journey, he produced one for a previous journey. As few of these sentries could read, the rubber stamps with which it was decorated were quite enough.

As Franco was now working round to the south-east of Madrid and threatening even the Valencia road, Lance had been ordered by the Junta of Defence to make a wide detour taking the Barcelona road as far as Torrejon de Ardoz and thence southward to the Valencia road at Arganda del Rey. It so happened that that very day Franco launched a fresh attack up the Jarama valley, which runs south-east and east of Madrid, and the convoy thus passed very close to the front when the battle was at its height. The shell-fire and the chatter of machine-guns was clearly heard on their right and, indeed, as they turned out at Arganda the Valencia road was being shelled only a mile or so behind them. Lance remarked to Margery that it all sounded very like a "push" and if it were successful they might never get back to Madrid. The Nationalist attack, however, did not get very far and was halted by the stout defence of the International Brigade.

After a nightmare journey of fifteen hours, they reached Alicante at five o'clock in the evening. There Lance and the two women found accommodation for the evacuees at five hotels in different parts of the town and by the time they themselves arrived at the Victoria Hotel for dinner they were exhausted. Lance said to Margery:

"This trip has put years on me already. How on earth are we going to smuggle sixty people out of the country?"

The first trouble occurred just as they sat down to dinner. A message was handed to Lance begging him to go round at once to one of the hotels where his charges were lodged.

There he found two police agents and three members of the Communist Committee who were running the hotel interrogating a very pale and frightened woman. It immediately occurred to Lance that he had forgotten to give instructions to the party what they were to say about their documents; for it was necessary at these hotels for every visitor not only to fill in a formidable questionnaire but also to produce an identity card or passport.

Fortunately one of the police agents was one of the men with whom, in accordance with his calculated practice, he had made friends on a previous visit. He recognized Lance at once and they greeted as old friends, turning an icy atmosphere at once into a warm one. Thinking fast, Lance said:

"It is all right, comrade. I have the documents for all these refugees. There are a lot more in other hotels—seventy-two altogether. I shall hand over all the documents to the British Consul tomorrow, and these people are then all embarking on a British warship."

This explanation went down well, but, in case there should be any awkward cross-questioning, he quickly excused himself.

"I really must go, comrade. There are two ladies waiting for me to dine with them. Come round to my hotel later on for a drink."

He rushed round to all the other four hotels and warned them what to say if the police called and to send at once for him if there was any difficulty.

He waited up at the Victoria till after midnight for his police guests. Dog-tired, he went to bed and was asleep when at last they came at two a.m., brought up on his previous instructions by Ernesto, the porter whose friendship he had secured. A bottle of whisky was produced, together with a dish of the grilled prawns for which Alicante is famous. They drank until four in the morning coming to no definite conclusions, as he told Margery the next morning, except that they were all jolly good fellows and would meet again the next night.

Notwithstanding this alcoholic ordeal and virtually two nights without sleep, Lance was up early next morning to reconnoitre. Alicante was bathed in winter mildness. He walked down to the waterfront, across the avenue of palms, and there, anchored just outside the harbour in the placid, blue stillness lay the ever sure symbol of quiet assurance and confidence—a British man-of-war.

Lance gazed at her with warm emotion, thinking of the clean, ordered, civilized life on board her, the air of brisk efficiency and the climate of quiet trust and confidence that pervaded her trim decks. So near she was, yet she might have been a thousand miles away for all the hope he had of getting his charges on board. It was quite impossible to get this phalanx of people, mainly women and children, past the Anarchist dock committee and other vigilant eyes, without some sort of authority.

For a very ugly situation had quickly developed in the town. The refugees, instead of staying quietly in their hotels, had unwisely come out into the street and were sitting at the pavement tables outside the cafés. They had immediately attracted attention by their unproletarian dress, their looks and their speech. The *Alicantinos* had become accustomed to Lance's British convoys, but, looking at these people, they stopped sharply in their footsteps and exclaimed:

"These are not *ingleses*!"

They began to collect and very soon there were angry cries and hisses of: "Fascists!" The crowds grew larger and more and more hostile.

In desperation Lance called on his old friend Valdes Casas, the Civil Governor, accompanied by Margery Hill and Fernanda Jacobson. They found themselves in a well-appointed office in the old Spanish style with gilded furniture and fine red upholstery, and Don Francisco rose to greet them from behind his desk. The two women sat down, Miss Jacobson in her kilt, Margery in plain skirt and cardigan and hatless to conform with the compulsion of the times. Lance, preferring to stand by the side of the desk, put his case.

Not knowing what else to say and following the precepts he had prescribed for himself, he placed his cards candidly on the table, told Don Francisco the full truth in confidence and asked him to help a friend out of a tight corner. It was a hell of a risk, but the least of several risks.

The Civil Governor was sympathetic. He did not, as he might well have done, say that he was sorry but it was a matter for police action. But he could offer no practical solution, except that all the sixty undocumented cases should be sent back to Madrid. At this obvious suggestion Lance mentally rebelled. He was darned if he would.

"Couldn't you," he suggested, "give an order to the port committee to authorize embarkation and give all these people provisional papers?"

The Governor shook his head. The Anarchist committee was all-powerful. "I'm afraid it is beyond my power, Capitán Lance. I'm afraid there's nothing at all that could be done to let them through, short of an order from the Minister for Foreign Affairs himself."

This, the Governor expected, would quite definitely close this tiresome matter; but he was never more mistaken. Lance, who knew perfectly well that in fact the Governor was scared stiff of the fanatical committees, astonished him by replying instantly:

"Very well, then, I'll telephone the Foreign Minister myself at once. Please ask your operator to get me Señor Alvarez del Vayo personally."

The Governor was very much taken aback. Clearly this *inglés* of the measured speech and deep laugh had powerful friends. Margery Hill, however, sitting quietly to one side, knew that it was sheer nerve. She smiled and thought: "Well done, Christopher!"

The priority call to Valencia came through quickly and Lance took the receiver. He greeted Alvarez del Vayo cheerfully and said:

"You remember our last meeting, Señor Alvarez del Vayo, after you had got me released from arrest at Alicante?"

"Certainly, señor: I was glad to be of help. I hope they have not put you in prison again?"

Lance laughed. "Fortunately not yet, but I'm in another little difficulty." He went on to remind Alvarez del Vayo that he had already taken several convoys of refugees for embarkation at Alicante—a fact of which the Foreign Minister was well aware—and that he had never had any trouble; that here he was again with seventy-two refugees and a British ship all ready for them, but for some reason was unable to get them embarked. The Civil Governor was willing to help but was not in a position to act without an authority from the Minister himself. Would the Minister have the great kindness to give the authority by three in the afternoon?

He paused for the reply, his heart in his mouth. Then he heard Alvarez del Vayo say slowly:

"I think I can probably help you. But first you will have to give me a list of all the names."

Again Lance had to think quickly. It happens that Spaniards have dual surnames, derived from both their parents, and, whereas in conversation and informal writings, the husband's or father's name only is used, in official documents both are required. Lance, thinking of some of these dual surnames on his list, groaned inwardly, for several of them, particularly Señorita Muñoz Seca, were of prominent right-wing families upon whom the shooting gangs would have loved to lay their hands. As he began to read out the names to a secretary in the Foreign Minister's office, however, he gave only one surname, avoiding any one that might be notorious. It worked. No question was asked the other end and he therefore continued in the same manner throughout the whole list, being careful, whether there was any danger or not, to give one name only, either the paternal or the maternal. He gave a sigh of relief when, after half an hour on the telephone, he at last hung up.

Alvarez del Vayo did not ask, nor did Lance volunteer the information, whether all these people held the proper documents. Once again audacity paid. By two-thirty that afternoon the

Governor received a telegram from the Foreign Minister giving the required authority for the party to embark.

Meanwhile, however, the position outside had become worse. The word had run quickly through the Anarchist-ridden town about this mysterious party of refugees and crowds had gathered round their hotels. Lance got them into the lorries and away to the port, but as they drove off the crowds were yelling:

"They are Fascists! Kill them! Shoot them before they get away!"

In the docks the unhappy people had to face an even worse ordeal. As they dismounted from their lorries they were confronted by seven or eight of the port committee. This junta of Anarchists, which now ruled the docks, was composed of youths of about twenty, the eldest not more than twenty-four. A wild-looking gang, unkempt, clad in the usual blue overalls and all armed, they glared at the refugees with hate and venom burning in their tigerish eyes. Lance tried his usual tactics. Approaching them with Margery, he said:

"Good afternoon, comrades. I have brought another convoy and the British ship out there is waiting for them. I have this telegram of clearance for them from the Foreign Minister and this order from the Civil Governor."

This time, however, his breezy manner did not work. They looked cursorily at the documents and burst out with angry imprecations. The Governor's order was invalid and the telegram a fake. The tirade of abuse and profanity rose to a towering climax while Lance and Margery wondered apprehensively where all this was leading. When the storm of words was spent, the refugees were ordered to follow the committee.

They were led into a shed and there were rigorously searched. There was little enough of luggage that the refugees carried, but on the persons of two women, in spite of the warning that Lance had given in Madrid, were found some articles of value. These the committee put in their pockets, then, to Lance's dismay, they walked off without a word, leaving the refugees high and dry. Lance went after them and asked what was to happen. One of them replied tartly:

"We are going because it will be dark soon and no lights are allowed. Anyhow, we have no intention of allowing you to leave. You are only a lot of damned Fascists and we've finished with you."

Things were now looking desperate. Many of the refugees were weary, hungry and forlorn. Wondering what on earth to do next, Lance left the party to the care of Margery and Fernanda Jacobson, and hurried back on foot to the Civil Governor, then the Military Governor, the police headquarters and the port offices, trying to get someone to do something. All voiced their sympathy, but none dared do a thing for fear of Anarchist anger and vengeance. More than once he was told that the party stood no hope of getting through and that they had better all go back to Madrid. Lance set his teeth and went on trying. Night had fallen in the uneasy silence of a frightened city, where none but the armed boiler-suits dared stir abroad at night.

At his wits' end, he returned to the darkened docks at about eight o'clock to find to his horror that, although the public were normally forbidden to enter, on this occasion they had been deliberately incited to go in by the Anarchists in order to provoke an incident which would justify them in taking violent action.

A hostile mob was fretting round the refugees in the dark, shouting insults, their surging dark shapes silhouetted against the grey background of sky and sea. The refugees themselves, exhausted and strained though they were, behaved with admirable calm but greeted Lance's return with tremendous relief. The mothers of some of the youngest children had collapsed from exhaustion and the indomitable Margery was sitting on a bollard with two babies in her arms and was giving a word of comfort to a woman in her party and in a miraculous way also humouring the menacing crowd. Close by, Miss Jacobson had another baby in her arms. The scene of fortitude and strength of character, which confronted him on his return, was one that Lance was always to remember. Even the two women, however, now thought that they would never get through and one of them said to Lance:

"It looks pretty hopeless. Wouldn't it be best to go back?"

Forcing a laugh, Lance answered:

"By George, no! We are not going to surrender to this lot."

In this dangerous situation the tramp of marching feet was heard in the darkness and a force of about fifty carabiniers arrived on the quayside. Dead silence. What did this mean? Was it a shooting squad? There were many who thought that the end had come.

Lance, however, with his usual buoyancy, went straight up to the officer in command, greeted him cheerfully and said:

"My word, I *am* glad to see you. There seems to have been an awful lot of fuss and bother about this convoy. I can't understand it."

He was vastly relieved when the officer replied:

"That is all right, señor. I have orders to see you safely embarked. We'll clear this crowd out for a start."

The mob themselves had fallen silent at sight of the carabiniers, equally uncertain what they would do. They were now left in no doubt and in a few minutes the quay was cleared.

Once more Lance and his party were summoned into the shed. As they went in at the door he whispered in Margery's ear:

"All O.K. now, Margery."

But he very soon found that it was far from O.K.

This time they found the committee, augmented to twelve in number, seated round a large table. A small crowd of sightseers had drifted back into the docks and were ranged behind. The scene was dimly lit by some hurricane lamps and in their pale, graveyard gleam the aspect of the committee appeared more menacing than ever. Their loathing impregnated the sombre atmosphere. They were, in fact, infuriated that Lance should have gone over their heads to the highest possible authority; for in the meantime they had learned that Alvarez del Vayo's telegram was genuine. Lance's running to and fro had borne fruit and behind the scenes someone had acted. Thus frustrated, the committee was determined to grill the party once more and, if they could, to find some victim for the altar of their hate.

Once more every man, woman and child was searched to the skin. The bag this time was naturally small, but Lance was extremely angry when, in spite of the warnings that he had given, one woman was found to have a sum equivalent to about £50 hidden in her corsets. There was a moment of sensation as the

Anarchist woman who was searching her pulled out the bundle of *peseta* notes, held them about her head and screamed:

"There! What did I tell you? Making away with the treasure of the Republic! What shall I do with it?"

Quick as thought, Lance supplied the inspired answer:

"Keep it!"

Thus prompted, the woman shot off like a shell from a gun, sprinting for the door and off into the darkness of the quay as fast as she could go. Two others immediately raced after her, shouting: "It's not hers! Stop her!"

The committee, who had half-risen in consternation at this diversion, sat down again with set faces, their self-confidence shaken and their anger against the offending refugee turned against one of their own people who had tricked them out of their share of the spoils.

Each of the seventy-two people was brought separately before the committee, and, standing in the dim circumference of the lamps' wan rays, with giant shadows silhouetted on the walls beyond, put through a harrowing cross-examination.

Quite early Señorita Muñoz Seca, a beautiful girl of about eighteen, came before them and Lance's heart was in his mouth. The name was notorious among the working classes and it was the one above all others which Lance had feared when he had read out the list to the Foreign Minister's secretary. He had accordingly given her the name Muñoz only, that being a fairly common name in Spain. Young and utterly blameless though she was, the girl was now also wanted, merely because she was the daughter of her father.

She stood now before the black-browed men, a small, pale, lonely figure, unskilled in the dealings of the world. The committee were in their most virulent form, and they seemed from the outset to be suspicious of her identity.

"Where," the chairman asked acidly, "are you trying to go?"

"To Paris," she replied.

"Why go such a long way round to the Nationalist headquarters?"

"I am not going to Burgos"—in a very small voice.

"What is the other part of your surname?"

Lance held his breath. The poor girl was visibly paling in the dim light, but, with great self-possession, she instantly invented a name. Then came the most dangerous question of all:

"Do you know Señorita Muñoz Seca?"

It was a bad moment for everyone, a moment of crisis and in the crisis it was Margery Hill who came to the rescue.

Still carrying the two babies in her arms, the little matron let fly at the twelve interrogators.

"How," she exclaimed, "can you be such brutes to a young girl? Can't you see that she is tired out after her journey? I was born in Alicante myself and I have always believed the *Alicantinos* to be *caballeros*. I have always thought so till now. How would you feel if you saw your own sisters or daughters being bullied in the way you are bullying this young and innocent girl? I shall be ashamed of Alicante for ever if you go on behaving like brutes."

It was a brave effort in the tense and dangerous atmosphere, with fear riding the night air. The rough and violent men around the dim lamps were suddenly mesmerized by this little woman who stood up to them so challengingly. With a shrug of the shoulders, the chairman said:

"Oh, let her go!"

At last the long, dark ordeal was over. Every man and woman was provided with an embarkation permit. Lance left the sombre shed with a sigh of relief and there, standing on the quayside in the dark, was the heart-warming sight of a young British naval officer. The ship's boats from the British man-of-war were alongside. They had indeed been patiently waiting throughout this long ordeal. Lance went up to the young officer and said:

"Thank God you're here. We've had the most frightful time."

The officer replied:

"Glad to be able to help, Sir. All ready now?"

"Yes, all ready, but for goodness sake get them away as quickly as you can. Everything's all right for the moment, but things can change damned quickly in Alicante!"

# CHAPTER EIGHT

# A CASE OF ORANGES

IN Madrid, where Lance and Margery found that the Republicans were justifiably rejoicing over their successful stand on the Jarama, the British community, like most other foreign communities, had been reduced to a handful. These used to gather frequently at the Anglo-American Club which had recently been opened near the American Embassy in the neutral zone, where, together with their Spanish friends they were free from the shelling and were able to some extent to make good the complete loss of the normal social life of Madrid. Lance, gregarious and very social, was naturally to be seen there often, and there he met many others who were active in the relief of Spanish distress, such as Charles Clayton-Ray, another public works contractor, Eric Glaisher and Harold Stowe of the British Chamber of Commerce, who, as Lance put it to Jinks later, "used his place in an ingenious and delightfully illegal way".

The Bank of London and South America also became a sort of club for the British community and their other customers, to whom they used to dispense cups of hot bovril that were a godsend to them all. Margery Hill was a frequent visitor there, and Lance, visiting one day, had the door opened for him by a six-inch shell that failed to explode.

There was to be a break in this now small community, however, for Glaisher got into trouble. He was a very generous man, who would have given the shirt off his back to anyone in trouble, and he had been helping Spaniards from his own resources almost to prodigality. One day he wrote a very indiscreet letter which angered the Republican censors. He was arrested and confined in a flat, formerly a "high-class brothel", commandeered by the police as a temporary place of confinement for special prisoners. On hearing of this, Lance instantly called on the Chief of Police and secured his release on the condition that he left the country at once. He then visited Glaisher in the flat to tell him the news, little reckoning that he was himself to be its unwilling tenant one day.

Margery had opened an out-patients' department for Spaniards and had endeared herself to men and women of all classes and all political opinions by her works of mercy. She had devoted assistance from Pilar Marin, her assistant. She also visited the Republican prisons, by permission, to do what she could for nursing mothers and babies who were shut up in them; and three of these she was able to get released.

Some of the Security Police knew perfectly well that the hospital was hiding Nationalists as "patients" and from time to time made formal searches of it, but they always gave notice of their intention and allowed Margery or Doña Pilar to lead the search party, so that the dangerous cases were able, on a prearranged plan, to move from room to room as the search proceeded. One of these patients was the Nationalist Colonel Antonio Herraiz, who assumed the rôle of a paralysed priest and for nearly three years was assumed to be such even by the other patients, who, when the day of release came, more than two years later, stood amazed to see him rise and walk out of his invalid chair. The British patients included two very venerable men, one aged ninety and the other a blind octogenarian.

So good were Margery's relations with the Republican authorities that officials would often pay her purely social calls, and engage her in perfectly frank discussions. More than once they asked her what her politics were and she would reply:

"Politics? I am not concerned with politics. My business is with people who are in sickness or in trouble."

"Why," they would ask her again, "do you give help and shelter to Fascists, as we know you do?"

"Because they are people in trouble. I will help any Spaniard in trouble. It does not matter to me whether they are Right or Left. I am a nurse."

In March came news of how Franco's Italian Fascist troops, attempting a drive towards Madrid from the north-east had been wildly routed, with their tanks bogged down and their aircraft grounded by sudden rain, in what became inaccurately known as the Battle of Guadalajara, their compatriots on the opposite side being partly responsible for their defeat. It was one of the Republicans' few major victories of the war and their rejoicing was well founded. The fall of Madrid seemed further away than ever; but so also did any hope that the Republicans, lacking any cohesive strategy and always quarrelling with each other and with the obstinate Russians, would do anything to relieve the strain on the city. At that moment neither side seemed within range of winning the war.

In this situation Lance decided very soon afterwards to go home to England for a while. He was under pressure from many sides. Jinks was very anxious; McDonnell, his chief in London, knowing how little he could now do for the firm, was advising him to return; and Margery also was urging him. She saw him running into dangerous waters, knew how much Jinks wanted him and was also concerned about his health, for he had got very thin and strained. Lance himself realized that things had now got a bit hot for him and gave way readily enough to these promptings, but had no intention of going home for good. "Back in two months," he told his "Duchess". He had not forgotten his *palabra*, nor all those who were dependent on him for help.

Neither had he any intention of going alone. The opportunity of getting a few people safely out under his care was too good to miss. Margery asked him to take out five. The first of these were her married sister and her two children. Another was Ana Maria Cobian, one of the five daughters of Don Edouardo Cobian, who had been in Paris when the war had broken out and knew that he would certainly be a victim of the gunmen if he returned. Ana Cobian, who was an extremely attractive girl, had been in serious trouble through her active membership of Catholic Action and had been thrown into prison, whence Ogilvie-Forbes had helped to rescue her.

She was by no means an easy person to get out, nor were the two men who were added to Lance's party. These were Dr. Enrique Agrasot, who had been medical assistant to Dr. Luque and Juaquin Amel, one of Fernanda Jacobson's ambulance staff, who had been disillusioned by the excesses of the so-called democratic parties.

Even this little party gave Lance some bad moments. He took them all off on March 20, with Pepe driving one of the two cars in the dark and early hours. He went this time not to Alicante but to the maritime city of Valencia, 210 miles to the east.

No plans had been made in advance, no warship could be expected for these people, and Lance had to search the port, which was beyond the city, for some ship that would give them passage. None was sailing, he was told, for ten days, by which time Ana Cobian's permit to leave Spain would have expired. Very disturbed, he began to search the dockyard cafés and in one of them learnt that the *Palacio*, a small tramp of only 1,300 tons of the MacAndrew line, was to sail next day, bound for Antwerp. He managed to secure passages in her for all but the two "Red Cross boys", Agrasot and Amel, but Ana Cobian gave him some terrible moments when he had to face the port committee for permission for her to embark, for they were as grim as the Alicante committee and more efficient, keenly on the lookout for escaping Fascists.

The two "Red Cross boys" the shipping company firmly refused to accept. Try as he would, he could find no means of getting them away, meeting opposition on every side. In desperation he went back to Gentry's flat, where he had quartered the two young men, and said to them:

"We're not going to be beaten. There's one more chance, but it means a risk. The *Palacio* is putting in at Alicante tomorrow and staying two or three days. That will give me time to go ashore myself and make some kind of plot. I can send you down there in the car with Pepe. Are you prepared to take the risk?"

They agreed without hesitation. "We are in your hands, señor," Agrasot said. It was the formula that so many of these refugees used to Lance.

"Very well, go to the Victoria Hotel and I will meet you there tomorrow."

He did not at all care himself for the idea of going ashore at Alicante, knowing that he would be spotted at once and watched by a hundred eyes, but if they were prepared to take a risk, so must he. He duly left Valencia with the others on the twenty-first. Forbes, who had a soft spot both for him and for Ana Cobian, came to see them off; he was due to leave Spain himself a few days later.

The next day, as the *Palacio* approached, Lance, leaning over the rails with Ana Cobian beside him, beheld the white steeps of Alicante, crowned by the stony summit of Santa Barbara, crystallize under the profound blue of sky and sea. His searching eyes fell upon a British ship lying in the bay and as they drew nearer to it a broad grin spread over his face. It was the hospital ship *Maine*.

"Just the job," he said to Ana Cobian. "What could be more suitable for two Red Cross boys?"

What followed was described with typical inadequacy in the brief pencilled note that he gave to Pepe for Margery:

> "I won't give you all the details now, but I got the two lads on board the *Maine* against strong opposition from the police and then they transferred to destroyer for Gib. as hospital ship was scared of search. It was a bit of a strain but worth it. We are sailing tomorrow, thank goodness, for London, not Antwerp. Your family A1. Love and best of luck. *C.*"

He did not stay in England long. The sea trip soon set him up. All he really wanted to do at home was to be reunited with Jinks. He was soon fretting to be back. Home and green fields and a fireside and the lights of Piccadilly could not wash out the memory of the human shooting-galleries and of the starving people hiding within the shuttered houses. He knew that he must go back.

He passed a brief and happy sojourn with Jinks at her father's house in Surbiton, was wined and dined in the West End with a distinguished politician by Angus McDonnell and put on flesh again. Jinks, of course, did not want him to go back, but was too good a wife to deflect him from what he considered to be his path of duty.

"Anyone would be grateful," he said to her, "for such a grand opportunity of saving life."

McDonnell told him not to be an ass and to stay at home, but he answered:

"I can't possibly leave all those people in the lurch."

He knew now exactly what he was going to do.

An unexpected invitation added weight to his decision. He was asked by Marconi's, whose manager in Madrid had been murdered by the Republicans, to take care of their interests there until things returned to normal. They had heard of him and his qualities from McDonnell. He accepted, though with some reserve, for it was not his line of country, and it was typical of him, and not very wise, that he would not accept any rate of remuneration fixed in advance, "as I can't possibly tell how much I shall be worth to you."

So he left again after only a fortnight in England and was back to the dreariness of Madrid by about the 22nd of April, back to the beans and lentils, back to the bombs and shells, back to the shuttered houses and the corpses in the gutters. His Spanish friends greeted him with relief and hope; his British friends with astonishment, thinking that he could scarcely be mad enough to return voluntarily and must have been away on some dark and secret mission. As de Caux said, he was always a mysterious person, regarded by the European community as a dark horse, and the springs that actuated his Quixotic actions were not easily discernible. He gave no hint to a soul of his new intent.

He returned to his old quarters in the hospital, where he was warmly greeted, and went round cracking jokes. "Still know how to cook lentils?" he asked of Valentina Hernandez, who for so long had been performing wonders with that unpromising vegetable. The fleeting Spanish spring had come and gone and it was already summer, though the sun's rays were not yet charged with malice. Lance, back again to open-necked shirt and bare head, revelled in the genial heat. Militarily, he found the situation unchanged and apparently in a condition of stalemate. The end of the war seemed far out of sight. Franco had given up his attempts on Madrid, but sharp bickering still continued along the front line in the Casa de Campo, the West Park and the battered husks of the New University buildings. The shells still flew to and fro, shaking the houses, and the "aery devils of the sky" still "rained down mischief".

On the other hand, Lance discovered that the Republicans, eternally quarrelling, had been carrying on a brisk civil war among themselves in Catalonia, though he could not yet see that behind the political scenes another kind of war was going on. Largo Caballero was being rapidly jockeyed out of the Prime Minister's chair by the Russians, for, Communist though he was in all but name, he was Spaniard enough to resent being pushed around by foreigners. However, the Russians were determined that he should go and after Rosenberg had been replaced by Gaikis as their Ambassador, the heat was turned on and Largo Caballero's days were numbered.

Such goings on, however, were still concealed from Lance and his friends behind the curtains of political secrecy, but other significant things Lance noticed immediately he returned to Spain. In Valencia and elsewhere outside the battle zones (as George Orwell also noted bitterly) the proletarian veneer was wearing thin. The boiler-suits were giving way to smart tailorings. Fat profiteers, sleek cars and elegant women were to be seen about. Hotels for the Republican upper crust were well victualled, while the working classes queued at the food shops.

On the other hand, Lance noticed that, under pressure from Largo Caballero, the insensate shootings by roving gangs had been reduced and the various ragged militias were getting some semblance of cohesion. Equally significant were the large numbers of foreign troops that had poured into the Spanish cockpit on both sides—Mussolini's Italians and Hitler's Germans on Franco's side and Stalin's Russians and the International Brigade, recruited by the Communists from the nations of the world, on the Republican. But, whereas Franco kept control of his own military machine, that of the Republicans was dominated and at times intimidated by the Russian General Staff under General Goriev.

It was with this general background in his mind that Lance, one day very soon after his return, while the Nationalists were flinging an occasional shell into the centre of the city, sat down in his office in the Commercial Secretariat, and pondered on the critical new step he was to take. He knew the ropes fairly well now, he reflected, but the nature of the people he wanted to rescue, especially those on Merry del Val's list, made those ropes into tight-ropes. He would have to be darned careful to provide for every detail, every possible contingency. Factor by factor, he examined the problem of escapes by sea.

One thing he had decided upon very early—no women. Women were not in nearly so much danger of being bumped off as men and they were also being quite well enough provided for by all the various embassies that were busy in the convoy trade, under the protection of their flags and sometimes under a protection less reputable. What Lance was mainly concerned with was not merely getting people away to an easier life but to save those who were in danger of death. To politics he was indifferent. He was not concerned merely with the people on Merry del Val's list; that was merely a formal honouring of a bargain unwillingly entered into. There were other people far more important to him, including some quite humble people.

Secondly, he decided that he must use Valencia and not his favourite Alicante, which, for the time being at any rate, had become much too hot for him.

Further, it was plain that the only chance of getting out his "bodies" safely in future was to take only one at a time, or perhaps a pair—never more. No more convoys. What he proposed was to get them on board one of the small British tramp steamers, of about 1,000 tons, that were nearly always to be found at Valencia. Whether or not the masters of these ships would be willing to take them was a thing he had still to find out, but he knew them to be a pretty sporting lot and, liking as he did the company of men of the sea, he had often made a point of meeting them casually for a drink and a talk.

It wasn't going to be very difficult, he reflected, to get his "bodies" down to the coast, now that he knew the hang of how to deal with the guards on the way. But, having got to Valencia, what was he to do with them? How get them into the walled-off dockyard past the sentries on the formidable gates, without passes? Especially if they were prominent right-wing sympathisers liable to be recognized by the police or by anyone else. How smuggle them on board a ship unseen? At night-time? That seemed to be the obvious thing, and yet. . . .

The night meant things clandestine, banking on being unobserved. Banking, in fact, on luck. Well, that might work once,

Alicante: the avenue of palms

Alicante with hill of Santa Barbara and harbour entrance used by Lance

but not repeatedly. A chance, a small slip, and it would be all up, not only with the chap he was trying to get away but with himself also. There would be no wriggling out if he were caught doing anything questionable by stealth. The old police-court phrase at home came to his mind—"being on unauthorized premises at night". To be caught doing anything fishy, at night especially, was a quick way to the firing squad.

No, not the night; nor anything else clandestine. No stealth. Nothing suspicious. Bluff, that was the thing. A bit of nerve. Everything open and obvious in the clear light of day. Be as conspicuous as possible. Wear the old check coat again. The very opposite tactics of those employed in prisoner of war escapes. Use main entrances always; no slinking in at back doors. Do what duly authorized people would do. No false beards, no bodies in coffins or any other theatrical nonsense of that sort.

Most definitely no false papers. Better no papers at all. Also, most definitely, no abuse of uniforms; respect for all uniforms and no masquerading of fugitives in British ones—that, in his code of thinking, was a matter of principle.

In fine, do everything above board and, as far as possible, do nothing illegal or against conscience.

That left one plenty to think about. A hell of a lot of gaps. The stickiest ones were how to get an obvious Spaniard into the guarded docks and then how to get him on board a ship—and a ship going to the right place. Not a ship that might be going to Russia! Several British ships, he knew, went to Black Sea ports, for example. Other gaps and snags would certainly appear, too, that he could not see yet.

Could he pull this thing off alone? Apart from the obvious need for secrecy, he did not want to drag anyone else into such a risky affair. He cast his mind over those whom he knew, but could not see the right man. He wanted a "sympathetic" person who understood the Spaniards thoroughly.

He lit a pipe, walked over to the window and gazed contemplatively over the bleak rooftops to where, in a light breeze, the Union Jack of the Embassy was flying freely. Away somewhere in the neighbourhood of the Telefonica, Franco's shells were dropping with a crash and a tinkle of glass. What was Jinks doing at home in England on this spring day? He wished she were with him to give him her advice. Was it fair to her to take these risks? What would she say if she knew what he was going to do? In his thoughts he could hear her say, as he knew she would:

"Dagger, whatever you decide to do, I shall back you up."

All these things, Lance resolved, he would keep entirely to himself, with one exception—Margery Hill. For one thing, he was anxious to clear the hospital of its refugees, for another he had tremendous faith in her knowledge of the Spanish mind and method, which he had seen so remarkably demonstrated on that last convoy to Alicante. He had no intention whatever of taking her with him on these excursions, but there was no one else he could trust so completely for sound advice and practical help in dealing with Spaniards.

He walked thoughtfully back to his frugal two o'clock lunch at the hospital. It was early May and the sun was beginning to hot up. The light breeze had dropped and the flags of the embassies drooped in pleated folds at their masts. A ragged child of fourteen, armed with a revolver, was scrabbling through the refuse that had accumulated in the gutter, searching for he knew not what. The shelling had stopped. High up in the deep blue sky, too bright to look at for long in comfort, an aircraft droned lazily. Russian, he thought, to judge from its blunt nose. At a lower level a stork flew with slow wing-beats in its laboured flight. All else was quiet and still. The sacred hour was approaching.

After lunch, when everyone else was relaxed in the siesta, Lance had a long talk with Margery in her office overlooking the acacias. He began by reminding her of their conversation just after the last Alicante convoy and then outlined the basis of his still rather vague plan. She was tremendously thrilled, but concerned for his safety.

"Do be careful what you do," she warned.

"As far as possible," he answered, "I'll do nothing that doesn't seem absolutely safe, because if I fail, whoever I take will be 'for it'."

"So will you be."

"I've an embassy behind me. The really difficult thing will be to get the 'bodies' through the dock gates and on board without suspicion. But I've kept my eyes open in the docks and I understand the ways of seamen pretty well. However, even before I can try to smuggle people on board I shall have to have a system of chekas."

"Chekas? What on earth are they?"

"I fancy it's a Russian word for some sinister sort of hiding-place. Also, isn't it the new Russian name for what used to be called the Ogpu? Anyhow that's the code name we'll use for them—chekas."

"But what will you want them for?"

"Because, unlike the convoys, I shan't be able to arrange a ship for these bodies in advance. I shall just have to beetle off to Valencia and take pot-luck and I can't expect to find a ship all ready waiting for me. I shall have to dump the bodies somewhere. They'll have to be hidden until I find the right ship and the right skipper willing to take them. They may have to hide for days. I shall need one cheka in Valencia, one in Alicante if I ever dare use it again and probably two in Madrid as well, because they'll have to be somewhere where I can put my hands on them at very short notice."

"What *sort* of places are you thinking of?"

"Preferably private houses, because the bodies will have to be fed and bedded down and so on. So we'll have to find houses of people who are absolutely reliable."

Her enthusiasm thoroughly aroused, Margery said:

"I know the very place in Valencia. Quite near the harbour. There is a very good-hearted woman I know there who is pro-Franco and who would do anything we asked her and be most discreet and reliable. Pearson, the Air Attaché, had a flat there and she likes and trusts the British."

"Fine! That gives us a good start. I thought you'd be likely to know of someone. You may think it odd, but do you know the very best place in Madrid? My old bombed flat! Antonio, the porter, is a Nationalist at heart and his wife is a wonderful cook. They would do anything for me. I've got a socking great Union Jack on the door of the flat. What could be better."

"You seem to have this all well worked out already."

"I've been thinking about it pretty hard for a long time—all the time I was home, in fact. But there are still a lot of gaps. I shall have to go down to Valencia as soon as possible to spy out the land—meet some of the skippers and see this woman there that you mentioned."

He got up and walked to the window, hands in pockets, and she could see that he was thinking of some new problem. She asked solicitously:

"What's worrying you?"

"Well, I was thinking in the first place that this woman might not accept me at face value unless you were there. Besides, I was thinking what a tower of strength you were last time. Look here, Margery, I don't want to drag you into this, but do you think you could tear yourself away for a bit and go down with me to have a look round?"

She reflected a moment, thinking of the hospital, then replied:

"Yes, I think so; I'd love to, if it's a matter of only two or three days. I can leave Doña Pilar with absolute confidence, but I don't want to ask too much of her."

"All right then. I'll have you back in three days. I should need a dress rehearsal, you know, in any case. So we'll pretend that you are the body I am trying to get away and I'll see if I can actually smuggle you on board a ship."

Margery was entirely willing.

Knowing the importance to the Republicans of pieces of paper, Lance, making a breezy round of the various offices, armed himself with a new pass, authorizing him to travel to and fro to inspect his works. Looking to the future, he had it made out for himself, two assistants and his secretary. The officials were very appreciative of his thoughtfulness in asking that the pass should be a permanent one, instead of a separate one for each journey, as was usual. "It will save you a lot of trouble, comrade," he said, to which they replied: "That is always a good idea." He did not add that it would also prevent the police from keeping a record of all his journeys.

They set out a few days later in the big black Chevrolet, driven by Pepe in his urgent way. It was a relief to get away from the bleakness and the sour breath of Madrid. They rose steeply by tortuous pock-marked roads to the dangerous Contreras Pass, where the most ferocious of the sentries jumped with pointed guns as the car twisted round the mountain bends. There was very little military traffic and few signs of war other than the frequent militia guards who, Lance thought, would have been much better employed at the front. From time to time a motor-cycle bounced past, but for the greater part all that they saw were the dawdling bullocks and the drowsy donkeys of a people who had little belief in getting a move on.

Leaving the plateau and the pass, they descended slowly to the fertile *huerta* that embraces Valencia on the landward side, passing through dense, glistening orange groves, plantations of white mulberries on which the silkworm spun his treasured cocoons, rigid vineyards where the leaf was sprouting vigorously on the lengthening canes and clusters of gnarled olive trees standing motionless in ranks.

Still descending, they came at last into the sombre intensity of Valencia, ran through its modern avenues and dived into the narrow, close-packed streets of other days, picturesquely sinister canyons between houses heavily protected with iron grilles and strong doors "garlanded with carven imag'ries", past the baroque, high-towered cathedral and the innumerable churches, now smoke-blackened skeletons in a world that had rejected God. Lance and Margery found that the city, now that the Government was seated there, was not so lifeless as Madrid, but the hot streets were filled with unsmiling crowds.

At length, under Margery's direction, Pepe drew up at the house which was the proposed "cheka". It was, Lance noted, in a quiet, narrow, back street in the old part of the town. There he left Margery and Pepe at the door and, keeping his eyes about him, drove alone to the long road which runs the length of the dockyard wall. It was about half a mile to the dock gates. There he got out and snooped about the bars and *fondas* and had drinks at several of them to get himself known to the *patrón* and to assess their usefulness to him.

In one of these he found a group of British merchant service officers and, choosing his man carefully, attached himself to the cheerful skipper of a tramp steamer whom he liked the looks of. After feeling his ground, Lance said to him:

"Look here, skipper, I've got a girl friend down here who has been having a rotten time in Madrid and it would do her a lot of good if she could go on board a British ship for a bit of a change. D'you think that's possible?"

"No difficulty at all, old man. Fetch her along."

Lance hurried off accordingly and brought Margery back in the car, with Pepe driving and the Union Jack flying. They met the captain, who got into the car with them, and they then drove the short distance to the big dock gates, guarded by sentries and watched by police. Lance was very interested to see not only whether he would get through but, even more, whether a woman would be admitted. In the event, it was utterly simple. They all got out at the gate and the captain, who was already known to the sentries, introduced Lance, who greeted the sentry with his usual breeziness and said:

"The captain has very kindly invited us on board his ship and I should like to introduce you to my friend, Señorita Hill, who is the Matron of a hospital in Madrid, where she has been having rather a rough time."

Margery then exchanged a few smiling words with the sentry and it was plain to see that he was immediately won over by this woman so obviously *simpática* and so far out of the rough world in which he lived. Two or three others of the guard came out from their hut to watch the unusual little episode, walked over to meet the English party and stood chatting with them.

Lance had succeeded in attracting the attention he desired and had tested the means of entry. It was at once clear to him that to be a friend of the captain was the touchstone. There was no word at all of passes.

Highly delighted, and his cheerful good humour this time entirely genuine, he passed in with the others and they went on board. Lance noted the sentry, rather bored and his rifle slung, at the foot of every ship's gangway, but again they had no difficulty in getting past. On some ships there was a sentry on board also, but Lance learnt from the captain that none of these sentries was relieved for meals, so that at such times there was no one there at all.

On board, the skipper produced rum and gin and Lance probed more directly. He told the captain that they had a "lot of pals" in a dangerous position and they might want to get one or two of them away. What were the chances of doing that by sea? The captain replied:

"Oh lord! That's a bit risky. You see, we have to advise the Security Police when we are going to sail and they come down and search the ship."

This was news to Lance, and very important news.

"What do they search for in particular?" he asked.

"Stowaways. They're very hot on stowaways, you know. We have to supply a list of the crew and sometimes the crew has to be paraded for inspection."

"There's no difficulty about that, surely? How thorough are these searches?"

"They vary. Sometimes quite thorough, but I don't think that, as a rule, they are chaps who really understand ships and it rather depends on how well they know the master, and how he treats them."

"Well then, that should be easy. Plenty of places to hide a chap in a ship." Thinking of that noisome, dark and dirty hole in the bowels of the ship, in which the anchor cable is stowed, he added: "Why not the chainlocker?"

The captain had to agree. "Why, yes, that ought to be pretty safe."

Pursuing the matter, Lance learnt that there would be little difficulty in finding British captains willing to take a refugee on board. There were a few awkward cusses, but generally they were a pretty sporting lot, who liked a bit of a lark. The crews, however, might sometimes be a bit awkward if they thought the refugee was a Fascist, as their Union at home was very pro-red. There would be a charge for the passage, of course, but usually £10 would suffice. A greater difficulty was what to do with the refugee on arrival at the port of destination, because he would have to get past the immigration authorities there.

All this was most valuable information, and the way was now much clearer. They thanked the captain and went ashore. Passing the open door of a warehouse, Lance saw a few crates of oranges and had an idea. Might be useful, he thought. Pepe then drove them back to the proposed cheka, so that Lance could inspect it and meet the *dueña*. He had been relieved to be told by Margery that she did not "have cold feet" at the proposal put to her, but on the contrary was eager to help.

Lance found that the cheka was an old-fashioned, unobtrusive little house, drab in appearance but spotlessly clean inside. Part of it was let off in flats but one of the floors was a boarding-house and it was over this in particular that the good Francisca personally presided. He found her to be a fat, homely, motherly soul —"a real old dear, an absolutely topping old girl".

Very pleased at this find, and well content with the trip as a whole, they started back for Madrid. Lance was feeling full of confidence. Everything had gone smoothly and he had got valuable information.

"It all looks easy now," he said to Margery as they jolted along. "I think I see the way to get a body through all the sentries— arrange to meet the master of the ship at a pub and then go through the dock gates in a crowd. The body, however, will have to look something like the rest of the crowd, and not like a Spaniard, so I shall try to get together a collection of blue reefer jackets and flannel bags if possible, from the wardrobes of other chaps in hiding, if the body himself hasn't got any."

Margery was thinking her own thoughts as Lance continued: "Of course, there's one thing we did not test, and I suppose we never can until we come to the real thing. Suppose you, as our test case today, had stayed on board and not come back with me? What would have happened? Would the sentry on the ship, or the police, have noticed and asked why you had not come off?"

"If I had been a man, wouldn't the sentry assume that I was just a member of the crew?" Margery asked.

"Quite so, that is the act we shall have to play; but if that happens time after time they may begin to smell a rat."

He then went on to broach to her with some diffidence his ultimate proposal. He had seen how thoroughly Margery had enjoyed the whole affair and he had been impressed again with her ability to deal with people. He saw how they all respected and appreciated her—"fell for her", in Lance's words. It was rare nowadays to see a respectably dressed lady in the streets, and the Spaniards were very susceptible to such things. He knew then that she must become "part and parcel" of the plot and he asked her outright if she would be willing to accompany him on his trips with the bodies.

The little matron was thrilled. "I can't tell you," she said, "how I'd love to come, whenever the hospital work allows." Eager to make a start at once, she asked: "Whom can we get away first?"

On this there followed an argument. The list in Lance's mind was a formidable one, embracing many people whom he knew himself, as well as those on Merry del Val's list. Some of them were exceedingly dangerous cases for him to handle, such as Don Domingo de las Bárcenas, a diplomat of very high standing and a future Ambassador in London, and there was another fearfully dangerous case on the Nationalist list, the very thought of which gave him a nightmare.

Margery, however, had other ideas. Naturally her thoughts flew at once to those "pals" of hers, as Lance called them, to whom she had given refuge in her hospital, particularly her special friends the Cobians. As Lance himself, like Clayton-Ray and others of the committee, was also anxious to clear the hospital, he found no difficulty in agreeing and it was decided that, for reasons of his health, the first "customer" should be young 'Roberto'.

Orphaned by the murder of his father, Roberto, who was a handsome young fellow of seventeen, had himself been saved from the gunmen by Lance in the nick of time and, going down with bronchitis, had been smuggled into the hospital one night when the shells were crashing. Both Margery and Lance had a soft spot for him, for he had heaps of guts and, now recovering, was burning to avenge his distinguished father.

Pepe brought the black car round to the hospital next week two hours before dawn. The unlit streets were black as pitch and the city was wrapped in that almost opaque silence that accompanies the darkest hour. Lance was feeling very much keyed-up, his perceptions keenly sharpened, and the exhilaration of adventure sobered by the responsibility laid on him for a life other than his own. However, he greeted Pepe with a light-hearted joke and the little chauffeur flashed a smile in return.

Roberto, who had not been outdoors for months, was very white, but was full of heart and eager for the trial that he had to undergo, though he knew well that the slightest slip on anyone's part or some mere trick of chance would mean his instant and violent death. It required some courage to leave the sanctuary of the hospital and face the hazards of a hostile world, but he responded well when Lance rallied him cheerfully.

"Be absolutely natural," he said, "and do exactly as you are told."

Again that familiar formula: "I am in your hands, Captain Lance."

They all had some coffee and moved quietly off in the dark. The trial was upon them and they felt all the tension of the moment. Lance was on tenterhooks as they were stopped at the first guard-post in Madrid, for fear his passenger would be recognized. In order that the double sentries should not be prompted to look inside the car, he got out himself, shone a torch into their eyes, greeted them with a jest and produced his impressive pass. To his relief, they accepted it without question and wished him *Buen viaje* in the friendliest manner.

With fresh confidence from this encounter, the little party drove on, successfully passing all the remaining guard-posts, left the city to the east, twisted round the circuitous deviation of the Jarama front across the bleak, eroded hills, past little sagging columns of tired mules and through the scattered encampments of a sleeping army. Under the keen Castilian wind of early morning they could occasionally hear the distant crackling of a machine-gun away on their right, but otherwise no warlike sounds broke the silence of a tired front.

As they gained the Valencia road, the sun, furrowing the eastern sky with gold and crimson, showed before them the long, rough way over the harsh and rocky plateau. Pepe put his foot down on the accelerator as hard as the pot-holes allowed. The four occupants of the car kept up a strained conversation, interrupted every few miles as Lance, in his now familiar conspicuous check coat, got out to chat and laugh with the guards. Sometimes

Margery would get out and smile with her head a little on one side.

Thus they passed safely through the thirty or more posts in their 210 miles drive, giving the Communist greeting each time and putting on a good face in spite of their inner anxiety. Even the ferocious guards of the Contreras Pass, leaping out from hairpin bends, did not delay them long, having seen the car for the third time. As they went farther south-east, the high-climbing sun waxed in strength until, after they had passed through the drowsy orchards of the *huerta* and slipped down into Valencia, the hot breath of the Mediterranean gave warning of the live coals on which they were about to tread and quickened their pulses as the moment for action drew near.

They drove straight to the cheka. The good Francisca opened to them and greeted them with rapture and surprise.

As they came inside she clasped the embarrassed Roberto to her generous bosom and, overcome with emotion exclaimed:

"Oh, thanks be to God that you have come here safely! You will be quite safe with Francisca. Francisca will take good care of you. Come right in all of you and we shall soon have some coffee going."

Entirely confident in this "topping old girl", Lance left Margery and Roberto in her care and made off on foot to the harbour to see if there were any British ships. He saw, in fact, several and stood awhile gazing at them and sizing up the situation. Now that it had come to the point, he began to feel very much on edge and strained and to ask himself pointed questions. Why was he doing this thing? Why take such a hell of a risk? What did this youngster mean to him? Should he get out of it while he could?

What pulled him round was the memory of those atrocious slaughter-pits. The very thought of them made him boil afresh with anger. It was *anyone's* duty to save people from those abominations.

Thus resolved, he made his way to the long dock road. He looked into all the bars in search of a gathering of British merchant service officers and found one at the corner of the approach road. It was not long before he got into the company of the seamen and swopped drinks. The liquor, as in all these bars in the dock areas, was pretty rough stuff—bad gin, inky *vino corriente* and a firewater that passed as brandy. Lance, however, had a strong stomach and could drink with the best. He always got on well with men of the sea and found these masters of small ships to be grand fellows—self-reliant, ready for anything, open and frank as their own wide horizons and with a great sense of humour.

He very soon found that some of these masters were bound for unsuitable ports, for he wanted ships going to Britain, France or Spanish Morocco. Thus he soon attached himself to a jovial and garrulous Scottish captain, dark-haired and sturdy, with whom he exchanged fiery brandies. After the second one, he said to the Scot:

"Why the hell do you drink this filthy stuff when you've got good Scotch and decent gin on board?"

"Och, just to get ashore, ye ken."

"You know, it's ages since I've tasted decent gin."

"Ye're not asking me to smuggle a bottle ashore, are ye?"

With a grin, Lance replied: "Not a bit of it; what I'm asking you to do, captain, is to invite me on board! Besides, I've something I want to chat to you about."

The Scot looked at him shrewdly. "Have ye noo? Well, ye'll be verra welcome."

"Grand! Let's get out of here, then, before this stuff burns up our guts."

In the main dock gates Lance recognized one of the sentries and stopped for a chat with him. Then, once on board, he put the proposition without equivocation in the privacy of the master's cabin. To his delight, but not to his surprise, the master entered into the spirit of the adventure with relish and agreed to take the passenger for the sum of £10.

"But mind," he added, "ye're to be responsible for the passenger until we sail. I'll no carry the can if he's found by the sairch party. Ye'll have to tak' responsibility for that."

To this Lance perforce agreed. The ship was to sail the next afternoon, bound for London, and it was accordingly arranged that they should all meet next day about noon in the same bar as before. Lance went back to the cheka, where he, Margery and Roberto spent the night.

The next day, driven by Pepe, Lance, wearing his check jacket, quietly left the cheka, with Roberto now dressed in a blue reefer jacket and flannel trousers, leaving Margery behind. Lance was on tenterhooks, but, knowing what a life-or-death ordeal it was to be for Roberto, he donned a cloak of cheerful confidence and said to the boy, who was sitting well back in the car:

"Now look here, my lad, you've jolly well got to play the part of a British sailor on the spree. You've got to talk English, laugh and drink English. Don't speak a word of Spanish. It's going to be quite easy. We shall probably all get thoroughly bottled but that will make it easier still."

Robert grinned cheerfully. "In fact, captain, a bit *loco inglés*?" he said, using the phrase for "mad Englishmen" by which Spaniards generally express their notion of the light-hearted eccentricity of the British.

"Absolutely!" Lance answered with a laugh, admiring the spirit with which the boy was taking it. "Like me, in fact! Well, here we go. Drive on, Pepe."

The plan that he had evolved in his mind was one of pure pantomime, and must surely have been one of the strangest escape stratagems ever devised. His decision to do everything in the open light of day, without false papers, misuse of uniforms and similar illegalities, while avoiding the more instant and violent dangers, incurred others. His purpose was not to cheat his way through, but to bluff it by acting the clown. It was a highly imaginative part that would require all his nerve, presence of mind and wit. But it was based on his knowledge of the psychology of the Spaniard, or at least of the type of Spaniard whose guard he had now to penetrate. To people of their innate, long-faced gravity, he argued, it would appear impossible that anyone who acted the fool could have a serious purpose. As we should say today, his stratagem was a "cover plan", an act of camouflage to cover up his real intentions. But it imposed on him, and on those whose lives he hoped to save, the need to act a part and now, in spite of the outward confidence that he had to display, he was suffering from stage fright, fearful for the life that was in his charge. So, he thought, must all clowns and jesters feel on their first appearance before a large and critical audience.

When it came to the point, Roberto, who spoke a little English, played his part well. They met the British skipper in the *fonda* at about noon and embarked on a studied campaign of drinking. Captain Browne, entering into the spirit of the thing, had had the shrewdness to bring along two others of his cloth, to add verisimilitude to the party.

The sailors, who had no act to play, were thoroughly enjoying themselves, but for Lance and Roberto the false conviviality was an ordeal of nerves. To Lance, who appreciated good wine, each drink was like sulphuric acid, but it was vital for him to keep his wits about him, to keep a wary eye on the door for the entry of any suspicious Spaniard and on no account allow himself to get tipsy. The fumes and the noonday heat soon brought him out in perspiration.

He was keeping a careful eye on his watch also, as everything had to be timed to suit the hour of sailing, and when at length the time came for the "act" he cried:

"Now then, down the hatch, everyone, and off we go!"

They finished their drinks and the five, deliberately hilarious but not drunk, rolled out of the bar together, singing English songs and now and then calling out some political slogan in deliberately bad Spanish to humour and amuse the people in the street. They reached the great gates of the main dockyard entrance. There before them were the two militia sentries, very severe looking and with rifles slung from the shoulder. A watching policeman stood just within. It was, Lance thought, frightfully hot all of a sudden. The critical time had come. Would they get through? Lance felt keenly for the boy at his side. He was very much on the *qui vive*, ready to take emergency action at once if they met difficulty. He had thought it all out and was arm in arm with Roberto on one hand and with Captain Browne on the other.

They all rolled in at the gateway, like cheerful trippers at the seaside. At a word from Lance they greeted the sentries with raised fists and cries of:

"*Viva la Republica!* Death to the Fascists! *No pasarán!*"

From beneath his mask of comedy Lance was watching the sentries closely. "Hell's bells," he thought, "how difficult it is to make some of these chaps smile!" He made some familiar "crack" and was relieved to see their faces soften, to show a glint of teeth between the black stubble.

The unfamilar noise and laughter had brought the whole guard out from their hut, to watch the *locos ingleses* making clowns of themselves. This was just what Lance wanted. He called out to them: "We are just going to have a little drink with the captain." He strolled over and offered them cigarettes. He was careful to appear merely hilarious, not drunk, in order not to lose their respect. Again they passed through and not a word was said about passes.

It was all, maybe, a little crude, but it was remarkably successful. Beneath the face of comedy was a strained and anxious mind. A hot sun beamed down on their antics from a deep-blue sky, hardening the granite outlines of the dockyard scene, and the warm breath of the Mediterranean intensified the atmosphere of menace and suspicion that overhung the city.

Not satisfied with this easy success, Lance, though longing to make straight for the ship and get the thing over before any of those mines he felt beneath his feet blew up, paused mentally and asked himself: "What else can I do for camouflage? How else to be conspicuous?"

Instead of going directly to the ship, he deliberately led the party away to the customs offices. There he found, as he knew he would, not only all the customs officials, but also the port committee, more guards, carabiniers and two secret police in plain clothes. They were a swarthy, sombre-faced lot, but he greeted them cheerfully and called on them all to join them on board the ship. "We are going to give Captain Browne a farewell party," he said, "and there will be some real Scotch whisky. Come along with us."

The sombre faces relaxed a little, but there was one black-browed, tight-lipped detective against whom all Lance's instincts warned him and whose keen, suspicious stare he was long to remember.

From the customs shed they came out again on to the quay, passing one after another the sentries who stood at the foot of ships' gangways, greeting them all in the same fashion. Men came from round about to stare at them. Would the sentry on their own ship count the numbers in their party and weigh up each member too carefully? Lance had arranged with the captain how to deal with him, too. At a word from Lance, Captain Browne took him by one arm and Lance by the other and, marching him up the gangway, said: "Now, comrade, you are coming on board for a little drink with us!"

So, under cover of another party on board, Roberto, his heart thumping beneath his cheerful grin, after a quick word of grateful thanks, was safely stowed away. The skipper was paid. The search party came and went, with yet more drinks and with cigarettes. Lance, a great weight lifted from his shoulders, had now to face the problem of how he was to leave the ship with his party reduced by one in numbers in addition to the skipper. Would it be noticed by those sharp eyes ashore? He bet that that black-browed detective fellow was watching them closely.

Thinking ahead as he always did, the notion had occurred to him as they had come on board that one fact may often be obscured by calling attention to another. With a quickness of wit that was typical of him, he had hailed a boat and ordered it to wait alongside the tramp steamer's seaward quarter. Now, after the search party had gone, he bade a quick good-bye to Browne, collected the two visiting skippers and, taking them down to the waiting boat, said to them:

"Play the fool for all you're worth."

There followed another piece of pure pantomime, again designed not to avoid attention but to atract it. Continuing the act of the carefree sailor, the three of them stood up unsteadily in the boat, contrary to the laws of seamanlike behaviour, shouting jokes and slogans to the crowd that had collected on the quayside some thirty yards away, while the unhappy boatman attempted to row and keep direction, his oars sinking deeper and deeper into the water.

"Sit down, señores," he implored.

With the boat rolling from side to side the boatman "caught a crab" and narrowly avoided collapse. From the quay the crowd began to shout advice. "You'll fall into the water," they cried, to which the *locos ingleses* replied with merely a laugh and a promise to bring them some fish.

"I beg you to sit down, señores," cried the boatman again, recovering himself.

The boat jerked on again, but as the foolery continued, the boatman caught an extra big crab, falling over backwards on the thwarts. One of the skippers leant forward to grasp the oars, stumbled and fell flat on his face on top of the boatman. The boat was rocking like a pendulum, while the crowd on shore looked on with a kind of suspended humour. How could there be anything suspicious in such irresponsible behaviour?

In this fashion Lance took each of the two skippers to his own ship in turn, and on the side farther from the quay. From the second one, forswearing any more liquor, he walked confidently ashore, satisfied that by now there was little fear that anyone would ask what had happened to the unobtrusive boy who had entered the docks with the revellers but half an hour ago. Before he reached the dock gates, he saw Captain Browne's ship putting out to sea. Roberto was safe.

Lance returned to the car, in which the faithful Pepe was still waiting, and sank into the back seat with a sigh of relief. He was drained of energy and clouded with the fumes of bad alcohol. He was perspiring freely and his head was swimming. The whole affair had gone unbelievably well, but beneath the façade of buffoonery there had been intense nervous strain. The slightest slip or mischance would have meant death for Roberto and perhaps for himself also. Would all the others be as easy as this had been? He did not like the look of that swarthy fellow. Thank God it was all over and the boy safe. But he still had one more thing to do. He said to Pepe:

"Drive me to the post office."

There he sent off a telegram to Jinks in England which said:

*One case of oranges despatched per S.S. Blank to London Docks stop Captain will radio date of arrival stop Important you meet and collect      Dagger*

Away in Surbiton Jinks read the telegram and was nonplussed. A "case of oranges"? Whatever did Dagger mean? She had no idea at all yet of the game that he was up to.

Nevertheless, on the date radioed to her by the master—the twelfth of May—she duly went off, alone, to the West India Dock in London one very bleak morning. She did not know the form about these things, felt very much at sea and did not know what she was in for. She found the ship, however, and when she asked the captain for her "case of oranges" he laughed heartily and brought to meet her a very reserved and suspicious Roberto, possessed of nothing but a brown paper parcel. She explained who she was and why she had come. But he would not budge. It was quite contrary to Spanish notions for a man to put himself under the charge of a woman. Moreover, he suspected a trap—that the Republican Government had discovered the plot and had sent an agent to lead him back into their clutches. In vain to say to him that such things did not happen in Britain. He refused to leave what he believed to be the safety of the ship.

Jinks returned to Surbiton very anxious and told her father and brother all about it. She realized that if Roberto would not land he would be sent back where he had come from and Dagger would be betrayed. Next day, therefore, her father, who also spoke Spanish, accompanied her himself to the docks and managed to persuade Roberto to place himself in their charge. Then followed an awkward discussion in the ship's saloon with an immigration officer, who could not, of course, allow a foreigner to land without passport or some other authority. He was naturally suspicious of a man who had no money, no luggage, no clothes but what he stood in. Finally, however, he accepted Jinks as a surety for the refugee, giving Roberto permission to remain in the country for a fortnight, subject to reporting to the police twice daily. As he walked off the quay Roberto kept looking over his shoulder, unable to believe that he now had nothing to fear.

Jinks took him home temporarily and later, through the help of Mr. McLundy, of Colonel McDonnell's staff, settled him in a boarding-house in Earl's Court until arrangements were made for him to leave the country. This resting-place was used by all the other "cases of oranges" who subsequently arrived in England, the expenses, like those incurred at the other end, being borne by the Lances personally.

# CHAPTER NINE

# THE ESCAPE MACHINE

EXHILARATED by the success of this first attempt, Lance at once planned to continue his mission.

The paradox by which such a man as Christopher Lance could enjoy the society of the roughest and most extreme militiamen whilst detesting their works was an apparent inconsistency explainable perhaps only by the fact that, to those of us who do not know Spain, much that happens there appears a paradox.

Many a time he had some testing of his conscience whether he was right deliberately to beguile men with whom he made friends, but always the recollections of the slaughter-pits, the mortuaries and the broken widows came back to justify and strengthen him. If he was obliged to bluff and mislead the guards for the export of his "cases of oranges", it was only the machine-gun he was out to cheat. He knew also that, friends or no friends, they would have shot him down, too, without a thought and without trial if he were caught off his guard.

No sooner, therefore, had he and Margery exported their first *cajas de naranjas* than they began plotting to send off their next. That, too, was successful, and was soon followed by a third. Thereafter they made the long, hot journey every ten days or so, though Margery went only when the "case" was one of her hospital inmates. When the case was one of those under his own wing, or one of those on Merry del Val's list, Lance went alone, for he never took anyone else at all into his confidence.

With such skill and resourcefulness did he organize these operations that for some six months he had an uninterrupted flow of successes. Extreme attention to detail and quick wit in emergencies were the bases of this astonishing record, and, although he could not have succeeded without a certain amount of luck, he never left any room for chance in his calculations. It was not part of his purpose to seek adventurous risk or colourful incident, but rather to avoid them. And it was because everything went so well for so long, thanks to these factors, that the escapes were to appear on the surface relatively easy and straightforward. So much so that there is no point in recording them here in detail.

The atmosphere in the Valencia docks, where the port committee was very much on its guard against unauthorized exits, was always deadly. "Suspicion" was "all stuck full of eyes", and every moment spent there was a trial, to be endured under a mask of confidence and good-fellowship. Well enough though he got known to them all in the docks, he was sometimes baulked by new faces, for the Government did not trust their own people, especially the police, among whom they knew that there were many Franco sympathizers and whom they accordingly moved frequently from one place to another.

Margery, who occasionally went inside the docks also, felt that every step she took there was like walking on live coals and, as Lance deliberately dawdled his way through, she kept asking herself: "Shall we ever reach the ship?" It seemed to her that Lance was deliberately courting danger, enjoying it, yet she knew only too well that he was consumed with anxiety for the life in his care. He had no other fear than that.

Nor, in spite of all outward appearances, were the hot and dusty journeys to Valencia any less charged with high tension. The pot-holed road knew them well as Pepe again and again drove them there and back and many of the guards became familiar with the black Chevrolet, but, to Margery at least, each stop brought its own agony as she asked herself: "What if they demand to know who this boy is?" Not until the guards had given a *Salud* and a *Buen viaje* was the agony dispelled, only to take form again a few miles further on. It was on these journeys that Margery learnt to smoke.

From early May onwards Lance kept up these journeys with his "cases of oranges", sometimes taking two cases at once, at others only one. He was always happiest when he had Margery with him, not only for her companionship but also for her positive value. Where some petty official or some way-denying sentry might have been induced slowly to open a door for Lance, for Margery he flung it wide open. Thus they kept up their steady freedom trade as the sun waxed fierce and the oranges set their fruits. The water-melon fattened in the fields and the mustard grew its yellow carpet again beneath the olives. The cicada awoke to a shrill new life and the stork flew to and from his huge nest precariously upon the house-tops. In the stuffy back streets of old Valencia, trapping the windless heat between their close-set buildings, the steady flow of escapists went on undetected. The good, fat Francisca opened her ample arms to them all and called upon the Mother of God to protect them.

Lance was not such a fool as to repeat the tipsy act each time. He assumed, to all appearances, the life of a light-hearted and breezy Englishman loafing about the docks because he liked ships and seamen and had nothing better to do, which was indeed scarcely removed from the truth. His check jacket and his wiry, rust-haired figure became a familiar spectacle and although the sentries, the police and the olive-green carabiniers very soon got used to his comings and goings, he never abused his position or took an unnecessary chance.

He was always particularly aware that he was being carefully watched by the black-visaged fellow of the secret police, whom he had spotted at that first visit to the customs house and whom he soon began to label mentally as Black Face. They never spoke to one another, but the fellow's gimlet eyes filled an uneasy place in the background of Lance's mind, fretting at the edges of his confidence. He was one of the policemen who were never changed.

Lance's "drill" at Valencia was nearly always the same. On arrival he would drop his "case" at the cheka, provide him with blue jacket and grey trousers, go off to the docks to see what ships were in, reconnoitre the firewater saloons along the dock road and strike up acquaintance with a skipper going to a suitable port. Then, at an agreed time, they would all meet and saunter into the docks together, a party of jolly sailors returning to their ship or giving their landsman friend a meal or a jovial drink on board before they sailed. Lance learnt early that passes were seldom demanded of anyone who went into the docks with a captain, but this was not always so, and the fates of all were balanced on a razor's edge when Edouardo and Carlos Cobian were twice so challenged.

Not all the escapists, however, were passed off as British sailors. Some of them looked too obviously Spanish and not all spoke English. His usual stratagem for these was to represent them as friends going on board for lunch or drinks, but as these were naturally expected to return from the ships he had to adopt various ruses to avoid having to account for their absence when he himself came ashore again.

In Madrid, as in Valencia, the cheka plan worked well. When the cases were from the hospital, where Lance himself continued to live, no difficulty arose. Other cases, however, had to be transferred from their hiding places to one of his two chekas— either his old, bomb-damaged flat, where Antonio and his wife looked after them, or else, very occasionally, the second cheka, which was the Embassy itself, where fierce old Dolores was his willing *aide*. Lance had no scruples about this, as the Embassy was now vacated, and as it was by no means the only embassy being used as a refuge for Spaniards who would otherwise have been done away with.

The transfers to these chekas in Madrid were always dangerous and Lance always took them himself, and on these occasions he did use the cover of night. On approaching the Embassy, at the gates of which were always two Spanish guards, he would put his headlights full on in the sentries' eyes as he drove up. He would then get out, shining a torch in their faces while he gossiped over a cigarette before slipping in with his charge.

When driving out of Madrid before dawn, however, he would often adopt the opposite course of showing no headlights, but, to the alarm of his charges, keeping the interior lights on, so that the guards would be able to recognize him as he approached and to foster the belief that there was nothing to hide.

By these and many other stratagems Lance built up a technique that seemed to provide for any risk. In the circle of his Spanish acquaintances he acquired an extraordinary reputation for infallibility. To them it seemed that there was nothing that he could not do, that he knew instinctively the right course to take and the right thing to say, could be either persuasive or briskly authoritative as occasion demanded. He had the quality of being everywhere at once, his responses were instantaneous and, however tired he might be, he got up at once to do whatever was necessary. Outwardly he appeared never ruffled, was always freshly washed and shaven and always neatly turned out. His wonderful kindness and his understanding of people in tragic circumstance won him their hearts, though they could not always understand his breeziness and even Margery found that his habitual joking got on her nerves when the air was most electric.

There were a few names on Merry del Val's list that Lance did not much care for, and he was not sorry when two of them flatly refused to take the terrible risks involved under a conductor whom they did not know. Two more he was unable to find. At other names he pulled a wry face, for they were dynamite. But Don Domingo de las Bárcenas, the future Spanish Ambassador in London, though as explosive a case as any, was one that he was delighted to handle. His was, indeed, one of the most audacious and barefaced of all Lance's escapes.

Don Domingo, like many aristocratic Spaniards, was much disposed to English ways and culture. He spoke perfect English, appeared to have been tailored in Savile Row and looked every inch the English country gentleman. Lance learnt that he was in hiding in the Norwegian Embassy and paid a call on him. He found him a charming and entertaining companion, and before long he "popped the question"—would Don Domingo like to be exported? Franco was very anxious to have him.

The Spaniard, who had plenty of nerve, readily accepted, quite prepared to face the perils and the discomforts to which he was unaccustomed. At very great risk and feeling extremely apprehensive, Lance outwitted the guards outside the Norwegian Embassy, and took his charge round to the British Embassy by night.

Don Domingo was not only a well-known figure; he was also a very conspicuous and distinguished-looking one. The risks of recognition multiplied in his case, but also it was obviously no use attempting to pass him off as a sailor at the dock-gates. "Altogether," Lance thought, " a darned risky case", but he was now in a confident frame of mind, feeling that he knew the ropes well. All the same, just because that was so, he planned ahead for this case in minute detail, devising an "act" of a different nature. The first thing that he did was to confiscate Don Domingo's black Homburg.

"Sorry, Don Domingo," he said with a laugh, "I shall have to confiscate that hat. Afraid you'll never see that hat again!"

They left the British Embassy, as usual, at about three in the morning, Don Domingo wearing a country gentleman's summer-weight tweeds. In Valencia Lance found a ship bound for Marseilles, without much difficulty, but did not arrange the usual rendezvous in the dockland *fonda* with the captain and mate. Instead, when the time came, he drove boldly up to the dock-gates in the car, with Don Domingo beside him, Pepe at the wheel and a large Union Jack on the bonnet. By prearrangement, Pepe crept up to the sentry without quite stopping, while Lance leant out of the window to give a cheerful salutation and Don Domingo turned casually to look out of the other window.

Having ascertained beforehand exactly where the ship lay, Lance directed Pepe to drive right up to the foot of the gangway, where the captain, by arrangement, was loitering about. With the car obscuring him from most of the quayside hands, and with his back turned to the gangway sentry, Don Domingo greeted the skipper, who very convincingly put on an air of surprised pleasure at meeting unexpected visitors, and the party carried on a deliberately casual slow-motion conversation for several minutes. When he thought it was time to go on board, Lance said in Spanish in a raised voice:

"Now, skipper, what about a little drink?"

The party then sauntered up the gangway and Don Domingo was promptly shut up in the captain's wardrobe locker, a place scarcely suitable either to his dignity or his size. Lance himself stayed in the cabin until the immigration officers arrived after searching the ship, and, praying fervently that the distinguished stowaway would not sneeze or be seized by cramp, he kept up a loud and continuous conversation while the captain served three rounds of drinks in quick succession.

Lance and the mate then boldly went ashore with the immigration officers themselves, to whom they bade a cheerful *Hasta la vista* at the foot of the gangway, where Pepe was still waiting. Though he felt a longing to leap into the car and tell Pepe to "step on it", Lance deliberately stayed chatting to the mate until it was time for the gangway to be stowed. Then at last he told Pepe to drive off slowly and casually, leaving the docks by another gate, so that no awkward questions should be asked about the non-return of the passenger who had accompanied him in at the main gate.

On one hot day there were two "cases" that had to be taken out to a ship, rather larger than usual, that lay a mile outside the harbour. To reach her Lance had ordered a fast motor-launch to be waiting at the main steps of the harbour at a fixed hour. The party met in the usual manner—Lance, his two charges, the master and his first and second mates in their best white rig.

They passed the sentry on the dock gate without difficulty and walked to the steps. There was the launch, with her engines running. There also was a guard of six militiamen, but they knew Lance and the ship's officers quite well and on this fact he relied.

The officers stepped on board the launch and Lance was on the point of following suit when he felt his shoulders gripped by one of the guards. He turned round in some surprise and was asked:

"Who are your friends, comrade?"

"Oh, they are just friends of mine and we are all going to lunch on board that ship out there with the captain. We shall be back in an hour or two."

"They cannot go without a pass from the Military Governor."

This was a poser, but Lance knew that somehow he must pass it off with good humour, and without argument. It was clear that the guard was very firm.

"That's a new one, comrade," he said. "Never had to get a pass before to have lunch on board. Never mind! I'll get one straightaway." Then to the British skipper: "Hang on a bit, skipper, will you?"

All the same, as he walked back up the landing steps in the fiery sun, he had no idea at all how he was going to get out of this fix. On the very doorstep of another success, the situation, so smiling a moment ago, was suddenly a very ugly one. If his two cases were turned back, not only might it break their nerve but also they would be marked men and awkward questions would follow. And what on earth had it to do with the Military Governor?

Reaching the top of the quay, he remembered that, in a shed close by, was a military post of some sort. Try a game of poker again, he thought; a spot of bluff.

Walking straight to the shed, he called in as if to pass the time of day, chatting with a junior officer for a few moments about trivialities. Judging the time, he walked smartly back to the landing steps, where he saw the launch still waiting and her engines throbbing. Walking down quickly and decisively through the guards, he said:

"It's all right, comrade. The officer on duty has telephoned headquarters and permission has been granted for us to go on board for lunch."

Without pausing he stepped over the gunwale and said to the boatman in quasi-naval fashion:

"Full ahead, coxs'n!"

Immediately the launch was off in a cloud of spray and Lance, as he stood up in the stern, felt his back itching in expectation of a sudden shot. But none came.

Having reached the ship, said good-bye to his cases and settled with the captain, he did not wait for lunch. Knowing that the guards on the steps would be off duty for their midday meal between twelve and one, he made straight back in the launch and got away with it.

An incident of a different sort astonished him by showing how unpredictable and unfathomable were the Republican police. Again Lance had two cases to dispatch. One was the architect, Pedro Muguruza, a man of distinguished appearance, culture and charming manner, but the identity of his companion is uncertain. For both of these Lance secured passages in the *Lesto*, bound for Immingham, and as soon as they were on board Muguruza was locked up in the captain's cabin.

Shortly afterwards two police officers arrived to search the ship. As they came on board Lance, to his consternation, heard the senior of them say to the other: "You do the top deck; I am going down to the captain's cabin."

When he was let into the cabin, there was Muguruza, not yet hidden away and his arrest seemed inevitable. The policeman, however, did not seem at all concerned and, instead of making an arrest, he took a letter out of his pocket and, handing it to Muguruza, said:

"When you get to Gibraltar, please post this for me."

Muguruza glanced at the envelope and saw to his horror that it was addressed to Franco's Chief of Staff. Naturally suspecting a trap, he replied evasively:

"I have nothing to do with this ship, you know, officer." He made to hand the letter back, but the police officer merely said:

"Never mind; have the kindness to post it for me all the same; it is important."

Lance could not help feeling that the policeman must have felt uncommonly sure of his ground to take such a deadly risk. "I bet," he thought afterwards, "that he knew perfectly well whom he was talking to." The thought was far from reassuring. It did not matter to Lance whether the fellow was a spy; but if one person in the police department knew what was going on, did not others also?

He was constantly worried by the lurking presence of Black Face, whose swarthy visage and beady eyes were nearly always to be seen in the background and he had a bad moment with him on an occasion when he had safely stowed his case deep down in the bowels of a ship. It had been a very tiring day. The August heat had been suffocating and Lance's nerves had been stretched by several small anxieties. He wrote a hurried line to Jinks, for posting by the skipper, saying: "How these jobs make me long to stay on board and go home to you! The police are on board now and I have to keep my wits about me." The search party came and went, the pilot was ready on the bridge and the skipper was waiting only for Lance to leave before pulling up the gangway, which was on the starboard side.

But still Lance waited. For near the foot of the gangway he had spotted that malevolent face. He seemed obviously to be waiting for Lance to come ashore. Sweating profusely and nervously exhausted, Lance felt now that he could not face the fellow. For once he departed from his principle of audacity first and chose evasion.

A boat appeared on the port side and he hailed it. Pointing out some landing steps on the far side of the harbour, he told the boatman to take him there. "You can save me a long walk," he said. In fact, it was the very opposite of the direction that he wanted, but the ship covered him from view as he was rowed over and he escaped the hateful face and the suspicious eyes.

Very different from any of these sea escapes was the curious affair of two of his own countrymen who unexpectedly appealed to him for help. Lance was working in his room in the Commercial Attaché's office one sultry day when he was told by the porter that two *ingleses* had come to see him. They were ushered in and he was astonished to see two "real toughs" from Glasgow in shirt-sleeves and khaki slacks. He frowned, feeling suspicious.

They told him that they had been serving in the International Brigade but were disillusioned, fed up and "never expected to be let in for such a packet". They had cleared out and sought refuge in some friend's house in Madrid, but, their host being scared stiff of having such dangerous guests, they had been obliged to take hazardously to the streets. By good chance, they had seen the Union Jack outside the British-American hospital and had been sent to Captain Lance. Could he help them to get home?

Lance, suspicious that this might be a trap, was very abrupt with them. "You got yourselves into this mess," he said, "quite unnecessarily, and you can jolly well get yourselves out of it."

The two Jocks looked dejected and one of them said: "We were led up the garden, you see, Sir."

Lance asked them how it had happened, and they told him that they had been invited to some club that ran dances in Glasgow and had been encouraged to join it themselves. The place, however, was obviously a Communist "cell", for they then started getting fed with a lot of Communist propaganda, got inveigled into signing a slip of paper and the next thing they knew was that, together with a lot of other small parties, they were working their way across France, finally joining a centre for Communist volunteers in the Pyrenees.

Lance grunted. "All I can say," he commented, "is that you are a couple of damned fools to allow yourselves to get taken in by that sort of poppycock. You come butting into a show which has nothing whatever to do with you or me and you've only yourselves to blame. I'm not going to risk my neck for a case like yours. You look quite capable of looking after yourselves."

It was the nearest that Lance ever got to saying no to any appeal for help. In every other appeal, whether from people he knew or from complete strangers over the telephone, and whether for escaping, hiding, bringing food or clothing, rescuing prisoners, finding dead relatives, burying firearms or any other kind of trouble, he said yes automatically, before he began to consider the hazards. On this occasion he said no firmly enough at first, but soon began to weaken, convinced by their manner that they were genuine. The two hapless young fellows, who, he felt sure, were all right at heart, told him that they had been sickened by things that they had seen and could not go on fighting for what they now knew were phoney slogans.

"We never knew Communism was like this," one of them said, "and we've had our bellyful. We're British still, Sir; won't you help us?"

Again that little tug at his heart.

"Very well," he said slowly, "I'll see what I can do, but I make no promises."

He drummed his fingers on the table, looking out of the window while he thought.

"Look here," he continued, "I'll help you on your way, but no more. I've got a lorry going down to Alicante next week and I could hide you up in my bombed flat until it is ready to go. Will that help?"

"Anything, Sir," they answered eagerly. "Anything to get away from this outfit. Perhaps we could sign on a British ship at Alicante?"

"Possibly, we'll see."

A week later, Lance hid the two men under some stores in a lorry and accompanied them to Alicante, without Margery. At the port he saw the British Vice-Consul, Mr. H. C. Brooks, and handed them over to him. "As British subjects," he said, "they

are your cup of tea. I'm jolly well keeping clear of Alicante docks."
Brooks, like the sportsman he was, accepted the charge, not
knowing what a packet of trouble it was to bring him. Before they
parted, however, one of the two Scots gave Lance the only present
it was in his power to give—a crude aluminium ring, set with
coloured glass, and two small coins. Ever afterwards it remained
one of his treasures.

Brooks, as a matter of fact, was engaged in the same sort of
export trade as Lance, though on a much smaller scale. He was a
very stout-hearted fellow, after Lance's own heart, and they
made great friends. At Valencia, however, the situation was
quite otherwise. Ogilvie-Forbes had been succeeded as Chargé
d'Affaires by Mr. J. H. Leche, and neither with him nor with the
Consul at Valencia was Lance on particularly good terms. They
also were said to be dabbling in the export business but Lance
was disgusted when one of the British officials at Valencia, whom
we need not name, arranged the escape of two Spaniards in British
naval officers' uniforms. To Lance, perhaps a purist in these
matters, this abuse of uniform, especially His Majesty's uniform,
was altogether deplorable, and he spoke his mind emphatically.
This, he thought, was against the rules; it was cheating, not mere
bluffing. It was the beginning of a coolness which was to stand
Lance in evil stead in the latter days.

Meanwhile, back in England, Jinks was being kept exceedingly
busy as consignee of many of these cases of oranges. After the
surprise of her first experience, she learnt, like Lance, "to put on
an act". To allay the suspicions of sceptical immigration officials,
she would greet her refugees like long-lost friends, throwing
her arms round their necks and exclaiming how glad she was to
see them again—though she had never seen any of them before.
In this guise she went far afield and at considerable expense—to
Liverpool, to Sunderland to meet the S.S. *Sheaffield*, to Newcastle
to meet the *Hebburn*, as well as often to London docks.

In August she had a call to collect two cases on the *Lesto* at
Immingham Docks and wondered where on earth Immingham
was. She made the tedious journey to that "bleak and awful
place", feeling somewhat forlorn in the wind and the rain as she

found her way to a desolate and almost deserted quay. She took shelter in a wooden shed at the far end and waited.

After a long vigil a small, dirty tramp steamer appeared and anchored in midstream. A boatman who appeared told her that it was the *Lesto* and he rowed her out to her. She climbed on board by a rope ladder and, following the drill she had now long adopted, greeted the two surprised refugees with outflung arms. They were the architect Pedro Muguruza and his companion. With his quick intelligence, Muguruza responded at once to Jinks's embrace, acting his part perfectly.

There followed a particularly awkward interview with the immigration and customs officers in the saloon, from which Jinks, now thoroughly experienced in the drill and being completely honest, emerged with flying colours. Nevertheless, the two Spaniards were extremely uncomfortable at being under the wing of a young woman on the long journey to London, the most painful part of all to them, as cultured Spaniards, being that she paid all their expenses, a thing totally alien to their upbringing.

Not all the cases of oranges were exported to Britain. Several went to Marseilles and a few to other parts. Edouardo and Carlos Cobian, who had had two very narrow squeaks at Valencia, went by the S.S. *Peckham* to Rotterdam. A cable to Jinks in London to seek the help of the steamship company's headquarters in London and a letter to the British Consul at Rotterdam ensured their safe reception. After the first case, all Lance's cables to Jinks were sent off from Gibraltar or other ports of call by the master of the ship, so that there was no evidence in Spain of his regular traffic. There was no detail, indeed, that he did not study and provide for.

By these means he succeeded in the rescue of thirty-one people in six months, in addition to what he flippantly called the sixty "illegitimates" of that awkward Alicante convoy in February. How he escaped discovery so long remains unexplained, except by the imaginative and audacious conception of the whole plan and the attention to every detail in its execution. Stealth, the cover of night, creeping in by back ways, scaling of walls, the use of faked papers, indeed all the commonly accepted methods of escape—these were the kinds of methods that sentries, police, carabiniers and all the rest might expect and be ready to deal with.

To walk in bold as brass, before the eyes of a crowd and under the very noses of those whose business it was to prevent such things—such a method, because it must have seemed impossibly foolhardy, was for that reason the most successful. It also satisfied Lance's code of ethics.

Pepe also became an integral element in the escape machine, completely devoted to its service. His skill, his understanding of a situation, his sang-froid, his disregard of the consequences to himself won both the admiration and affection of his British companions. One day, on return from a successful trip to Valencia, Pepe, with his broad, humorous smile, asked:

"When does my turn come, *mi capitán*?"

Lance saw that he spoke half in jest, but replied:

"Ah, Pepe, never for you, I hope. I know that you are the last person who would ever think of leaving the señorita."

But the day was fast approaching when both Lance and Pepe were to be in grave danger.

The fishing boats of Alicante. The lower picture was taken
at the spot where "Pablo Sanchez" was taken off in a boat
similar to the one shown. Jinks seen on left

Valencia harbour, showing one of the entrances used by Lance

# CHAPTER TEN

# THE FRIGHTENED MAN

THE summer of 1937 came and went. The war still dragged on, showing no sign of ending and the purely domestic issue was blurred by the quantities of Italians, Germans, Russians, Frenchmen, Americans and British who fought on one side or the other. In Madrid, life grew more and more grim, Franco's air raids often so quickly succeeding one another that the warning sirens stopped sounding. In July, as Lance and his friends learnt, the Republicans had loosed a well-conceived attack to the west to relieve Franco's pressure on the city—to become known as the Battle of Brunete—but with a negative result.

Lance, still living at the hospital and still using the offices of the Commercial Attaché, was feeling the pressure of events. In the muddied waters of the time the affairs of his two companies were moving at dead slow, their engines at minimum revolutions, and nearly all his days and evenings were now devoted to rescue and relief. He was, however, in spite of his outward buoyancy, feeling the strain of the past few months and wondering how long he could keep going. The winds of chance, he knew, would not for ever blow in his favour. Some time or other the people in Valencia, such as the nasty-looking Black Face fellow in the secret police, would begin to question the validity of the colours under which he sailed. There had lately been several small signs that caused him to watch his course more carefully. In Madrid also he had become known in the foreign communities as very much of a dark horse. Awkward and pointed questions were put to him in the Anglo-American club, so much so that, sociable and gregarious though he was, he had been obliged to keep away. He missed very much this companionship and began to feel lonely and cut off.

He went over in his mind those whom he still particularly wanted to get out. There was one case of oranges in Madrid.

Then there was Hilario, the handsome butler, who had looked after him in the marquesa's house; he was now employed by Leche at the Embassy, which had been moved from Valencia to the picturesque village of El Perelló, and was thus in no danger, but Lance had promised him that he would get away.

Next, there was a fearfully dangerous case, which he had long been shirking, hiding obscurely in Valencia itself and now in imminent danger of arrest and execution; this was young Alvaro Martin Moreno, son of no less a person than Franco's Chief of Staff, General Francisco Martin Moreno. These three cases he was specially anxious to get away quickly, especially Moreno, whose life was balanced on a knife-edge.

"Well," he thought, "I'll get that out 'by the usual channels,' all in one go, then I'll go out myself. It's high time."

For himself, he knew quite well that he could have gone openly and legitimately by sea, but another thought came to tempt and fret at his imagination. With these three gone, the total of his escapes, counting the sixty "illegitimates" of Alicante in February, would have reached ninety-four. Why not go on and complete his century? He felt like a batsman at the crease watching the scoreboard. "100 not" would be a most satisfactory way of retiring to the pavilion.

There were, indeed, six other cases weighing on his mind, one of which was the last name on the Burgos list. He couldn't face another three or four of those Valencia ordeals, however, and the thought occurred to him of a land route through the opposing lines that he had heard of from Antonio, his old porter. It was in the direction of Manzanares, one hundred miles to the south. He knew that country well and if he could find the right spot he could take these six out, all in one bunch. "So only one more trip to Valencia," he thought, "then I'll reconnoitre this route, take those chaps over and not come back."

He began to plan carefully for this last and specially dangerous Valencia expedition. The case in Madrid, who for the purposes of our story will be known as 'Ramón', he would dispose of in the ordinary way at Valencia. For Moreno, he would have to improvise on the spot as best he could after seeking him out. He grimaced at the very thought. Then, if he could pull that off without being nabbed, he would run out to El Perelló, twenty miles by road to the south, to fetch the excellent Hilario, for whom he had a soft spot.

The operation began one Saturday night. Lance brought Ramón cautiously out of his hiding place to the Embassy cheka, using the headlamp trick for going in. Margery was not to accompany them and Lance, Ramón and Pepe dossed down in the Embassy for a short night's sleep. Two hours before dawn on Sunday they set out. Lance, having washed and shaved as usual, engaged the sleepy Embassy guard in conversation and cigarettes while Pepe drove out slowly with Ramón and parked a safe ten yards away. Then with a casual *hasta la vista* to the guard, Lance joined them.

It was relatively cool and all the city was dead quiet as they drove through the neglected streets, past the shuttered houses and the gaping bomb-holes. Not a soul was to be seen except the lurking guards who from time to time stepped out from behind a roadside tree or a shadowed doorway. As he approached them, Lance put on the car's interior light, so that the guards could recognize his check coat. One of them commented on the absence of the señorita and Lance replied that her hands were too full at the hospital. Thus they left the sleeping city and drove on over the long, rough road to Valencia, beneath the myriad stars and the young moon, past the innumerable, drowsy guards, the wan, shadowy villages and the ravaged churches that took shape in the searchlight glare of Pepe's lamps.

The sun at length rose in splendour as, in the cool of Sunday morning, Pepe hurried on as best the road would allow through the awakening countryside. They drove through the fertile *huerta*, in the full pride of "autumn's golden quittance", and very soon all the air was touched with the sting of the Mediterranean sun.

Arrived in Valencia, Lance went straight to the cheka and there had his first surprise. The narrow street was littered with debris and the windows of the old houses blown out as by a violent explosion. Francisca, on seeing him, threw up her plump arms and burst into a torrent of words.

"*Madre mia, señor!*" she cried. "The things that have happened! We have been bombed, señor! I, Francisca, have been hurled from my bed by a great bomb that burst at my feet. Ah, Mother of God, what are things coming to?"

Lance grinned broadly. It would have taken a mighty big bomb, he reflected to blow the good Francisca out of bed.

"You look remarkably well after it, Francisca! No bones broken, I see."

"God protected me, señor, or else I should have been blown to little pieces. But my room, señor! It is a calamity. Come, you shall see for yourself."

Chattering volubly, she led him to the top of the old house, ominously cluttered with the detritus of a violent shaking, and there, in the roof, was a hole of the same size as that made by the small bomb which had interrupted his conversation with Mrs. Norris in the flat of the Embassy annexe. Broken timbers, wrecked furniture, plaster and a thick layer of dust lay over all and the bed stood tipsily on two legs. Lance bantered her with gentle good humour. His chief concern had been whether she could carry on the cheka, but Francisca would have carried on if she had had no more than a hole in the ground. The first floor was intact, though strewn with dust and plaster. Accordingly he stowed Ramón safely away and gave him the usual warning not to go out and not even to show his face at the windows.

He then went down to the docks to make his usual enquiries about what ships were sailing and there had his first check. There were no Red Ensign ships sailing till Thursday. What now? He had three cases to export and could not afford to hang about in idleness for three days. He slipped into one of the *fondas* and over a glass of very astringent sherry decided that, though he didn't at all care for the idea, he must try Alicante; perhaps he could get at least the butler away from there and be back by Wednesday, or earlier, to deal with his two Valencia cases. He walked back to the cheka and before calling for Pepe told Ramón not to worry if he was away for a day or two, "as I have another little job to do first."

He and Pepe then drove the 110 miles of the winding coast road to Alicante, which he himself had helped to shape and maintain. He went straight to the Victoria Hotel, using, as he invariably did, a back entrance, and had a talk with his old friend Ernesto, the porter. By this time there was very little shipping at Alicante, for the war had seriously upset the normal activities of export and import, but on looking out over the harbour he was very relieved to see two ships wearing the Red Ensign.

Except for his quick trips with the two "Red Cross boys" and with the two men of the International Brigade, Lance had not used Alicante since that critical day in February when he and Margery had got away the big convoy. Because of the stir that that incident had created he knew he must be very wary, but he learnt in conversation with Ernesto that the Anarchist committee that used to control the port had now been replaced by "a bunch of Communists", in keeping with the general pattern all over Republican Spain since the Russians had begun to exert their influence. There had also been several changes among the police. Moreover, very few of the former port officials were left. This greatly relieved Lance, for, although Communist control was usually more strict and efficient, it meant that he was unlikely to be recognized in the docks and denounced. "Most people," Ernesto said, "have forgotten the February affair by now."

With reasonable confidence, therefore, Lance walked across the familiar avenue of palms to the dock entrance (there was no gate then) and got past the sentry and police on presentation of his impressive pass. He called first on the master of the smaller of the two British ships, but found that he was bound directly for a Russian port in the Black Sea. No use.

He boarded the larger of the two ships and found that, although she also was bound for the Black Sea, she was calling first at a port in French Morocco. She was not sailing till Saturday, however— seven days hence. Another very awkward complication. However, liking the looks of the master, who was a Welshman, he put his usual question: would Captain Jones be prepared to take a passenger and thus save a human life?

The skipper grinned broadly. "Why, sure, Captain Lance," he said. "No need to explain, you know; I've heard about you from Jim Browne! A bit of fun will relieve the monotony."

That, thought Lance as he strolled back to the hotel, not knowing in what unexpected way the monotony was to be relieved, would be all right for Hilario, who was in no danger, but it meant another change in his own ideas. He would now have to go back again to Valencia to get Moreno and Ramón away by Thursday as best he could, then collect the butler out at El Perelló and smuggle him on board at Alicante on Friday afternoon.

Meanwhile, although Alicante was now a drab and dreary place, a grim contrast to the bright and sociable town that he and Jinks had known in happier days, the weather was wonderful. The delicious cool breeze came in punctually at six o'clock, a pleasure that no sour-faced politicians could change. The atmosphere still enjoyed that diamond luminosity and that wonderful crisp clarity by which you could count the stones of the old castle walls away on the top of Santa Barbara, more than half a mile distant. As he looked seaward, he saw, some three miles out, a British warship at anchor, engaged upon the enforcement of "non-intervention" which the other European powers had declared. Further out in the sea Lance could see some dark, triangular specks of fishing boats; they would be back at their old place on the waterfront, beyond the yacht club, he knew, by ten o'clock that night, their guardian eyes leading them through all perils.

Some guardian had also surely been guiding him, he thought, for how else could he have avoided the shoals among which so many other escapers had been shipwrecked? As he looked out over the placid sea, the sea that he loved so much, he wondered how men could call it cruel. Was not the land, Whitman's "unendurable land", far more cruel, the land that nourished so much hate and greed and savagery, where men, in the strait and cabined cells of fevered minds, sought means to cheat, to torture and to slaughter on so vast a scale?

So he thought; and thought, too, how soon he himself would be out on that sea, bound for sanity, for a fireside beneath a grey sky and for his dear Jinks. Next week maybe, or the week after, if he could tidy things up in Madrid in time and get his big party across into Franco's lines.

He dined, well enough considering the times, with a half-bottle of Valdepeñas, and called on the Navarros, who were living in close confinement in a flat on the seafront nearby. He missed Margery's company and had gone up to his room for an early bed, when, to his surprise, Ernesto knocked at his door and showed in Captain Jones, the skipper with whom he had made arrangements that day, accompanied by his two mates. They were in a very agitated state. Could Captain Lance please go out to the docks at once? There was a fearful row going on with the locals and it looked as though everybody in the ship was going to be put in jug.

Dagger asked: "Hell's bells! What's up, skipper?"

"My second engineer," Jones answered, "has fallen over the quayside in the dark, struck his head on the quay wall and been drowned. As if that wasn't bad enough, the locals seem to think that we bumped the poor chap off; or else they're squabbling about who is going to have the loot. They're swarming all round his body screaming their heads off and of course we don't understand a damned word."

"All right, let's go and sort it out."

Lance got up immediately, as he always did, and they all walked over to the docks in the dark. As the skipper had said, there on the quayside was a crowd of gesticulating Spaniards—police, carabiniers and dockyard officials—and in the middle of the mêlée a couple of stolid British sailors stood as it were on guard over the corpse of their shipmate. Lance, however, summed up the situation at once. The Spaniards, far from threatening or quarrelling, were in their emotional way merely expressing their sympathy and discussing how they could help!

Though fears were allayed and excitement abated, Lance found that a very awkward problem remained. The Spanish police would not accept the fact that the nasty head wound had been caused by a fall over the quayside. Someone, they said, either British or Spanish, must have killed the man. Lance became more and more alarmed for his friends; if the police were not disabused of this notion, he knew, there would be interminable enquiries and the ship would be detained. He had a word with the skipper, now very much alarmed, and out of his quick thinking offered a solution, one which went against the grain but was the only quick way out. He turned to the police officers and said:

"The captain says that the man was undoubtedly drunk and that was why he fell in the sea. He is sure no one attacked him."

"Ah, that is a different matter," answered the senior of the policemen. "That explains the whole thing."

The easy explanation was accepted without further question. Sensitive about such things, Lance hated the idea of libelling a dead man, but he could see no other way out of the dilemma and felt further justified by the thought that other lives might be at hazard if he became involved. He went back to bed, but next morning, which was Monday, found himself again heavily involved in the affair, and in a manner that would have had all the elements of comedy if it had not been basically so tragic.

With the prohibition in Republican Spain of all forms, ceremonies and objects of religion, including burial, extraordinary difficulties arose over the disposal of the engineer's body. The crews of the two British ships naturally desired that their countryman should be buried with decent reverence and Christian rites and in the difficulties with which they were now faced they again appealed to Lance for help.

The first problem, in this city of 100,000 people, was to find a coffin. No, the police told him, under the Popular Front government there were no longer any undertakers; they were all Fascists and stooges of the church and those who had not been "executed" had fled. However, the police went out of their way to give him all the help they could. They approached the Communist "committee" that ruled the town's carpenters, but the committee would have nothing to do with an object so reactionary and bourgeois as a coffin.

Lance, police and skipper continued to scour the town till at last, with police sanction, a shuttered undertaker's shop was broken open and a coffin found. The rightful owner could not be paid but before the police would let the captain have the coffin they made him pay a subscription in support of the "Red Aid".

The actual burial raised even greater and more delicate difficulties. A site was offered in a field, but this the sailors firmly refused, as it was not consecrated ground. At length, after many consultations, permission was somewhat reluctantly given for burial in the disused cemetery and the police undertook to have a grave dug ready for the next morning. The cemetery, however, raised its own problems, as it was several miles out of Alicante, no cars

168

were to be had for hire and horses were as scarce as coffins. Thus the whole of Monday was taken up by this affair, of which he had by no means seen the end, but before its conclusion another totally unexpected emergency arose.

Wearied out with all this chasing to and fro in the heat, this arguing and haggling, Lance went back to his hotel in the evening, hoping for a quiet night at last but not very convinced that all would be well on Tuesday morning. He had lost a day out of his proposed programme already but was resolved to see this funeral through for the sailors' sake. It was rotten enough to lose a shipmate and it meant a great deal to them that he should be laid to rest with reverence and pride. Without help from someone who spoke Spanish and knew the mood of Alicante, Lance knew that they were only too likely to suffer distress and outrage to their feelings. He therefore made their cause his own.

So thinking, he entered the hotel by the back door with relief, mopping his brow. But his hope for a quiet evening was once again to be shattered by an interruption that put even the troublesome affair of the funeral in the background for a while.

Summoned to the telephone just as day had dissolved into night, he was surprised to hear the voice of one of the Navarros. They wanted to see Señor Lance at once on a very urgent matter. Could he come round to their flat?

"I'm awfully tired," Lance answered. "Couldn't you come round here? We could talk in my room."

"That would be terribly dangerous for us after dark, Señor Lance. It isn't safe to go out at all."

"Hell! What about me then?"

"It's different for you; you are English."

"You seem to think we are bullet-proof. All right, I'll come."

He went out by the back door and along the front behind the dangerous palm avenue and gained the Navarros' safely. Theirs was a large flat furnished mainly with the comfortable red-plush furniture of which the Spaniards were so fond. Don Gines was there with Raphael and José. Lance was, of course, pretty certain that they wanted him to get away some friend of theirs, but he thought he would get his oar in first and, after greetings, he said:

"Now then, what about getting you two out of the country?"

At the direct question they looked a little taken aback and one of them said:

"It is not for ourselves we are anxious, Señor Lance, but for a special friend who is in great danger, so much so that, if he is not got away this very night, he will be shot tomorrow. In fact, they may come for him tonight, so there is not a moment to lose."

"The usual grim story," Lance thought. Although he already had three cases on his hands, he did not hesitate a moment. In those cases when there was an immediate threat of death, all his instincts arose at once to save and defend life. He had, indeed, trained himself to say yes first and to think afterwards, because he knew only too well that if he reversed the process he would let slip a life.

"All right," he said. "Where is he?"

They told him the address, which was quite close. "Pablo Sanchez" had been hiding there for several months, but they had learnt that the Communists had discovered where he was and were "going to get him", as he was very Right. Taking leave of the Navarros, whom he was never to see again, Lance went out again into the dark streets, alone, feeling anything but bullet-proof. He found the address with some difficulty—a small, dark, dirty place, in which Sanchez occupied one room. His reaction to Lance's entry was one of complete terror. He looked a little worm of a man, completely down and cowed and very sick. At Lance's entry he shrank back trembling, not knowing who he was, having had no warning of his coming and supposing that this was the summons to death that he had been fearing for so long.

Worm though he seemed, Lance was filled with pity. Why shoot a poor creature such as this? What good would his death be to any political cause? It was, however, only with the greatest difficulty, and not until he had given an ultimatum, that he persuaded the poor fellow to accept him as genuine.

"Pull yourself together, man," he said. "Can't you tell that I'm not even a Spaniard, let alone a Communist? Either you come with me and take a chance, or stay behind and get bumped off for certain. Come along, for I'm not going to stay any longer."

This moved him out of his timid hesitation, but when he had to face the open street, he shrank back again in abject terror, as though he saw the firing squad in front of him. Lance took him firmly by the arm and marched him out. They reached the back door of the hotel and Lance took him straight up to his own room.

Not until he had got him there did Lance begin to think, and think hard. What on earth was he to do with the fellow? Tomorrow, in addition to this trying funeral affair, he simply must get back to Valencia to get off his two cases there. He could not dream of taking the poor, frightened little Sanchez with him, because his hands would be full enough already. Young Moreno alone was headache enough. Having got rid of his two Valencia cases, he must then collect the butler, bring him to Alicante and get him stowed away in Jones's ship by Friday night. No doubt Jones would take Sanchez also, but he could not take him before Friday night and, meantime, to leave him alone in the hotel for three days or more was unthinkable.

From this bristling entanglement, with men's lives hanging by such slender threads, he could see only one way out. Somehow he must get Sanchez away this very night. Now. At once. He must do an immediate reconnaissance. He would have to abandon all his carefully evolved principles and resort to the cover of night and the chancey tactics of stealth and evasion.

Having done his best to reassure Sanchez, whose nervousness had thawed a little under the influence of some food and wine, Lance locked him in the room and went down to see Ernesto. Knowing well that what he was about to do was extremely dangerous, he gave Ernesto the key of the room and said: "If I am not back by the morning, Ernesto, go round at once and see Señor Navarro."

He went out again into the hostile night. A partial moon had joined the thronging congregation of stars, giving a faint light in the canyons of the shuttered and deserted streets and seeming, in the manner of moonlight, to intensify the silence. It was about nine o'clock, but, where once there had been so much bustle and noise at this hour, a tomb-like stillness reigned. Lance turned the corner and gained the sea-front, where he and Jinks used in happier times to stroll in the cool of the evening. Here the famous double avenue of palms would have been garlanded with lamps of every colour, beneath which, in an everlasting carnival acted to the music of the orchestras, the sparkling Spanish women paraded up and down to display their beauty. Now, as the bright memory flashed across Lance's mind, those gay avenues were sinister black tunnels in which the unshaven gunmen lurked unseen.

Avoiding those dark and dangerous tunnels, Lance made out on to the open waterfront, where a low sea wall met the beach only two or three feet below. Old memories came back to him and his enquiring thoughts went to the little yacht club which lay some distance along the front. Once crowded with yachts, skiffs and holiday diversions of every kind, it was now headquarters of the carabiniers and no craft remained there except a few rowing boats. Beyond the yacht club stretched the long, low sea wall where the picturesque fishing craft were drawn up and where he and Jinks used to wait for them to come in at ten o'clock and have a chat with the fishermen. He knew nearly all of them.

Two thoughts were now in his mind. Provided he could get Sanchez safely past all the boiler-suits lurking behind the palm-trees, could he seize a rowing boat at the yacht club, right under the noses of the carabiniers, and row this man out to the British warship that was anchored three miles out? A long pull there and back, but he thought he could do it, provided he could make a getaway undetected in the light of the half-moon. An unlikely provision and one that he did not like at all, but he was prepared to try. He knew that British warships were no longer allowed to take refugees without proper documents, but he knew of a ruse that would defeat that official prohibition surely enough—throw his man overboard close to the warship and shout for help! The Navy would always go instantly to the help of a drowning man; and, once he was on board, they would never dream of sending him ashore again to certain death. Of that Lance felt quite certain.

A hare-brained plot and very chancy indeed. Quite against the rules he had set for himself, depending far too much on the uncontrollable factors of luck and involving the illegality of pinching someone else's boat; he could be put in jug for that alone. But it seemed the best way out of a tight corner. There was, however, one alternative, even more risky—the fishing boats farther on.

He knew that some of them would put to sea between three and four in the morning; but would any of the fishermen be prepared to get a refugee away? They were, Lance knew, all very Red, and it was a darned risky thing even to mention such a proposition to them; though he had been friends with many of them in the old days, it was only too likely in the new state of things that they would denounce him at once to the police.

So scheming, Lance went on his lonely walk, stepping noisily, smoking a cigarette and making no pretence at stealth. He was challenged repeatedly, both by men who sprang out from the palms, rifle presented, and by others who called out without revealing themselves. This sort of thing, however, did not worry him in the least when he was alone; he was quite accustomed to dealing with sentries. He answered them cheerfully in his confident voice, telling them truthfully that he was an engineer of Gines Navarro out for his evening stroll. As one sentry jumped out on him with rifle presented to his stomach, he exclaimed gaily:

"Look out, comrade! Mind my belly-button!"

Such an expression could have been used only by a *loco inglés* and sounded laughable when spoken in literal Spanish. The sentry's rifle dropped and his face broke into a wide grin as Lance explained.

Lance could not at first understand what on earth all these sentries were there for, until at length he realized that it must be part of the private war going on everywhere between the rival political parties of Republican Spain; for a Communist would just as soon murder and loot an Anarchist as a Fascist, and vice versa. How these chaps liked killing! How much better would have been the Republicans' chances of winning the war if all these gunmen and guards lurking in every town and village had got themselves properly trained and gone off to the front! It was characteristic of Lance that, far from being perturbed by these dangerous sentries, he welcomed the opportunity of making a careful mental note of exactly where they were all stationed.

Thus, before long he saw the dark bulk of the yacht club ahead. It was a wooden structure, standing out from the esplanade, built on piles above the water in the manner of a pier. He went more

173

slowly as he neared it, his senses keenly alert. He was disconcerted to see carabiniers and militiamen strolling about and chatting all over the place. Clearly it was impossible to reach the yacht club openly from this side.

Changing his tactics, he now adopted those of stealth. Walking quietly, cigarette out, he made for the shadow of the palms on his right hand, since there were not likely to be any sentries lurking at this point, and so passed on beyond the club. At a safe distance he turned, made over to the low sea wall at the water's edge, dropped over it on to the beach on hands and knees and cautiously crawled back to the club.

The beach was only a foot or two below the level of the sea wall, but the small moon-shadow was just enough to give him cover as he crept along. As he drew near he could distinguish the wooden piles that supported the staging on which the club stood, clear at the waterline but disappearing in the dense gloom overhead. A yard or two from the staging there was an indentation in the wall where the shadow was deeper. He paused here awhile, lying on his stomach.

Far out on the moon-polished water he could see the pin-point lights of the British warship that he so much wished to reach. She looked an awful long way off. Close to him the tideless sea lapped quietly against the stout piles. From his animal position they looked like the trunks of trees in some tropical forest swamp, gloomy and lethal. Above him he could hear the carabiniers pacing about on the stage and others were on the pavement a few yards away. From just above someone spat into the sea.

What interested Lance most, however, was that, in the gloom beneath the outer edge of the staging, but only just beneath, he could discern the shapes of six or seven rowing-boats. How could he hope to reach them and get away unseen? "Damned *infra dig*," he thought, "to get caught here." What an ass he would feel! What the devil should he say? Already, according to his usual habit, he was thinking ahead how to get out of any difficulty into which he ran.

His mind made up, he crawled at last underneath the staging. Groping about, he found the painter of one of the boats. Very, very gently he pulled her inshore. With the utmost possible quiet he stepped on board, but he could not avoid stepping into the water and the drip from his shoes as he got in sounded in his ears like a cataract. To be heard, or to cause ripples that might be seen on the moonlit water from above or from the pavement, would be disastrous.

Once on board, he lay on the thwarts and he felt about for oars. There were none. What now? He must try the other boats, hoping that someone had been careless. Still lying down, he was just able, by stretching his arm outboard, to reach one of the piles and, pressing with great care on it, managed to propel the boat very gently within reach of another.

To move from one boat into another without floundering about is at the best of times an unsteady operation. To do so at night, noiselessly, keeping a low silhouette and without making visible ripples, is nearly impossible. Studying the feel of the boat, Lance seized the gunwale of the second firmly and, keeping head and shoulders very low, transferred himself with infinite pains, but inevitably there was some rocking of each boat as he shifted his weight.

As he feared, the second boat also had no oars. He continued the operation from boat to boat, his spirits falling lower and lower as he found each one empty. Every move was a trial of balance and patience and nerve. Some of the boats were scarcely within arm's length and once he all but fell in the water. He was about to move into the last boat when he heard fresh footsteps on the pavement, very close. He froze at once, but was just able to see two carabiniers stop ten yards away. He clearly heard one of them say:

"I don't see anything, comrade."

"Well, I certainly thought I heard a noise, like boats bumping up against each other."

"Old Garcia thumping the deck, I suppose."

"They should supply us with torches."

"They should supply us with lots of things, comrade. Come, I've had enough standing about, or they will have to supply me with new legs."

Remaining stock still, Lance watched them go. After a long wait he transferred his weight cautiously into the last boat and completed his search. In all seven of them there was not an oar to be found.

What an ass he had been, he thought. Damned silly idea to imagine that he could row two or three hundred yards over moon-lit water without being seen. And he ought to have known that all the oars would have been taken away.

Desperately disappointed, and feeling very low in spirits, he painfully reversed his operation, crawling back from boat to boat. With the same infinite caution as before, he regained the beach and waited under the staging, lying on his stomach. A few soldiers were still walking about on the pavement not many yards away, but he had a good chance of escaping observation from these if they did not come right up to the edge of the sea wall. But what was happening on the staging above him? Was anyone up there looking out over the beach? If so, it would go hard with him. But there was no means at all of knowing, so he must take a chance.

He crept out again into the narrow band of shadow at the foot of the wall, his nerves taut, feeling how very much more unpleasant it was to creep away from an enemy than towards him. At any moment he expected a challenge and his back tingled at the expectation of a shot. So far, he reflected, it had been anything but his lucky night. "Hell's bells," he thought, "I'm too old for this sort of lark." Two or three times he lay dead still as footsteps or voices seemed to be approaching. Bit by bit, however, he gained ground, lizard-wise. At about the distance of a cricket pitch he thought it safe to get up on hands and knees and a little farther on, having peered round carefully, he stood up with relief, dusted himself down and walked on, his wet shoes and socks squelching uncomfortably. Not since that little war in Russia, he reflected, had he walked sodden-footed.

The fishermen were now his only hope. In fact, after the grim outlook under the staging, they seemed a better bet. He looked forward to meeting them, for he had many friends among them, and had always found their company refreshing. He drew reflec-tively on his newly lit cigarette as, wondering what change he would find in them since the old days, he drew near and saw the long, low shapes of their boats darkly outlined ahead. They were drawn up in a long line, close up to the sea wall, their white, eye-painted bows showing up in the blue-grey night with sharper meaning. One boat was just creeping in, wrinkling the moon-glazed surface of the sea. Ashore the fishermen bent over their gear or stood about in dim groups on the pavements.

Lance knew that these were the crews who would be going out in the early hours next morning and that, after preparing their boats, they would go home for a few hours' sleep. He had caught them just at the right time.

He went up to the first group and began chatting casually with them as he and Jinks had done in the old days, asking them what fish were about and what sort of catches they had had. To his bitter disappointment, he was received with apathy and lukewarm monosyllables. Never had he seen men more changed. Once so cheerful in their temper, so carefree in their way of chatting and joking, so matched in spirit to the sun-drenched bronze of their skin, they were now morose, taciturn and sour. His attempts to jest with these old friends met not with hostility, to be sure, but with the indifference and astringency of men whose hearts had been emptied of all warmth and colour. Here was the signature of Communism, chilling and acid in its influence. Better far, he thought, the hot emotion, violent though it might be, of the Anarchists. You could deal with that, but the stiff concrete of Communism was hard to permeate.

For a full hour Lance wandered up and down the dark quay, going from group to group, from boat to boat, testing the temper of each, but finding no relief to the sullen atmosphere. There was not a single man who responded with any warmth or friendliness or whom he felt he could trust with confidence if he put him the critical question. His hopes fell lower and lower. Time was pass-ing. The fishermen were beginning to drift away to their homes. He must do something quickly.

Desperately, he decided that he must again take a chance, pick-ing the most likely man there was among that unpromising lot. It was a fearful risk to take, for in their present temper a hostile answer seemed the only likelihood, and that would without any doubt at all be followed by denunciation to the police.

Nevertheless, some chance had to be taken. He thought of the little frightened rabbit in the hotel and knew that he must risk his fingers to release the trap. He remembered how, once before driven into a corner, he had taken a chance by putting the straight question to the Civil Governor to save his road convoy, and had got away with it.

One man there was, part-owner of a fishing boat of about twenty tons, whom he had known better than the others in pre-war days. He remembered his sense of humour and his healthy smile and decided that he would put his fate in his hands. He sought out his man and began in a quiet undertone to lead up to his main question with a long rigmarole, when the fisherman interrupted him and said quite bluntly:

"How much?"

Quite taken aback, Lance almost gasped with relief. Instinctively he named the same sum as he paid to the British captains:

"Four hundred pesetas."

Instantly the fisherman countered with:

"Eight hundred."

It was far more than Lance was prepared to stump up, but he had no choice. For this sum the fisherman agreed to run the case of oranges over to Oran in French Morocco, a distance of about 160 miles. The boat was to put out at four a.m. and Lance was to bring Sanchez down an hour earlier, when there would be only one other hand of the crew present.

Very pleased with his bargain, hard though it was in terms of cash, Lance turned back to the Victoria Hotel with wet feet, a tired body but a lighter heart. As he went he checked the positions of all the sentries, almost like a duty officer on his rounds, and found them all present and correct, but with the addition of two others he had not spotted before.

Not the least difficult of his tasks that night was to tell Sanchez of the plans for his own escape. Back in the hotel bedroom, he found him such a piteous spectacle that he was at first quite unable to face the painful task of telling the unfortunate fellow what was expected of him. Sanchez was as pale as parchment and as thin as a skeleton. His eyes seemed to protrude with fear. He had been shut up in a small room for fourteen months, with no fresh air, no exercise and very little food. For all these months he had been listening for the door bell to ring and every time it rang he had gone through the sensation of being dragged from his hiding place to be murdered. How could he face the ordeal that Lance had prepared for him?

Lance, himself tired and strained, felt so unnerved by the prospect that he "almost had the jitters" himself and he went and sat down in another room for a while to pull himself together. He was fearfully concerned how the fellow would behave when challenged by the numerous sentries, for any jitters would certainly give the game away; in any case, the sentries were bound to be extra suspicious of anyone who was about at such an hour. The hotel itself was now dead quiet, like all the world outside.

Fortified by his rest, Lance went back to Sanchez and put the matter to him as gently as he could, as though he were talking to a child.

"You must have absolute confidence in me," he said, "and do exactly as I tell you. When we meet the sentries, don't on any account show any fear and leave the talking to me."

They left the hotel at about half past two in the morning in deathly quiet, Lance holding Sanchez firmly by the arm. The moon had declined a little, but the stars still thronged the night sky. The two men walked out on to the front, with the pale lilac-grey sea on their left and the long, velvet-black belt of the palms on their right. The night was cold, cold enough to shiver a little. In the stillness their footsteps seemed to ring on the paving like castanets. The antennae of Lance's perceptions were stretched to their uttermost, alert to all signs of danger and ready to meet them. Sanchez was so weak that he stumbled several times and would have fallen headlong if Lance had not supported him. He hardly answered as Lance chatted away inconsequentially to keep up his companion's spirits.

Lance now knew exactly where to expect every sentry, but to his surprise he was not challenged once. Obviously the comrades had all gone home to bed, realizing that at this late hour they were unlikely to find any sport for their rifles. Their departure was a tremendous relief, for Lance had no confidence in Sanchez's ability to face them. He knew, however, that there were bound to be a few carabiniers awake on duty at the yacht club, since it was their headquarters. These few he could see stencilled against the night sky as he approached carefully.

"Quiet here, my friend," he whispered to Sanchez.

With the same stealth as before, he made away to the right through the palms and beyond, to come out safely on to the esplanade again. His luck seemed to have returned and his spirits rose higher.

He was quite prepared, however, to find the police all ready waiting for him at the boats, to catch him red-handed, and the same fear had occurred to Sanchez, for, stopping in his stride, as Spaniards often do when about to talk, he clutched Lance by his lapels and said in a husky voice full of apprehension:

"Señor, we shall be trapped, I know. The police will be there. They have told the police and we shall be trapped."

Not at all sure himself, Lance answered in robust voice:

"Not a bit of it, Sanchez. I told you to trust me. They are my friends. Brace up, man. Everything is going fine."

The luck continued to hold. They reached the boats at last without difficulty and there were the fisherman and his mate ready for them, stowing their food and wine. The fisherman, however, was in no better mood than he had been earlier and spoke brusquely.

"Get him on board at once." Then to Sanchez: "Come on."

He helped him on board, Lance following. He took the fugitive down into a small, sinister and completely dark hold, reeking of years of stale fish, and then immediately closed the hatch, scarcely giving Lance any chance of saying a last word of encouragement to the distracted fugitive and of handing him his usual letter to the British Consul at Oran. "Poor devil," thought Lance. "I'm damned glad I'm not in his shoes." He would have liked to stay a while and chat with the skipper, but was told:

"You must leave at once, señor. You must not be here when my crew arrives. So give me the money and leave."

Lance, however, had no intention of quitting the scene alto-gether until he had seen his charge safely away. He withdrew and hid in the darkness of the palms. At about four o'clock, when it was very dark, he watched from his hiding-place as the boat put out at last. He followed its dark shape as it moved slowly over the grey water and listened to the chug-chug of its diesel engine gradually growing fainter. Then with a sigh he turned for his lonely walk home.

# CHAPTER ELEVEN

# DANGEROUS CARGOES

TUESDAY morning, after a couple of hours' sleep, brought back the distressing matter of the sailor's funeral.

Eighteen hands from the two British ships turned out to attend the funeral, in their best rig. It was very hot, with the dry, dusty heat of Alicante. As they assembled in silence, they were stirred by a sense of frustrated reverence. They were not allowed to make the burial a purely private and British one; a Spanish police officer must go with them. Moreover, they were told there must be no religious ceremony, but Lance asked if there would be any objection to a few simple prayers being read at the graveside. For this permission was given, but with the stipulation that they must be read in Spanish; there must be no clergy, no "ritual", "rites", singing or other observances contrary to the law.

They made their way out to the distant cemetery by a lorry that Lance had managed to hire from another firm of contractors and he himself accompanied them in his car. It was a harsh and forbidding scene. Desolate and untended, the forsaken cemetery lay away on high, exposed ground, barren, desiccated, stony, the grass withered and brown. No fit resting place for a sailor.

The coffin, draped with the Red Ensign, was carried to the graveside by six seamen and laid down beside the grave that the police had undertaken to have dug. To the distress of all, it was found that the grave was only two feet deep and that it was too short and too narrow to hold the coffin. There was nothing for it but to enlarge the grave there and then and accordingly, feeling upset and angry at this unseemly distraction from the decorum of their simple ceremony, the sailors began to cast about for tools. All they could find, in a shed some distance away, were a shovel and a crowbar. With these they set to, working in silence in short shifts, for it was now extremely hot.

It was a full hour before the grave was ready and Lance then read out an extempore translation of a few prayers from the Church of England Prayer Book, a task that taxed to the uttermost his knowledge of Spanish. But he read from the heart and, as the sun poured down on the bared heads of these simple men of the sea, he felt a strong community of spirit with them.

On his advice, the sailors filled in the grave themselves, as the brass fittings on the coffin were of some value and he knew that the grave would be liable to desecration and looting.

Finally, one of the ship's mates stepped out with a camera to take a photograph of the grave for the engineer's family. The police officer at once came forward and said that no photograph could be taken without a written permit from the Military Governor, but Lance had thought of that, too, and said to him with satisfaction:

"It's all right, comrade, I've got one. Here it is."

Immediately after the funeral Pepe began the drive back to Valencia to resume the affairs of Moreno and Ramón. Very tired after his all-night outing, Lance dozed for a while but the thought that he still had three cases to export weighed heavily on his mind. He anticipated no unusual difficulty about Ramón, whom he had brought from Madrid, but it was young Moreno who really worried him.

The young man was dynamite. As the son of Franco's Chief of Staff, he was dangerous enough, but, in addition, he was a hostage for an officer of high rank who was in Nationalist hands. Lance knew that arrangements for an exchange had failed and that Moreno's days were numbered unless he were rescued. The police knew perfectly well where he was and were keeping him under close observation. Two foreign embassies and two individuals had already attempted to rescue him, all without success.

Their failures, Lance felt sure, were due to their plans having been too elaborate. His own would be perfectly simple, and would be based, as all his other rescues had been, on the simple theory that the Spaniards would never dream that anyone would try to get so dangerous a customer away right under their noses, least of all an irresponsible, good-time chap like himself. On that he rested his hopes.

With these reflections, and chatting to Pepe, Lance hurried along the tortuous coast road. The day was hot and drowsy and the little coastal villages, grilled by the Mediterranean sun, lay asleep, for it was the period of the siesta, and scarcely a soul was to be seen. Occasionally Lance could see in the distance some patrolling warship, either a Spanish one or a foreign one engaged in the enforcement of non-intervention, witnesses to the passions and rivalries that had been aroused all over the world and to the risk that all Europe might at any moment find itself plunged into a disastrous war of rival ideologies.

Passing on through the region of flat rice-fields, Lance arrived in Valencia late in the afternoon and noted that a British warship was lying outside, perhaps the same one that had been at Alicante the day before. He went straight to the cheka. Ramón was safe and in good spirits but very glad to see his guardian back again. Having warned Francisca to expect another guest on the morrow, Lance went out and dined early at the Marcelina, where he learnt from one of the Embassy staff that Admiral Somerville was on board the warship that he had noticed and that next day he was attending an official luncheon party, to which the leading British residents had also been invited, to be given by Leche at El Perelló. Feeling very tired, Lance returned to the cheka early and went to bed.

After breakfast next morning, which was Wednesday, he went off to his dockyard haunts and soon found himself among a crowd of British sailors, for there were half a dozen Red Ensign ships in harbour. They greeted him as an old friend, for by now most of them knew him, calling out:

"Here comes the Scarlet Pimpernel! What's it to be, Captain?"

"For the love of Mike cut that out! It's the same word in Spanish. Give me a *vino rojo* for my nerves."

Very soon he had learned the date and sailing hour of each ship. With this information he picked his skipper—another Welshman, the fair-haired, genial and piratically named Henry Morgan. He was sailing at six o'clock that evening. Under cover of a brisk conversation, Lance asked him in a low voice:

"Can you take a couple of customers this time, skipper?"

"Sure, captain, what's the plan?"

"A slight variation of the usual. Look here, can you get one of the *other* skippers to invite us all on board for lunch? As a blind, you know."

Morgan grinned. "Always ready for a bit of a blind."

"Not that sort of blind! A false trail, you know."

"Nothing easier," Morgan replied. Turning to a skipper on his right, he asked: "Jim, what say you ask us all aboard for lunch? The captain here wants to sample your gin and sausages."

"That will be fine, Taffy. The gin's all right, but the sausages will probably be Spanish dog!"

Thus, about an hour later, under Lance's stage management, five or six captains and mates, all of whom he had primed for their parts, accompanied him through the dock gates in high spirits. As he had done before, Lance went from place to place with them, greeting all the port officials, guards and police whom he knew, to advertise his presence to the full. Then they went on board the second ship and over lunch discussed their plans together. The sailors entered into the plot with the greatest zest.

As he came out on deck after lunch, Lance noted that the air had become oppressive, as with the threat of imminent rain. That, he reflected, would suit his purpose well. On his orders, Pepe had brought the car right into the docks, alone. It was a thing Lance had never asked him to do before, for it involved a terrible risk for the chauffeur. But it was a vital part of the plan he had devised for this special occasion, designed to drop into the Spaniards' minds the idea that the car was to be expected to be seen again going in and out. The loyal Pepe did not turn a hair. The big black Chevrolet, wearing the Union Jack, was as familiar a sight outside the docks as Lance's check coat, and Pepe, though stopped by the guards, came through successfully.

Ostensibly, the car had come only to collect Lance after his luncheon party on board, but his real intention was to advertise the fact that he would be coming back later in the afternoon for another party, in a different ship. As he drove away from the ship's side with all the signs of good cheer, he continually stopped the car, therefore, to greet some acquaintance, tell him what a wonderful luncheon he had had and say how much he was looking forward to *yet another merry party* that evening.

185

Now for Moreno.

Lance had never met him but had got his address from Clayton-Ray. He told Pepe to drive there and to go past the house very slowly, so that he could reconnoitre. It was siesta time, a time that Lance had so often found useful, for Spaniards' perceptions are then at their lowest. He found that the house was in the old quarter of the city, in a narrow street of tall stone houses, a place of ancient splendour, handsome and dirty. Here, through the ages, hate and lust and love had enacted their tragedy and their romances.

Lance knew that, even as he passed, the agents of the S.I.M. were observing, from some curtained window opposite, every movement in the house where young Moreno lay in hiding and every person who went in and out. Swiftly he made his plan.

Going back to the cheka, he dismissed Pepe. No need to get him implicated in such a risky mission. He then took the wheel himself and drove thoughtfully back to Moreno's hiding-place, knowing exactly what he was going to do. He had noted that the house had every appearance of being like his own cheka and other houses in the locality, having one floor as a boarding house and the remainder as flats. That would mean that a person not under suspicion could go in and out freely. Moreover, it had begun to rain and he seized instantly on this fact for the advantage of his plan.

He stopped the car dead in front of the door, where the glistening pavement, as he had noted already, was very narrow. There had been no loitering observer in the street when he had passed before, nor was there now, so that he knew that the only watch was from the windows opposite. Luckily the rain would serve to obscure vision. He got out of the car casually, rang the bell and walked in without waiting, as was customary.

The house, he found, was arranged very much as he expected. The *dueña* met him in the hall with the utmost suspicion.

"What is it you want, señor?" she asked.

"I have come to call on Señor Alvaro Martin Moreno, señora."

Her kindly face set in firm lines. She replied, sharply:

"There is no such person here."

She stood like a rock in his way and Lance took an instant liking to her. She was joined by two young women, her daughters, who stood behind her, fully blocking the passage. He said gently, placing his hand lightly on her shoulder:

"Señora, I am a British captain and not an agent of the police. I have come to help the young man."

His manner, more than his words, reassured her and her face relaxed.

"Very well, señor, come with me."

She turned to lead the way upstairs. As they did so, Lance's observant eye caught sight of an umbrella in the hall stand at the foot of the stairs. "I'll have that," he thought, "just what I want."

They stopped at the door of a flat, the *dueña* knocked, but, there being no reply, she unlocked the door with the key that she was carrying. Moreno was lying on the bed, asleep but fully clothed and Lance observed with satisfaction that he was already wearing a dark-blue double-breasted suit. Roused by the *dueña*, Moreno sat up, bemused and completely taken aback. Lance assessed that he was very startled, but not frightened, like most of the others had been. To put him at his ease at once, Lance said with friendly formality:

"May I come in? I have some good news for you."

Moreno looked doubtful and suspicious and asked:

"Who are you?"

Lance told him and went on: "Have you got somewhere where we can sit down and talk? It is quite all right. I have come to help you."

Without a word, the young man led the way into an adjoining small sitting-room and, before they sat down, Lance asked:

"Are you under observation from the house opposite?"

"I don't know for certain. I have never dared go near the window; but I think it is almost certain."

Lance cautiously approached the window and intently studied the house opposite from behind the lace curtains. As the windows opposite were similarly curtained, however, he could see nothing and he said:

"I know, in fact, that there is a watch being kept from somewhere; so no smoking please."

When they had sat down, he went on:

187

"I have heard from the other side and from friends on this side of the dangerous position you are in, and it will probably surprise you very much that I have come to get you out."

"Get me out, señor. It certainly does surprise me. I do not understand. How can you possibly get me out? How do I know that this is not some trap?"

"I shall tell you and you must then decide for yourself. It will be difficult and dangerous and I shall not attempt to press you if you are unwilling."

In contrast to the manner in which he had treated other fugitives, Lance proceeded to lay special emphasis on the very great hazards that Moreno would have to run. He put the case as hard as possible, with the deliberate intention of testing Moreno's nerve, for the risks would be very much multiplied if so dangerous a case, whose description must be known to every policeman in Valencia, should call attention to himself by appearing frightened at a critical moment. He ended by saying:

"If we are seen going out of here, or if you are recognized going into the docks, or if anything should go wrong, it will mean certain death for you."

Moreno listened in silence and then, after a pause, asked:

"And yourself, señor?"

"Oh, of course, for me, too."

A further short pause and then Moreno said quietly:

"Very well, señor, I will place myself in your hands. You are a brave man."

Lance was pleased to see him take it so well. Here was no frightened rabbit. He got up and said:

"Let's go, then. At once. Remember, you must do exactly as I say always."

"I shall do that, señor."

"The first problem is to get into the car undetected, but the rain will help us and the pavement is very narrow. The car itself will partly mask us as we go out. We shall go downstairs together and you will then wait in the hall. I shall go out into the car and have a careful look round. If you hear me slam the door that is a danger signal. Do not come out. If I don't slam the door in about half a minute, you will take the umbrella that is in the hall, put it up before you come out of the door tilt your hat down and slip straight into the car, the door of which I shall have open. When you have got into the car, sit sideways facing this side of the road."

Moreno nodded. "You have it all thought out, señor."

"One must, you know. Come along."

They went down into the hall. Lance then sauntered out of the door, paused on the threshold and, turning up his coat collar, looked upwards and to right and left, like a man summing up the weather but in fact keenly searching the windows opposite.

Seeing nothing, he got into the car casually and looked up and down the street through the veil of rain. In this siesta time he knew that anyone whom he might see about was suspect. He searched all the doorways in sight, but there was not a soul to be seen.

He closed his door quietly, started his engine and windscreen-wiper and opened the passenger door an inch. The rain poured down as he waited. How would Moreno behave? Would he funk coming out into the street he had not trodden for so long? Would he rush out excitedly?

Was that a curtain moving that he could see out of the corner of his eye? He stretched out his hand, ready to slam the door, but there was no further sign, and as he waited Moreno appeared out of the shadowed hall. Perfectly cool and natural, he stepped out briskly, head down and umbrella tilted forward so that it was impossible to see his face from the windows opposite. Two steps took him to the car. He turned, closed the umbrella with a quick snap and backed into the car.

"Good man," thought Lance with relief, "he'll do." He slipped into gear and drove straight to the cheka. Stage One completed.

This was certainly a promising start, but there was no time for delay. If Moreno's disappearance were discovered, every police and S.I.M. agent in the town would be out; especially in the docks. In the cheka he introduced Moreno and Ramón to each other and then got Moreno quickly out of his blue trousers and into a pair of the grey flannel ones from his stock. Satisfied that he now looked the part, he instructed both fugitives carefully in the act that they had to play. Finally, he insisted on Moreno's taking a large glass of wine, "because, my dear chap, you look miserably sober."

Pepe drove them all down to the *fonda* facing the main gates of the docks and in the reeking atmosphere they met Captain Morgan and a cheerful gathering of merchant servicemen, as Lance had arranged. They were, of course, all in the know, and their jovial company infused a new spirit into the affair and gave Lance fresh confidence.

Together they had one or two quick drinks to lend verisimilitude to the parts that they had to play. Lance was watching Ramón and Moreno very closely and he knew that, beneath the surface, their pulses must be beating quickly; but he knew also that the sailors would carry them along on the current of their confident and resourceful spirits. He was watching the time also and keenly examining every fresh entrant from the street.

At the right moment he gave the word and they all got up. Because he spoke perfect English, Ramón stayed in the rear in the safe custody of two skippers. The remainder walked out in noisy and cheerful goodfellowship. Pepe, primed for his part, was ready waiting outside with the car. As many as could piled in— Lance in front beside Pepe, and Moreno at the back sandwiched between two skippers. Two mates stood on the running-board, placing themselves to hide Moreno from view.

This was the critical Stage Two, the stage when the great fear was that Moreno would be recognized by police or guards. It was for this reason that Lance had schemed to pack him into a crowded car, and for this reason that he had that morning advertised the presence and purpose of the car to everyone in the dockyard.

The successful act of early May was repeated again in different form. While those inside the car chattered and laughed and the wingers on the running-boards sang snatches of song, the car glided into the docks and came to a halt by the sentries. Lance leaned out and cried:

"Here we are back again, you see!"

The sentries, their normal Spanish gravity melting into slow smiles, answered:

"*Salud*, comrades, good appetite."

They stood back and Lance ordered Pepe to drive on at once. Only the briefest halt this time, he decided. Without stopping further, but greeting acquaintances cheerfully as they passed, the car went through at a casual speed. Lance's eyes darted to and fro. Yes, there was Black Face, watching from a little distance without a smile. Devoutly Lance hoped, having no premonitions of the future, that it was the last time he would see that swarthy visage and those black, unsmiling eyes.

Unchallenged, the car drew up at the gangway of Morgan's ship. They all went on board quite easily, Ramón and his two companions following on foot. Lance felt exultant. The ship was due to sail in an hour or so. Stage Three was completed and the task nearly done. Only some totally unexpected incident could now stand in the way.

The whole party sat down to a cheerful supper, during the course of which, however, Lance learnt that the ship's sailing had been delayed until the next morning. The news caused him some slight concern, for he never felt really at ease on any mission until he had actually seen the ship sail.

After supper he saw his two cases carefully stowed away in the chartroom and, merely as a precaution against the unexpected, gave Morgan the address of the cheka, where, as usual, he would spend the night. It was fortunate that he did so.

At seven o'clock on Thursday morning, while he was still in bed, he was sharply roused by Morgan's first mate, accompanied by a suspicious Francisca. He sat up, immediately alert. Very agitated, the mate said:

"The skipper has sent me to tell you that the police seem to have got wind of the stowaways, and he has got the breeze up properly. Can you come on board at once? The skipper says for God's sake get those chaps off as quick as you can, because the police will be there any minute."

Lance was already out of bed and dressing.

"How does he know?" he asked.

"We saw a lot of blokes dashing in and out of the harbour police office at six-thirty—long before the usual time. So we asked the gangway sentry and he told us that the police were coming on board at eight instead of nine."

His thoughts racing, Lance said composedly:

"I think we can sort that out all right. But look here, that gangway sentry must be got out of the way. So as soon as we get on board, arrange to cart him off to the galley and give him a jolly good tuck-in of bacon and eggs."

"Aye, Aye."

"We shall do it, all right, I think."

Taking the mate with him, but without summoning Pepe, Lance fetched the car himself from the yard and drove fast to the docks.

He drove through the entrance without difficulty. At the gangway he bade a cheerful *"Buenos dias"* to the sentry and said:

"The first mate says he would like you to come on board for a nice breakfast of bacon and eggs. Come along, comrade."

The sentry was only too willing and the mate took him off to the galley, while Lance went straight to the Captain's cabin. He found that Morgan had already got Moreno and Ramón there and he said to Morgan:

"Sorry about this, skipper; I'll get them away at once," and to the two Spaniards, naturally looking a little ill at ease:

"No time to talk, I'm afraid. We've got to go quickly. It will be quite all right; don't be anxious."

With the two Spaniards in the back of the car he drove away from the ship's side at a casual speed, slowing down as he passed the sentries on the gate to wave an arm out of the window and say: *"Hasta luego"* (Till later).

Without incident, he drove them back to the cheka by a roundabout route, looking carefully to see if he was being followed. At the cheka they slipped quickly inside, where Francisca, surprised and concerned at their return, exclaimed on seeing them:

*"Madre mia!* Something has gone wrong?"

"Nothing serious, Francisca," Lance answered, wishing devoutly that that were true; "what we really want is some coffee."

He could not conceal from himself, however, that he and his charges were in a pretty pickle. He learnt later that day that the police had in fact boarded and searched Morgan's ship only fifteen minutes after he had left. It was quite clear to him that the S.I.M. had discovered that Moreno had disappeared from his hiding-place and immediately suspected that he had been stowed away in a ship about to leave the port. No doubt (as later turned out to be the case) the detective assigned to watch Moreno's hide-out had either gone to sleep or absented himself while Lance was getting him away. The astonishing thing was that Lance himself was still not associated in any way with the attempted escape, otherwise they would have been on him as soon as he had appeared in the docks that morning; and it was certainly rank inefficiency on their part not to have spotted him driving them out. "I'll bet," thought Lance, "that Black Face was off duty this morning."

What was he to do now? He had to get these two away somehow that very day, for tomorrow he must get the butler away at Alicante. Again, as he had done for Sanchez at Alicante, he went out on a reconnaissance.

He drove out northwards and his questioning eye fell on the British warship lying a little way out. He recalled that Admiral Somerville would be coming ashore at about noon to attend Leche's luncheon party, and he began to speculate. A last chance there, but he hated the idea of embarrassing the Royal Navy.

He drove on up the coast road, searching every little port as far as Castellón, forty miles to the north, for some glimpse of the Red Ensign. There was none and he would trust no other.

Back he came, passed again through Valencia and drove south as far as Gandia, the same distance to the south. Again no luck. Time was getting on. Regretfully, he would have to take that last chance.

He arrived back in Valencia docks just about noon, hot and perspiring. As he went in he saw a naval pinnace approaching, immaculate and gleaming, and at the head of the main landing steps was a group of British civilians, dressed as for an occasion, headed by Leche. Feeling very dishevelled and somewhat the outcast, he joined the group and began chatting with Leche while they all watched the pinnace approaching. He had made up his mind just what he was going to do.

The launch came alongside, officers and ratings immaculate in their white tropical rig. The group at the top of the stairs watched the Admiral come ashore below them, gold lace gleaming on cap and shoulder. This was the moment for which Lance had been waiting. As soon as the Admiral's foot touched land, he bounded down the stairs, leaving the official party in consternation at such a breach of decorum. Meeting Somerville midway, Lance said:

"I'm terribly sorry to bother you, Admiral. My name is Lance and I badly need your advice. I'm in a fix."

Somerville, not in the least put out, answered:

"Oh, you're Lance, are you? I've heard about you. Couldn't we talk it over at lunch?"

"I'm not going."

"Not going?" The Admiral knew quite well that meant he had not been invited. "Well, look here; I shall be going back at four. Meet me here and we'll go on board and have a talk."

He moved on up the steps to meet Leche and Lance withdrew, hope renewed. What a sportsman! The invitation to go on board was a clear indication that he was willing to help. All the same, there might be some obstacle, or some slip. And every minute that these two chaps, especially Moreno, remained on his hands was like holding a grenade with the pin out.

His thoughts went to the two men back in the cheka. They must be suffering agonies of suspense and doubt. Had they lost confidence in him? It would not do to wait till four o'clock and then perhaps still not be successful. He must make shift somehow to get at least one of them away earlier, particularly Moreno, whom he felt sure the police were now looking for. Where, he wondered, is that dangerous, swarthy-faced detective?

Lance was not a man who got rattled. He had, indeed, a considerable confidence in himself. There seemed nothing for it now but to attack without reconnaissance, taking his luck in his hands. He went back to the cheka, resolved now to bring Moreno out immediately and put him on to the first British ship there was. It was the custom for ships to draw out of harbour at sunset and anchor a mile or so out in order to avoid any air raids and, if he could be got on board any of them, Moreno would be safe for that night at least.

Hot, thirsty and hungry, he got Francisca to give him a glass of wine and a hasty meal of grilled prawns. He was now feeling very nervous and on edge, having for the first time no fixed plan, but it would not do at all to communicate his anxiety to Moreno. He spoke to Moreno reassuringly therefore, looking him up and down thoughtfully.

"Take your tie off," he said, "and leave your hat behind. Run a comb through your hair, too. Much too tidy. Let it flop down over the side of your face."

As Moreno obeyed, Lance laughed to conceal his own anxiety, admiring the young fellow's steadiness and grateful for his confidence.

"You'll do," he said, "let's go now."

He took Moreno straight down to the waiting car and told Pepe to drive to the docks.

"Don't stop at the gates this time, Pepe," he said. "Just slow down, so that they won't think we are trying to rush them, but don't stop on any account. I want to give the impression that we are just in a hurry."

"And you, señor," he added to Moreno, "when we get to the sentries, look out of the window on the other side and stroke your chin to cover the lower part of your face."

It was a far greater risk than they had taken before, but it had to be done. As the car entered the gates, Lance put his arm well out of the window so that his check coat would be recognized, and gave the Communist salute in the usual style. There was a terrible moment as one of the sentries stepped forward as though to halt the car and Pepe came almost to a dead stop. "Get on, Pepe," Lance whispered urgently and to the sentry he called cheerfully, leaning his head out of the window:

"Sorry, comrade. In a hurry. Be back shortly. *Hasta luego.*"

Then came a tremendous piece of luck. Lance spotted a British ship at the quayside just preparing to get under way. He recognized her as the *Stanholme,* and he knew that she was bound for England and that her master, whom he had met several times, was a first-class chap. Hands were actually preparing to take in the gangway.

"Quick, Pepe!" he ordered, "run the car in behind that shed."

This was the side farthest away from the ship, and from there the car was shielded from a group of officials and guards who were watching her departure. As the car came to a stop, Lance took from a locker a large and official-looking envelope, which contained in fact nothing more than the car's documents. He gave it to Moreno and said: "Hold on to these till I come back."

He then got out of the car, went into the shed and, through a crack between the double doors, carefully watched what was going on and noted where all the onlookers stood. He waited till he saw hands in the ship actually begin to haul in the gangway.

This was the moment he had been waiting for. Darting back to the car, he said to Pepe:

"Fast as you can round to the ship's side!"

Pepe needed no pressing. He darted out, swung round the end of the shed and, with a squeal of tyres, drew up where the gangway had been and under the very noses of the watching officials. While he was doing so, Lance had snatched the car's papers, leaving the large envelope in Moreno's hands and hurriedly instructing Moreno in his part. As the car stopped, he jumped out and, waving his papers in the air, shouted up:

"Ahoy, there, skipper! Let it down again."

The astonished skipper called back:

"What's up now?"

"Got some important papers for you. Must see you at once."

From that moment, while the gangway was being run out again, he kept up a running conversation without pause, with the intention of giving no opportunity to the watching officials to butt in and ask embarrassing questions.

The moment the gangway was down, Lance put his head inside the car and said to Moreno in a low voice:

"Up the gangway quickly!"

Moreno, under cover of Lance's continued flow of loud talk, stepped out of the car and, the large official envelope under his arm, walked calmly and importantly on board, under the very eyes of the officials and guards.

The captain met them both at the top with a broad grin and asked:

"What's this all about? What mischief are you up to now?"

"Let's all get into your cabin quickly and I'll tell you. Get one of your chaps to warn us if anyone comes up."

This must be got over quickly. No time for drinks or pleasantries. Moreno, who had behaved splendidly through the whole ticklish affair and never shown the least sign of nervousness, must be hidden away at once and Lance himself must get ashore again as quickly as possible. He would not be happy till he had seen the gangway in again and the ship away. As soon as they were all in the cabin he said shortly:

"You remember our friend of yesterday? I had to haul him off Captain Morgan's ship in a hurry. Take him for me, skipper, will you? You're my last chance."

The captain laughed. "By gum! You're a caution, Captain Lance, and no mistake. All right, course I'll take him."

"Splendid! Awfully grateful to you. But there is one special caution. You are calling at Gib as usual, I suppose?"

"Yes."

"Well, on no account whatever allow him to go ashore there. He must go right on to England. No time to explain."

"That'll be all right."

To Moreno, Lance repeated the warning with the utmost emphasis not to land at Gibraltar. "Don't even show your face at a porthole. It's terribly important."

Having paid the skipper and explained the procedure about cabling Jinks, Lance had a few quick parting words with Moreno.

"I am very sorry," the boy said, "that I have no money."

"Don't worry," Lance replied. "All fixed. The captain is the Bank of England."

"I can't thank you enough for all you have done. It seems like a dream. I never expected this."

"Only too glad to have been able to help. If you want to do something for me, it is this—never mention to a soul how you got away. Not even," with a broad smile, "to the Generalissimo!"

Lance hastened to leave the ship, but again he was faced by the problem of returning in front of all the officials minus the man he had gone on board with. It must be glaringly obvious on this occasion. With his usual resourcefulness, he said:

"Come on, skipper, you and some of the boys come and see me off."

They crowded down the gangway with him, five or six of them, all talking at once. Ashore, they clustered round the car door and noisily saw him in with waving of hands. As Pepe drove unhurriedly away, Lance saw with relief the gangway begin to go inboard and before he had reached the dock gates the *Stanholme* had already begun to edge away from the quayside.

With what vividness he was to remember those last minutes when, a few days later, he learned that his vital last request had not been honoured.

There remained Ramón, who was patiently waiting for his turn in the cheka. Equally patiently, Lance waited for Somerville's return from his luncheon party.

As the time drew near, not wishing to hang about unnecessarily in the strained atmosphere of the docks, Lance stationed the car some little way off in a street outside, where he could watch the entrance of the docks and even see the landing steps within. Directly the Embassy car appeared, carrying Somerville, Leche and others, Pepe drove straight in behind it. There was a little parting conversation piece on the steps and Lance was scared stiff that Leche and the attaché were going on board the warship too, but fortunately they did not.

Somerville had recognized Lance at once and, as he had promised, took him out to his flagship. There, in his cabin, they talked over drinks for an hour and a half. The Admiral's nephew had been adjutant of Lance's own battalion of the Somerset Light Infantry and Lance had been present when he had been killed on the Somme in 1916.

Mainly, however, they discussed Lance's exploits, in which the Admiral was keenly interested. He had heard a good deal about Lance, but, of course, knew little of the detail. Lance reflected how much better British naval intelligence was than the intelligence of the Spanish Republicans.

Somerville bade him goodbye at six-thirty and said pointedly: "Oh, by the way, there will be a launch going ashore again tomorrow. It will leave the landing steps to return at twelve noon."

Grinning broadly, Lance took his leave.

Ramón was safely on board in time for lunch next day.

# CHAPTER TWELVE

## "YOU ARE PLAYING WITH FIRE"

THERE was still Hilario to be disposed of, and only just time enough to get him away at Alicante.

With a smile of relief, Lance packed a few things on Friday afternoon and told Pepe to drive off. He lay back in the car, wishing that it was not so hot and stuffy. He could have done with a siesta. For nearly six days he had been careering about, dealing with totally unexpected predicaments and sudden alarms. It had been a fatiguing time physically and the episodes of those few days had taxed his resourcefulness and his wits. Yet, he found himself thoroughly enjoying these electric situations and the exhilarating atmosphere of tight corners. He had saved three people by a hair's breadth and Sanchez had brought him one nearer to his century than he had expected. He foresaw no difficulty with the butler. Everything was laid on.

Less than an hour's drive brought them to the picturesque seaside village of El Perelló, where the skeleton British Embassy was now situated. Hilario himself answered Lance's summons. He was a splendid figure, tall, athletic in build, handsome and aquiline in countenance with a most charming smile. He greeted Lance with the utmost pleasure and Lance said:

"Come along, Hilario! I've come to take you away."

Surprised and delighted, the butler's face lit up.

"Oh, señor!" he said. "That is wonderful. But I was not expecting you. I am not ready."

"Never mind, come just as you are. Grab a toothbrush and razor and a change of underwear. Only what you can stuff in your pockets. No luggage. Meanwhile, I'll have a word with Señor Leche."

"He is out, señor."

"Well, anyone will do." He went in and spoke to one of the attachés, asking him to tell Leche that he was taking the butler away and to apologize for any inconvenience that he might be causing him.

In a very few minutes Hilario returned, looking very much the well-bred manservant in black suit, tie and hat. This suited Lance's purpose very well, for time was now so pressing that he would not be able to take his man to the Victoria Hotel and to arrange the usual sailor act with Captain Jones. He would have to improvise again, going straight to the docks, taking his man-servant with him. He had merely to be natural, and to a man of Hilario's training that meant that the first requirement was to be unobtrusive.

It was dark when, having covered the remaining eighty miles of the twisting coast road, they arrived at Alicante. Pepe drove straight to the docks and Lance stopped him some twenty-five yards short of the carabiniers' office at the main entrance. He intended, as usual, to make his entry completely open and above-board and, indeed, well advertised. He went into the office and there saw five or six carabiniers and some police, some of whom he recognized from having been concerned in the affair of the drowned engineer. He announced to them:

"I have to pay a visit to Captain Jones again about the death of his engineer. Would some of the comrades like to come with me for a little party? I am sure Captain Jones would be delighted to see you."

Accepting his invitation, several of the Spaniards crowded into the car and, with a police officer standing on one running board and Lance himself on the other, they proceeded into the docks for the drive of four hundred yards. On arrival at the ship it was a perfectly easy matter for Hilario to go on board with the crowd. Lance led them to the saloon and then, after a whispered word with the master, quickly took the butler off to the captain's cabin, where he stowed him away in a locker under the captain's bunk.

The party went on and on. The rum was good and the Spaniards were very much enjoying themselves. Lance's thoughts all the time were of the unfortunate butler cramped up in the locker. He was a tall man and must have been extremely uncom-fortable and the air must be getting very foul. In an agony of suspense, Lance longed for the police officer to go. It was upon him that he had to keep a special eye. Not till very late did he at last leave, agreeing, under the influence of the rum, that Lance himself should stay on board till the ship sailed at four in the morning.

With relief Lance and the captain went back to the cabin and released Hilario from his coffin-like refuge. There was nothing to do now but wait till the ship sailed. So, at least, they were all entitled to think.

For almost the first and only time, however, there then occurred one of those small, totally unexpected interjections of chance which upset all calculations. A steward, not fully in the know or not realizing the state of affairs, opened the door of the cabin and announced the arrival of another police officer. The officer, in fact, walked in immediately behind him. He had come, he said, to pay a call on the captain before he sailed—really, for a free drink.

That was a nuisance, but no tragedy. A bottle of rum came out and Hilario was introduced to the policeman as Lance's man-servant. The old business was started again and Flatfoot simply would not leave. Under the stimulus of the rum he became more and more friendly, more and more *simpático*. Lance, keeping as cold a head as he could, fretted more and more, thinking of some way out of the corner. The fellow looked like staying to the bitter end. If he did, Lance would have to leave the ship with him, and Hilario, too. He remembered how twice before he had got out of a dead end by quite simply revealing the true facts and appealing for help; he had done so with the Civil Governor of the town and with the fisherman. This policeman, full of rum and friendliness, should be equally easy, and as the night wore on Lance decided that he would have to take that course again if the fellow would not leave the ship alone.

After a few words in English with Jones, he said to the police agent:

"The captain says he is about to cast off now if you will excuse him."

"Certainly, comrade; the best things must end."

He got up to go and, after paying his compliments to the captain, turned for the door, Lance beside him. With his hand on the door and his head half-turned, he said to the butler, who was holding back:

"What about you, comrade?"

This was the moment when Lance knew that he must take the last chance once more. He said casually:

"Oh, he is going off to England to get things ready for me. I'm going myself in a week or two and I want him to go on in advance."

There could have been no greater mistake. In that extraordinary manner in which the Spanish countenance can, in the twinkling of an eye, be transfigured from tender affection to the most tigerish hatred, the policeman's face blackened with fury. Very coldly the policeman said:

"On no account can any Spaniard, whether for an Englishman or anyone else, be allowed to leave the country at this crisis. This ship will not sail until he leaves, and under police escort."

Lance did his utmost to hold his ground. "Look here, comrade," he said, "this man is in my employment. He has been true and faithful. He has done nothing against the Republic nor anything else to concern the police. There is no reason at all why he should not go. After all I have done for Spain, the authorities could never have any possible objections to my servant going on in advance of me."

The policeman's face grew darker and darker.

"Those who employ servants," he said viciously, "are all Fascists, and those who work for them are Fascist stooges. You will both have to come ashore with me."

Lance did all that he could to cool the fires of wrath, but he knew that it was all up. He turned to Jones and thanked him for his help.

"I am damned sorry," he said, "but I am afraid it is a question of our both leaving the ship."

The captain was sorely troubled on Lance's behalf. Taking out his wallet at once to return the £10, he answered:

"I'm sorry, too, Captain Lance. A rotten piece of bad luck. I wish to goodness I could help you." Then he added fervently: "For God's sake, Captain Lance, do be careful; you're just playing with fire."

"I shall wriggle out all right, skipper. It's Hilario I'm worried about."

All this time Hilario himself was behaving with complete calm and composure, not showing a trace of the bitter disappointment that he felt, nor fear for the dread punishment that must surely be in store for him. In those moments Lance liked and admired him more than ever.

The police officer, arriving at the gangway, called down to the sentry at the foot and between them they escorted Lance and Hilario to the car. Pepe, who was dozing in the car, was ordered to drive back down the dark and deserted quay to the carabiniers' office. It was about three o'clock in the morning, and the early morning breeze touched them with chilly fingers. Lance, concealing as best he could his bitter feelings, re-entered the office which he had so lately left in cheerful and friendly mood and saw it for the stark and mean place that it was, its darkness lit by a weak electric globe. Two men lay asleep on the floor in a corner of the room and one or two others stood about listlessly with that half-moribund detachment of an all-night office. Lance was shortly but closely questioned, the butler being ignored, and a telephone call was made to some higher headquarters.

To the astonishment of them both, they were not put under arrest. Indeed, on informing the police that he stayed habitually at the Victoria Hotel, Lance was even allowed to return there, together with Hilario, but accompanied also by the policeman. Lance knew perfectly well, however, that it was only his status as a foreigner that won this leniency for them both.

It was but four hundred yards to the hotel and in that brief journey Lance looked out of the window with a wry smile at the scene that he knew so well and was never to see again. The city lay wrapped in a thick, opaque silence, and, over the white semicircle of buildings that climbed to the heights behind, the thin moon, gleaming palely from the multitude of stars, shone a dim and sombre light.

From this dark scene, so soon to become a memory, Lance, Hilario and the policeman, passed into the main entrance of the Victoria Hotel, half-lit, exhaling the dreariness of all hotels in the dead hours of the night, silent and deserted except for the drowsy night porter at his desk. Lance, taking one look at his oily face and shifty eyes, did not like his looks. A pity that Ernesto was not on duty.

Pepe also came in to sign the hotel book, expecting afterwards to put the car away and go to bed. But Lance told him to go back to the car and wait.

The policeman stood beside them while they booked in for the night. Automatically, without thinking, Lance wrote Valencia in the "destination" column of the tedious form. The policeman had now thawed by several degrees and seemed quite satisfied that his charges could safely be relied upon to stay for what remained left of the night; for it was now half past three.

"I shall be round again in the morning," he said, "as there are other matters that have to be enquired into. You must not leave for Valencia before then."

As soon as he had, as he thought, seen them safely booked in, he bade them a not unfriendly good night and went. They were all still standing by the night porter's desk. The moment they were alone Lance said to the butler:

"I'm terribly sorry about this, Hilario."

"Please don't mention it, señor; it is nothing."

"Well; let's go out now and tell Pepe to put the car away."

They turned away from the night porter's desk and made for the front door. Had they looked back as they went out, they would have seen the porter quietly reaching for the telephone. Why was it necessary for both the señores to go out for instructing the chauffeur?

For the first and only time, Lance had made a bad slip. Had he entered in the hotel registration book that their destination was southwards to Murcia, instead of northwards to Valencia, they would have been spared much. But the night was nearly spent and Lance was worn out.

Outside Pepe was still waiting anxiously in the car and was surprised to see both Lance and Hilario come out and get quietly into the car. He was even more surprised when Lance said:

"Pepe, I hope you are not too tired, because I want you to drive like the devil back to Valencia."

Pepe's infectious grin broke out. There was no order he liked better than "drive like the devil".

"Never too tired for that, *mi capitán*," he said.

"Quietly out of the town though, Pepe, and sidelights only, but as soon as we are out of the town, let her go."

This was a business that Pepe understood well. The big Chevrolet slid away quietly by silent back streets, with the great bulk of Santa Barbara obscuring the stars on its left. They seemed to have the world to themselves. Nothing stood between them and Valencia, where Hilario would go straight into the safety of Lance's cheka. There would be no difficulty, he felt sure, in getting one of the British ships there to take him at short notice. Tired out, Lance, in the back seat, sunk his head on his chest for such sleep as he could get while Pepe, leaving the last houses behind him, put on his headlights, opened the throttle and shot forward on the twisting road.

They had not gone far, however, before Pepe exclaimed:

"Is the captain awake? There is a car behind us and I think it is following us."

Lance jerked himself erect and looked out of the rear window. There, still a long way behind, he saw the glare of powerful headlights. He studied them appraisingly. Headlights were very rarely seen in these troubled times. He seldom saw any others than his own. Equally unusual was it to see any car about at such an hour, except for some slow-moving troop transport in the war zones.

"What do you make of it, Pepe?" he asked.

"I cannot be sure, *mi capitán*, but they have been in my driving mirror for a full minute now and I think they are going faster than we are."

"Well, whoever they are, I don't want to meet them, Pepe. Put your foot down as hard as you can."

Pepe obeyed with gusto. Lance could imagine the smile on the little fellow's swarthy face. Fast as it had been going before, the car surged forward with an eager access of speed, its tyres screaming round the sharp bends. High, rocky banks on their left obscured vision and jutted out to make dangerous blind bends, but Pepe took them all at speed, knowing nothing could be on the road ahead. On their right the sea gleamed pewter-grey, its surface brightly silvered as the shaft of Pepe's headlamps swung round a bend. He was driving with splendid skill and nerve, his speedometer needle on the short straight stretches swinging round to seventy-five miles an hour.

Yet the car behind gained steadily on them. Often hidden by the corners of the high-shouldered road, each time it reappeared it was a little nearer. The headlights of the two cars swung and flickered, lighting up now the rocky hills, now the leaden sea, now the straight road ahead. Lance glanced at Hilario to see how he was taking it and in the half-dark was happy to see that he was relaxed and composed, even, he thought, smiling a little.

Taking a long concealed curve at full speed, Pepe struck a small rock that had fallen from the hillside. The car rocked and trembled. Pepe, keeping control with wonderful skill, was forced to slow a little and at that moment, looking across the dark countryside, Lance saw the car behind once more and judged it to be not more than half a mile away. He said to Pepe:

"By God, that is a damned fast car! It must be a police car and they are certainly after us."

"Yes, it is a police car, *mi capitán*; there are no other cars in Republican Spain so fast."

"Could you drive without headlamps on the straight, Pepe?"

"I think so, *mi capitán*; I will try."

He shut them off at once, turning them on again only when a bend obscured them from their pursuers and still maintaining a marvellous speed. The engine sang on a high note and the cold morning air whistled on the car's projections. The body swung and rocked on the chassis as the car screamed round corners, bounced and trembled as the car careered over the innumerable pot-holes. They were thrilling and desperate moments, in darkness one minute and with headlamps on the next. Still the police car gained, the glare of its headlamps getting nearer and nearer until, after another few miles, they were faintly illuminating the rear of the Chevrolet. Only four hundred yards now, losing a little when Pepe had the advantage of a straight, catching up again at the next corner. In another few minutes Lance's car was racing its own elongated shadow.

There came a point when, on the two legs of a hairpin bend, the two cars were racing on opposite and parallel courses, scarcely a hundred yards of broken ground between them. At that moment Lance, gazing with fascinated detachment, saw a spurt of machine-gun flashes burst from the police car and a long trail of red tracer bullets streamed ahead, splintering the rock at the roadside. He laughed and drawled:

"Well, that's certainly a police car all right! Damned rude of them, Pepe, eh?"

In spite of his buoyancy, however, it was clear that the end could not be far off. He thought seriously of abandoning the car at the roadside and making off across the country on foot, but at that moment it flashed across his mind that the Consul in Alicante lived in a delightful villa at a hamlet only a mile or so ahead. It was right on the coast, with a garden running down almost to the sea, and was approached by a mere cart-track issuing from the main road at right angles. He said to Pepe eagerly:

"Do you remember Señor Brooks's house?"

"Yes, *mi capitán*; just a little way ahead."

"Could you find that turning without lights?"

"I think so. I know just where it is."

"If you can make it we are safe."

The hairpin bend had slowed down the police car and Pepe shot ahead on the straight, gaining a little, with headlamps off. In half a mile, he shut off his sidelights also, suddenly spotted the cart-track and braked fiercely. The brake-shoes screamed and the car skidded violently, nearly turning over on its side as he took the right-angle bend. Twenty yards on, on Lance's order, he stopped. The roar of the police car was heard immediately and in twenty seconds it flashed by like a blazing meteor.

Lance laughed aloud and clapped Pepe on the shoulder.

"Well done, Pepe!" he cried. "That was the most wonderful drive of my life."

Pleased as Punch, the little chauffeur was half-turned round in his seat, smiling with pleasure.

"It was a near thing, *mi capitán*."

"Thanks to you, it has been a safe thing. You should be driving on the race-track. You would beat all the stars."

"I prefer the roads, *mi capitán*. They are more dangerous."

"Spoken like a true matador! Now we can take it quietly. But no lights still, in case they look back and spot them."

Another hundred yards or so brought them to the villa. Brooks was no longer there, but they were let in. They rested for a few hours, had some breakfast, filled up with petrol and went on again cautiously, fearful that their pursuers of the night might meet them on return, or that the road posts, which had all been manned at daybreak, had been warned and ordered to arrest them. But no such thing occurred.

Two hours' drive brought them back to El Perelló and there, feeling very down in the mouth, Lance said good-bye to Hilario, telling him how bitter and self-reproachful he felt at the shipwreck of the butler's hopes. He was, indeed, very near to breaking down, so keenly did he feel his failure.

"To think," he said, "that I should have let you down, after the complete faith you had in me. It does not bear thinking about. You are my only failure and I cannot tell you how sorry I am."

Hilario took it wonderfully, thanking Lance for his efforts.

"I know it was only bad luck, señor," he said, "and I shall be ready for the señor when he can try again."

From El Perelló Lance and Pepe drove right through to Madrid, not stopping in Valencia, and taking turns at the wheel while the other rested but dared not sleep.

It was a very tired pair who at length arrived back at the hospital after their last trip together.

# CHAPTER THIRTEEN

# THE NEW SPANISH INQUISITION

MARGERY, when he told her that evening about the extraordinary events of the past week, was filled with concern.

They were in her hospital office and had just finished their frugal meal of beans and oranges. A touch of autumnal mildness softened the air and, beyond the dilapidated garage across the road, the acacias were stirring to a light breeze. From the Casa de Campo, three miles away to the west, came the occasional crack and rattle of desultory artillery and machine-gun fire. The "evening hate", thought Lance. Dog-tired, he had lit his pipe and had told Margery the story in simple terms in his slow-spoken way.

"You've been terribly rash, haven't you?" Margery said. "Don't you think you've got a bit over-confident?"

Lance grimaced. "I had to do something," he said, "the poor chaps had to be got off somehow. But I feel pretty sore about Hilario. I feel that I let him down badly."

"You mustn't think about it that way. What you've got to think about now is your own safety. You'll have to give up this escape business altogether, you know. I hope you realize that?"

"You're probably right, but by George, it goes against the grain to do a bunk and leave all these people to face the music. Leaving you, too, you know. I don't like that either."

"All the same, you ought to go, and go at once. You may have the police after you at any moment."

"I suppose so; but I don't think I've done anything I can't wriggle out of with Embassy help, which I suppose they are bound to give me, whether they approve of my stunts or not. Anyhow, I promise to lie low for a bit."

He rose from his chair, yawned sleepily, tapped out his pipe and stood at the window, looking thoughtfully down at the derelict garage. Margery, divining the struggle of emotions that was going on within him, was filled with a sense of apprehension for his safety. She was still more touched when, with a wry laugh, he said:

"Well, that's goodbye to the Man in the Check Jacket!"

For two or three days, as he had promised, Lance lay low in the hospital. There he felt fairly safe from arrest. His natural buoyancy and resilience were such that, after a day's rest, he was already planning what he might do next. He felt, as he said, "full of beans" and had confidence in his ability to get himself out of a scrape. He was pretty certain that, provided no orders were given for his arrest, he himself would be able to get home from Valencia in a perfectly normal way with the regular documents as a genuine British subject if he wanted to do so. But he badly wanted to get out that one last party which would complete his century and to which he had more or less pledged himself, but which he refrained from mentioning to Margery.

The sea routes, however, were now out of the question for them. He would therefore have to reconnoitre the overland escape route through the front lines to the south of Navalcarnero that he had heard of from Antonio. He would cross the lines with them and not come back. There was some chap living in a hut there who acted as guide, but you had to be jolly careful, he reflected, about these organized overland escape routes, because it was through some of these that people had been betrayed and trapped. Accordingly the route would need careful reconnaissance before he could hope to complete his century of escapes.

Such were Lance's thoughts as he rested in the hospital. After two or three days he was out and about again, going to the offices of Gines Navarro and to the Commercial Attaché's office where he ran his underground movement. He then paid a call on the War Office and, on the excuse of his contract work, got the promise of a guide to the Navalcarnero front to show him exactly where the lines were. "I got pinched near there once by Franco," he said, "and don't want the experience again." Negotiating some shell fire, he returned to his office highly satisfied and full of confidence.

That confidence, however, was now rudely shattered. To his

horror, he heard on the radio an announcement that Moreno, contrary to all his warnings, had landed at Gibraltar and, furthermore, had advertised the fact by sending a message over the air.

This, Lance realized, was damned serious. Far more serious than the matter of Hilario. Deadly serious, in fact. He swore roundly. Why the devil had the fellow gone and done the one thing he had specially asked him not to do? Or had something else gone wrong? He knew that the Republican authorities would be furious and would order the S.I.M. to sift the matter to the bottom. How long would it be before they began to connect Moreno's disappearance with the conspicuous activities of the Check Jacket? How long before Black Face at Valencia recalled that the Check Jacket had been there that day?

It was not very long.

On October 8, just after a light breakfast, Lance was in his office at the Commercial Secretariat wearing his old check jacket, over his open-necked shirt, as the morning was rather cool. The sounds of some brisk small-arms shooting came faintly from the University City two miles away. His pipe was going well, but it was about time, he reflected as he looked at its worn-down bowl, that he had a new one. Not long now. He had fulfilled his *palabra* as best he could.

The telephone on his desk rang. It was his Gines Navarro office calling him. Two police officers were there enquiring for him; what should they do?

"Is this it?" he thought. To the clerk at the other end he said in a confident voice: "Send them along here."

It was only a few minutes before the porter at the secretariat announced their arrival. "Tell them to come in," Lance said to him. He was not at all concerned. Several days had elapsed and the officers might be calling on some entirely different affair. If they were Madrid police, he would probably know them.

He was less confident when the porter returned to say that the policemen would not come in but desired that Captain Lance should go out to them. That was significant. If the call was a friendly or a routine one, they would have no hesitation about coming into Embassy premises, but they could not enter the premises to make an arrest.

"Do you know them?" Lance asked the porter. "Are they from Madrid?"

"No, señor, I have never seen them before. I would advise the señor not to go out to them; they do not seem at all friendly."

Lance stepped to the window and through the net curtains looked up and down the street as far as he was able. He could see no vehicle. If the police had come on foot, they would almost certainly be only local officers.

"Go out to them again," he told the porter. "Say that I am engaged at the moment, so can't see them just yet, but ask them to come in and sit down till I'm free. At the same time, have a look out in the street and see if there is a car parked anywhere near."

After a minute or two the porter came back again looking very much concerned.

"Señor," he said, "they absolutely refuse to come in and demand that you should go out to them. Also, there is a big black car parked a little down the street. It has a Valencia number plate and the rear window is curtained. I implore the señor not to go out to them."

"Oh lord," thought Lance, "this really is it then." But he thought of it only as a nuisance to be overcome and did not doubt his ability to get out of an awkward spot, as he had so often done before. The usual technique when police officers intended to make an arrest was to have the telephone cut off first. So Lance tested it at once.

He called the British Consul, and got through to him at the Consulate a little way down the street. That was encouraging. He told the Consul what had happened and was not very happy when the Consul replied:

"I am not surprised. I should go out and see them if I were you and ask them their business. I'll come along later if I can."

"Why, when I know already?" Lance rejoined.

"Well, what more's to be said? When you are in jug I'll bring you some cigarettes."

Flabbergasted, Lance observed coldly: "That will be kind of you."

Keeping his temper, he then asked the Consul, who lived in a flat in the building where Lance was, whether he might "doss down" in the flat for a few days. "I'll provide my own food," he said, "and guarantee to clear out in a few days."

The Consul replied: "Nothing doing. I didn't know you were afraid."

White with anger, Lance banged down the receiver, got up and walked out. In the hall the porter grabbed his arm and begged him not to go. Lance shook him off and strode to the front door. There, immediately outside, were the two policemen. One of them, he was not surprised to see, was Black Face.

Immediately he crossed the threshold they both stepped forward grabbed him by the arms and marched him firmly but without violence to the big black car. It was a Packard seven-seater. Lance observed with misgiving that the blinds were drawn down not only on the rear window but on the side windows too. The police were wearing large revolvers and on the front seat was a sub-machine-gun. Humiliated and angry, Lance none the less kept his temper and attempted to employ his usual light-hearted raillery; but it fell on deaf ears and stony faces and all they would say in reply to his questions was that they had orders to take him to Valencia, where he would be asked "a few questions" and then he would be brought back to Madrid.

"In that case," he said, "I should like to get my things for the night from the hospital." He was terribly anxious about Margery, wondering whether she was being arrested too.

"That," they replied, "will not be necessary."

He was put into the car, which made off at speed, the horn sounding repeatedly. Lance resigned himself to the thought of the long, uncomfortable ride to Valencia, but instead he was taken to the former "high-class brothel" from which he had liberated Glaisher. Evidently it was one the special police chekas. With aloof correctness, he was taken up to a luxurious double bedroom with private bath, the obvious ribaldries impassively ignored. Again he was told that he was to be taken on to Valencia but would be brought back to Madrid next day. Here he was left all day with no food but his thoughts. These were not very despondent. The policemen's repeated assurance that he would be brought back next day seemed genuine enough and, in any case, a British subject would not be detained in this manner for more than a month.

He got very hungry, having had nothing to eat since his breakfast of imitation coffee and a slice of toast. He went to sleep quite composedly on the luxurious bed of infamy and was woken up at four o'clock. He asked again about his night things and was this time allowed to send a message to Margery by telephone, asking her to have them ready, as well as some food.

It was seven o'clock before they started and they went straight to the hospital. Lance was infinitely relieved to see Margery herself come out to the car carrying a small bag for him. She had done so in the face of a warning from the anxious Pepe, who had been watching from a window. Lance greeted her cheerfully, saying that there was nothing to worry about and that he would be back next day. What he was very afraid of, knowing her, was that she would follow him to Valencia to be near at hand and to help him out of any trouble. He begged her not to do so, and she, dreadfully uneasy though she was, agreed with some reluctance. They drove out of Madrid at last and Lance, very hungry, opened Margery's parcel. He found it to contain not only his night things and plenty to eat but also a bottle of whisky, a hundred cigarettes and matches. What a brick she was! She had thought of everything.

The policemen also took an interest. Here was manna from heaven for them. They stopped the car just outside the city and joined in the feast. The good Scotch whisky was much to their liking and served partially to soften their frosty relationship.

There followed a dreary night journey over the road that Lance knew so well. Driving pretty fast over the villainous road, they reached Valencia at three in the morning and Lance, carrying his small bag and feeling very drowsy, was taken straight into an exceptionally well-furnished house and led up to a comfortable, dimly-lit room. Here he was received by a good-looking, well-spoken, smartly dressed young Spaniard of the sort one would have expected to see in good society in the old days. He offered Lance a comfortable seat and for a while they discussed things of no importance in a perfectly friendly way. Lance was by now very sleepy and, although he did not yet realize the fact, all these timings had been carefully arranged so that he should be so. The treatment was about to begin.

After this pleasant chat, the smooth-spoken young man got up, saying:

"I've got to leave you for a bit. I shall be back in an hour or so and have got a few things I must ask you about. You will then be free to go back to Madrid and I've arranged to have a car at your disposal."

He then switched on an exceptionally powerful electric lamp directed straight on to Lance's face and left the room.

Lance knew nothing then of what has since become notorious as the normal Communist technique for "asking a few questions". Longing for sleep, he said, "Damn the thing," and got up to look for the switch. He could not find it, so turned the lamp itself away from the settee and composed himself for sleep, with his legs up. No sooner had he done so, however, than a man came in and directed the beam of the lamp again on to his face.

"Why are you doing that?" Lance asked. "Do please turn the thing off. I want to sleep."

"Comrade," the fellow replied very civilly, "my instructions are that it is to be kept in that position. You must not touch it, please."

As soon as the man had left the room, he got up again and, instead of turning the lamp round, left the settee and seated himself in the armchair away from that horrible glare. Once more, however, the fellow, obviously watching from some spy-hole, returned and swung the searchlight on to him. This little act was repeated several times till Lance, wondering what on earth could be the purpose of this tomfoolery, gave up and resigned himself to enforced wakefulness. It was all, as he learnt later, part of the treatment for making the victim tired and strained before he was put on the grill.

After another hour or so, a policeman came in and said "they" were ready for the interrogation and he asked Lance very civilly to "step this way". Still carrying his small bag, Lance was shown into another large room arranged as for a conference. The moment he went in, however, he was brought sharply up against something that he had never experienced before. The room was heavily charged with hostility, a tangible emanation from the eight men who confronted him behind a long table. All were youngish men of the State Intelligence and conspicuous among them was a large monolith of a man who, as Lance learnt subsequently, was a Russian notorious as "The Boxer", his function being to apply physical persuasion, such as knocking out a few teeth, when other means were inadequate.

For a while no word was spoken. Lance was motioned to a lone, upright seat at the table confronting the eight. They then began fidgeting at their stomachs and buttocks as though lousy and simultaneously produced concealed revolvers from their persons and laid them ostentatiously on the table. It was so obviously a drill done "by numbers" that Lance, in spite of his weariness, his trial of nerves under that abominable lamp and his realization that a severe ordeal was now upon him, could not repress a grim smile.

The revolvers having been displayed, the devilish searchlight was brought in from the other room, placed on the table and once more directed on Lance at point-blank range. So completely was he dazzled that he could see nothing whatever of his accusers, nothing else at all in the room, nothing anywhere but the blinding white glare that penetrated his eyelids and seemed to burn into his brain. From somewhere beyond this impenetrable burst of light, this white nothingness that seemed more empty than the blackness of chaos, the voices of his unseen inquisitors came through to him as the interrogation began.

They got down at once to a volley of questions and the matter that they pitched into was the affair of Moreno. So it *was* that, Lance reflected, that had caused the trouble. He had expected so. The inquisitors made it obvious that they were furious at Lance for having made fools of them by getting the young man away right under their noses. They made no bones about disclosing that Moreno was being watched day and night and that Lance, by a stroke of luck, had caught them napping.

It was also obvious that they were in no doubt that it was Lance who had done the trick; they were not making a shot in the dark. The check jacket, the disappearance of Moreno from his known hiding-place and then from the first ship just before it had been searched, the sudden dash later in the day to the second ship just about to sail—all this and much else was clearly known to the unseen eight beyond the blinding light.

This examination Lance faced with an air of easy confidence, but the moment that the extent of their knowledge began to be apparent to him he became inwardly disturbed about how much his inquisitors might know about his friends and helpers, particularly Margery, Pepe and Francisca. These he was determined should not be involved if he could help it. He, therefore, under pressure, admitted the essential facts, taking full responsibility for them and hoping that this would satisfy them.

It did nothing of the sort, however, and very soon they were pressing him on dangerous ground. Who had been his accomplices? Absolutely no one at all. What about the chauffeur and who was he? No, no chauffeur was in it at all; he had driven the car himself. Was anyone at the British Embassy involved? Certainly not. What about the master of the British ship? He was entirely ignorant who the stowaway was, and so on.

All this, except about the chauffeur, was true enough of that particular incident. Lance answered all their questions with an easy conscience. They did not believe that he could have been working without accomplices and bluntly told him that he was a liar. As he answered the rattling barrage of questions under the paralysing light, he made a small prayer that no force, no guile, no unguarded word would induce or suffer him to betray his friends.

So far, the inquisition had been concerned only with the affair of Moreno and, although he was dog-tired and the whole affair was hateful, he had kept his composure and had done his utmost to put on an air of easygoing confidence. He could take it, as long as it concerned himself only. The inquisition went on for hour after hour. Outside, the sun had risen long ago, but the blinds of the room were kept close drawn and the fierce beam of the lamp beat upon his face.

Quite suddenly, the eight inquisitors dropped the matter of Moreno and began to bombard him with questions on other incidents. His visits to the *fondas*, the rowing episodes in the harbour, the dates and times of his visits to the docks, his meeting with Somerville. All these they knew. To Lance the hand of Black Face was only too evident; that stony, inscrutable visage had all the time been diligently observing and making notes against the time when they might be of value.

When the eight began to get on to his relations with other people, Lance's mind became more and more tortured. He knew by now that he himself was "for it", so he might as well be in for a pound as a penny and admit no responsibility but his own. The interrogation became more and more gruelling as the inquisitors strove to drive him from corner to corner; but he put as brave a face as he could to the blinding light, trying not to appear worried or to have anything serious to conceal.

The inquisitors knew so much that Lance was surprised that they did not know all. What most astonished him was their exact knowledge of his personal antecedents. They told him, in detail, not only of his British Army career, but also how he had fought in the Russian White Army's Karelian regiment against the Bolsheviks and been wounded. They knew about his sojourns in Chile and the Argentine and all their dates and names were uncannily accurate.

What was less accurate was that they accused him of having been a spy in Russia, a spy in South America and now a spy in Spain. All this biographical detail was brought out by one of the two Russians on the board of inquisitors and it was obvious that it had been extracted from the fabulous Intelligence files that are kept by Moscow.

After about five hours of this searching enquiry under the infernal lamp, Lance felt nearly dead. His brain was upside-down. He felt he could stand the thing no longer. He began to turn dizzy and to slide away into semi-consciousness; when a means of temporary salvation suddenly occurred to that resourceful mind of his. He remembered the little bag that Margery had given him. It was at his side now and there was still a good half bottle of whisky in it.

"Excuse me, comrades," he said, "I am not feeling very well and I must just take my medicine. It is here in my bag and after I have taken it I shall be able to be more helpful to you."

"If," answered the granite-faced chairman, "it will help you to tell the truth, take it. You have been telling a pack of lies so far."

When, however, the inquisitors saw the nature of the medicine and when their victim passed round a fat packet of cigarettes, which were worth their weight in gold, the atmosphere changed like an April sky. A bell was rung, glasses were brought in, the damnable searchlight switched off, the blinds drawn and the blessed sun, so long obscured, allowed to pour into the room. It was as if an evil spell had suddenly been exorcised.

Lance quickly took advantage of the brief opportunity. Even in these circumstances, he was quite irrepressible. He got up and began chatting in a friendly manner with his inquisitors about family and personal matters, while everyone sipped the vanishing whisky and puffed at the cigarettes. Having broken the ice, he went a little further in and made a proposal of the most extraordinary temerity. To one of the eight who had been particularly aggressive he said:

"You say you do not believe that I have embarked a few Spaniards without any accomplices and that it isn't possible. Very well, I'll prove it to you if you give me the chance. I'll undertake to get any of you comrades away from Spain within the next few days, on two conditions—that you let me get my car from Madrid and that you don't alert the people in the docks. Who would like to go? Only *one*, please,. I assure you I mean what I say and will comply with your conditions when we get to England. What do you say?"

Dead silence. The comrades must have been completely taken aback at this exhibition of "nerve". Lance looked round and saw several of them glancing sideways at each other. "I bet a dollar," he thought, "that they'd give quids to go if they dared." He handed round the cigarettes again and held up the nearly empty bottle of whisky.

"Just enough," he said, "for a *copita* (a nip) each." He stood and offered a toast to Spain and her government and their friends *Gran Bretaña*, but no one got up with him or joined in. "A dead flop," he thought, "they are not interested in Spain, they are only interested in their beastly Communism."

However, the evil spell had been broken. The inquisition was over, though what followed was awkward enough. A typed statement was brought in, purporting to be a record of what he had said, which had obviously been taken down by stenographers outside the room through a microphone. It was a highly edited account, recording faithfully all his admissions and leaving out everything that tended to be in his favour.

He argued as best he could with the inquisitors, objecting to the way they had twisted and misinterpreted many of his statements and omitted others. But the more he objected the more hostile they became. They would not accept a modification of a single comma and declared venomously that the only things omitted had been his innumerable lies. The account was a true one and he could not be released until he signed. In any case, they added, it was only a formality and of no real importance. They were not prepared to continue this tiring enquiry any longer than necessary. In desperation, Lance "signed the damned thing".

This was just what they wanted. They had got him.

This over at last, Lance was driven under police escort to an hotel in Valencia, somewhere about ten a.m. and locked up in a bathroom with the usual revolting w.c. In the bath itself was a mattress. This was to be his residence for four days, with a guard stationed day and night immediately outside the door. He was fearfully hungry and tired, not having had a proper meal for thirty-six hours, but, with his usual habits of cleanliness, he shaved and washed before going down to the restaurant with his guard for a meal.

Afterwards he had a long sleep, but removed the mattress from the bath to the floor, which was not only more comfortable but also had the advantage of blocking the door so that no one could come in without waking him. He very soon got on good terms with his guards and the food, compared with what those in Madrid had to put up with, was good.

Except for meals, he was kept locked up in the stinking little room all day and had nothing to do but think. His thoughts of Moreno were bitter. "Hell's bells," he said to himself, "I risked my skin to save the young blighter's neck, and this is what I get in return. Why the devil couldn't he have done as I asked?"

Apart from such acid reflections, however, it would have been quite contrary to Lance's nature to surrender himself to dejection.

He fully accepted the assurances given him that he would be returned to Madrid very shortly. It was in this frame of mind that he was visited while lunching with his guard by a representative of the Embassy, who came to enquire if he wanted any official help. Very foolishly, he declined.

"Oh, no," he said. "Apart from the beastly stink, I'm quite all right, you know, and they've promised to send me back to Madrid any day now. Thanks all the same."

"Isn't that just part of the technique?" asked his visitor. "How d'you know they mean what they say?"

"Oh, I'm sure they do, old boy. In any case the worst they could possibly do would be to order me to leave the country."

It was a decision that he was ever afterwards to regret. He had not yet learnt what the Communist "technique" in these matters really was and he took some pride in standing on his own feet and in getting himself out of his own scrapes, the more so as his relations with certain of the Embassy staff were not cordial.

His confidence seemed to be fully confirmed when, after four days, a police agent came one evening to tell him that he was to go to headquarters for a few final questions and he would then be driven back to Madrid that same night. Lance was delighted and at once began shaping his plans for the future, dwelling eagerly on his intention to get away those last six in Madrid. Should he lie low for a while? For how long? Would those he knew in the Madrid *Seguridad* and at the War Office be informed of the "confession" he had just signed? How could he find an overland route of escape without their help?

In the flood of such conjectures he was escorted from the hotel and driven in the complete darkness of the black-out to what he took to be police headquarters. He stepped from the car, followed by the policeman, and entered the dark void of the building. The moment he had stepped inside he was violently seized by hands that sprang out upon him from the dark. His arms were pinioned behind his back and quickly tied at the elbows. A powerful and foul-smelling hand was clapped over his mouth from behind him, nearly breaking his neck as it wrenched his head back. He was swung round, thrust out of the door and forced into another car, which went off at speed into the darkness.

221

After a few minutes in the car, his arms were released but there was no relaxation of the hostile attitude of the armed guards on either side of him. It was characteristic of him that he began to chat amicably to them, only to be met with a frigid silence. He offered them cigarettes, but they refused with curt monosyllables. Refusal of a cigarette by the tobacco-starved Republicans was the worst of omens and Lance stirred uneasily in the dark between his guards. He would make a further test.

"Well," he asked, "do you mind if I have one?"

"No," he was coldly told, "this is not the time to smoke."

He was convinced then that he was being taken for his last *paseito*—the "little joy ride" which he had seen so many others suffer in Madrid and from which no man returned.

Some eight miles outside Valencia, as far as Lance could judge, the car suddenly shot off the main road into a lane and its lights were turned off. "Well," thought Lance, "this certainly looks more and more like the *paseito*." To suppress his fear of showing fear, he began asking "damned silly" questions: Where are we going? Why have the lights been turned off? Shall we get back in time for some dinner? Are you sure you won't have a smoke? And so on.

In the icy silence into which his questions trailed away unanswered, his eye fell again upon the sub-machine-gun beside the driver's seat. He knew all this drill so well and did not doubt what lay before him. He prayed quietly that it would be a quick end and that the savage revolver shot so cynically called the *coup de grace* would not be necessary.

The car slowed down and Lance saw in front the shadowy outlines of a large country house. The car stopped in front of it and Lance was ordered out. Six armed Assault Guards moved forward and closed round him. He was marched rapidly round to the back of the house. This undoubtedly was the end. They halted, however, in front of a door dimly discerned in the gloom, and two of the guards seized Lance by the shoulders and hurled him inside, following with a vicious kick in the buttocks. He fell sprawling on to a hard floor and heard the door slammed and a key grate in the lock behind him.

Shaken and sore, Lance slowly got up into a sitting position. He was in complete darkness, but his brain seemed to be irradiated with flashing red lights and whirling galaxies of dim stars. He thought: "The devils are trying to frighten me, and, by God, they've succeeded!" The place he was in was damp and cold. He began tentatively to explore it with his fingers, feeling over the concrete floor and brick walls. Near the door he touched an electric light switch and, to his surprise, it worked. He found himself in a small dirty cell, festooned with cobwebs. A heap of rubbish had been swept up into one corner and the only furniture was a primitive bed of canvas strips on a wooden frame.

Those Assault Guards, with their tommy-guns and the revolver for the final shattering of the skull, were only too obviously a firing-squad. But something seemed to have gone wrong to delay the execution, some last-minute hitch of which he could not guess the cause.

To change his thoughts, Lance went through his pockets. The sum of his possessions amounted to a pen and pencil, a cigarette case containing four cigarettes, a lighter, a wrist-watch, a treasured signet ring, 800 pesetas and the same red handkerchief that he had waved aloft when he had been captured by Franco's troops. He looked at it ruefully and stuffed it up his sleeve again. Shivering from the damp cold, he sat down on the edge of the bed frame and smoked away the four cigarettes.

When he had finished the last one, it was four o'clock. He got up and started banging on the door. There was no response. He went on banging and shouting, determined to achieve some kind of action. After several minutes the door was opened by a squat, square-shouldered fellow of repulsive countenance. He asked:

"What the hell are you making this row for?"

"I want to know what I am being kept here for. Why don't they get on with it?"

"How the devil should I know? I'm only here to obey orders."

"Am I going to be shot?"

"I hope so. I'd like to shoot you myself."

"Well, if you don't know, kindly go and ask your officer. Tell him that if I am going to be shot I want to be shot as soon as possible. Tell him I can't wait."

"Oh, go to the devil. You must be *loco*."

The door was slammed and locked again. Chilled to the

bone, Lance lay down on the bed frame and fell into an uneasy sleep.

The merciful, quick end did not come. He was kept in the cell for two days without food, blanket or human contact. Cold, dirty, unshaven, famished, he asked himself whether this was some form of cat-and-mouse torture. His thoughts roved far, to Jinks, to those unhappy souls in Madrid who had been dependent on him and ultimately, as he saw that his end was inevitable to Almighty God whose Word had never failed to give him strength and comfort in adversity.

On the third night he was roused by the unexpected unlocking of his door shortly after midnight. This, as he knew, was the favourite time for summoning a man to the little *paseo*. Though faint with hunger, he sat up at once alert and expectant. There entered, however, not a shooting party, but three of the Valencia inquisitors and their demeanour was outwardly far from hostile. This time it was they who provided a cigarette, which he smoked with some relish, though his system was crying out for food.

What they were after was the matter of his "accomplices" in which hitherto he had so successfully baffled them. They wanted two names in particular—a chauffeur and a señorita. Others also. They promised him leniency if he could help them to arrive at "the truth", but threatened that the consequences would be very serious if he refused to do so.

It then began to dawn on Lance that, in what had seemed to him a desperate situation, he still held some valuable cards. He had some information that they badly wanted and they were not likely to bump him off until they got it. He realized then that the purpose of his clandestine imprisonment and starvation had been to break him down so that he would be in a fit state of funk to spill the beans. He felt tremendously bucked, the pains of hunger for the time being forgotten. They could darned well go on waiting. Quite politely, he parried their quickfire questions and stuck to his previous story. He had had no "accomplices"; wouldn't have trusted anyone and felt much safer on his own. The inquisitors retired baffled.

Next morning there was a further fillip to his morale. A guard brought in a bucket of water, in which was floating a piece of dirty sacking, and ordered him to wash the floor. To a man so fastidious of his personal cleanliness, this was an opportunity not to be missed. The water was dirty, there was no soap or towel, but he stripped and washed himself down with his red handkerchief, while the astonished soldiery collected outside the open door and abused him again as "a dirty Fascist". Feeling much refreshed, he sluiced down the floor, but the effort fatigued him, for he was weak and dizzy from hunger. Then, at noon on the third day, they at last brought him some food—a bowl of bean soup and some water in a tin mug. With some of the water he rubbed over his teeth with his handkerchief.

On the fifth night, again just after midnight, the same three inquisitors paid him another call and again they were superficially friendly. What specially pleased Lance was that they now brought him the bag which Margery had packed for him. Besides his toilet gear, the bag also contained twelve cigarettes, a Prayer Book, a triple photoframe with pictures of Jinks, a second hand-kerchief and a second pair of socks.

Once more the inquisitors pumped him about his accomplices, once more without avail. When they saw that they could get nothing out of him, instead of leaving him in his cell, they told him this time to go with them. They gave no explanation but walked him out into the night and round to the front of the building, where all four got into a car. By now Lance felt a good deal more buoyant and hopeful. The vision of the firing-squad had dimmed and in his five days of solitary confinement he had disciplined his mind and undergone a spiritual experience that fortified his resolve.

He was now taken in the small hours to the convent of St. Ursula in Valencia which had been closed by the Republicans and turned into a prison. Immediately on arrival he was handed over to three jailers and was forthwith searched and stripped of all his personal possessions, including those which the inquisitors had just returned to him.

So, at least, was the jailers' intention, but some quick-thinking saved a few things from the pillage. His wrist-watch and his money went, but, in counting out the money, he palmed a one hundred-peseta note, to the wrath and mystification of his searchers, who knew that he had eight such notes instead of the seven that they counted out. His Prayer Book, the photographs of Jinks and his shaving stick he quickly put into a pocket that had already been searched. His signet ring he pulled off as he stooped down to open his bag and slipped under his tongue. After about a dozen subsequent searches in which he hid the ring in as many different places, he observed that he was never required to take off his socks, so, on the innumerable occasions that he was afterwards searched, he kept the ring safely between his toes.

These, however, were but minor triumphs. He was informed that orders had been received to treat him as a "very dangerous prisoner" and he was thrust at once into a small, dark cell in solitary confinement. The cell measured eight feet by five feet, with walls of dirty whitewash and a brick floor. The window had been boarded up, except for a small, square hole at the top. There was no bed or furniture of any other sort and no electric light.

In this black hole Lance spent a terrible seven weeks under rigid surveillance. Escape, he quickly realized, was out of the question, for, even if he could have got out of the place, he was a marked man. He was allowed out only to visit the latrine or to go, once every three days, to wash as best he could under a tap with his handkerchief and shaving soap. His diet consisted of a tin of rice or lentil soup twice a day and a tin of warm water with a little condensed milk in it. He soon managed, however, to supplement this diet from the garbage heap alongside the latrine. From this he managed to pick up a few pieces of orange peel and cabbage stalk, which he added to his soup after cutting them up with the lid of a small tin can, also salvaged from the garbage heap. Meanwhile, his hair grew long and wild, his beard tough and ragged, his clothes frayed at cuff and trouser-hem.

But the solitariness was the worst thing. Knowing now that the purpose of this treatment was to get him down, he determined to defeat it by keeping up his spirits and his natural gaiety, especially in the presence of his enemies. To occupy himself, he set himself to take such exercise as he could in his tiny cell. Three short paces in the dark took him from end to end of it and two even shorter ones across its breadth. Taking great trouble over the measurements, he set himself the daily task of walking five miles and he kept the score by marking up every hundred circuits by a scratch on the wall made with a splinter of wood pulled from the shutter across the window. After a day or two he found this too much for his strength and reduced it to four miles, but as he grew weaker and weaker, he cut it down more and more, finally giving it up altogether as he realized that the first need was to conserve what strength he had, so that for the last week he spent nearly all day, as well as all night, lying on the brick floor. His loss of strength was quickly accelerated by lack of sleep. About sunrise and sunset each day, in common with other prisoners in these night-black cells, he turned almost blind, a phenomenon apparently due to starvation.

Far more efficacious in maintaining his spirits was his Prayer Book. For short periods, by standing and holding up the book to the pale shaft of light overhead, he was able to read it, and before long he knew a great deal of it by heart. In the Psalms especially he found an inspiration to strength and inner happiness and as in thought he lifted up his eyes to the hills or walked beside the waters of comfort he felt fortified against all material ills and against all assaults of the enemy.

Thus stayed up and his natural resourcefulness kept awake, he began to look outwards and to wonder what was going on around him in all those other dreary cells. Were there, he wondered, any other Britons there? How could he find out? He began the habit, as he walked to the latrines or the ablution tap, of whistling or humming snatches of "Tipperary". Two or three days later, as he was passing one of the cells, he heard a sharp Cockney voice, evidently speaking through the keyhole a foot or so from him, say:

"Are you English, chum? Have you got a fag?"

Lance immediately stopped his whistling and sang aloud:

" 'It's a long way to go'."

The next day he signalled his approach in a similar way and saw a tiny piece of paper appear at the keyhole. He plucked it out as he passed and when he was alone read its message, scribbled in pencil:

*See you at the lats 6 tonight.*

227

They met accordingly and had a short, muttered conversation. Lance found the other man to be a little fellow, with a shrewd, quizzical face. He said to Lance:

"Name's King, mate. What's yours?"

Lance told him.

"Oh, heard about you. Any fags?"

"Sorry, all gone."

"You can make some, you know, from them orange leaves in the garbage heap."

"Sounds foul."

"Better than biting your nails."

It was the beginning of a strange, clandestine friendship built up under the most difficult circumstances in the next fifteen months, for wherever Lance was sent King also was there, even to the end. King was a typical little cockney with a great sense of humour. Lance never knew exactly what he was "in" for, except that in some way he had fallen foul of the Communists.

When, after about a month, the Communists thought that Lance's spirit had surely been sufficiently broken, they roused him out of his cell, again just after midnight. He got up wearily from the brick floor, bleak-eyed, chalk-faced under his stubbly beard, but still wearing an easy smile, and was led out of the building and bundled into a car. What now?

It was, in fact, another grilling. He was taken to some sort of office, where, having lived in darkness for so long, he was blinded and confused by the unaccustomed light. Worse still, the horrible lamp was brought out again and he was put through a gruelling inquisition from three a.m. to six a.m. He was pretty dead-beat and the dirt had got him down as much as anything, making him feel a social outcast, forgotten and shunned by all his friends. Their damnable questions and charges twisted and tortured his tired mind, yet he faced them with a quiet smile, getting tied up in words at times, but clinging for all he was worth to the life-line of his faith. It was once again with the matter of his accomplices that they challenged him and this time they nearly broke him down. Twisting about in a mental maze, he felt himself being forced to give at least some answer.

"Well, comrades," he said at last, "I admit I did get a little help. It was Señor ———." He gave the name of one of those whom he had got safely out of the country.

The inquisitors leaned forward eagerly and the chairman said: "Ah, so you've changed your mind. We shall find out before long whether you are telling the truth this time. If we find you to be lying again, things will not be very pleasant for you."

The inquisitors then suddenly switched the axis of their attack, trying to force him to admit that he was a "spy". They made him give an account of his time as Franco's prisoner and when he gave them the approximate date of his leaving Irun for Hendaye, before returning to Republican territory, they whipped out his passport from among their papers and showed him the date on the passport stamp, which was completely different, and declared angrily that this proved him to be a liar and a spy.

Flabbergasted, Lance said:

"That is quite incorrect. Someone has altered the date by a month."

This infuriated the inquisitors and one of them jumped up and began to manhandle Lance, but he was called off by the senior, who, however, drew his revolver and slammed it down menacingly on the table.

Largely on this evidence Lance was later condemned to death.

The inquisition ended there and Lance was put into an adjoining room to wait for his escort. At a desk in this room a girl was typing letters. She was a handsome girl and smartly dressed, with good features, black eyebrows and platinum-dyed hair. She glanced up as Lance entered and rattled on with her work. No word passed between them until she had finished her page and pulled it out of the machine. She then turned upon Lance a look of such unspeakable malevolence that even he, accustomed though he was to these manifestations of Spanish hatred, was dumbfounded.

"So," she said, her eyes flashing, "you are the English spy! We shoot spies. Do you hear? We shoot them. But if you do get away, we shall see to it that your health will be so ruined that you will not live long, you brute!"

Never had Lance seen an ebullition of hate so violent, boiling with murderous meaning. Compared to this typist, he thought,

*La Pasionaria* was a tame saint. He was relieved to be taken away by his jailer and still more relieved, after those gruelling hours, to find himself back again in the black night of his cell, alone. He prayed for a while and when the sun rose and sent a narrow shaft of light through the hole in the shutter he read from his Prayer Book for strength and reassurance.

He was not alone much longer, however. Very shortly a fellow-prisoner arrived to share his tiny cell. Lance looked upon him with mixed feelings. Any human company was welcome, even in such crowded confinement, but there was the uncomfortable thought that the newcomer might be a stool-pigeon planted there by the police. The other obviously had similar doubts and at first they regarded each other warily and spoke guardedly. It was not long, however, before they were friends, especially as the new arrival brought with him a cigar and a few cigarettes, which he shared equally with Lance.

He had been foreman in charge of a dockers' gang at some small port, was an Anarchist and member of the CNT and at the beginning of the Civil War had joined with his comrades in exterminating the entire "aristocratic" community of that district, which Lance knew perfectly well meant chiefly middle-class professional men. He himself, he declared without the slightest reservation, had murdered twenty-one and he took the greatest delight in giving an intimate description of each outrage, which he thought would amuse and entertain his fellow-prisoner.

He was not in prison for these murders, however. No one ever was. What had got him into trouble was his own carelessness when he shipped off to France the money and jewels that he had looted from his victims, for he had committed the crime of failing to give a rake-off to the local police.

Yet this confessed murderer and robber had an exceptionally tender spot for his wife and children and often broke down in tears when he speculated on their fate in his absence. He was, like many Anarchists, a cheerful and likeable rogue and, as they moved from prison to prison, often sent Lance precious little gifts of food which, having money, he bribed the guards to bring in.

# CHAPTER FOURTEEN

# INTO THE DEPTHS

ONCE again a summons just after midnight.

As he stumbled out into the dark, cold night of 22 November, Lance found that this time he was one of a party of about twenty, including a few women prisoners, herded together beside a lorry under a strong escort of tommy-gunners. Lance was now in a very low condition. Seven weeks on a diet of thin soup and milky water, together with orange skins and cabbage stalks picked from the latrine garbage heap, had left him drained of strength. His stick of shaving soap was exhausted and he had had no change of clothing, day or night, since leaving Madrid two months ago. His hair was growing down his neck and over his ears and his beard was tough and shaggy. He was not alone in this, for many of his fellow-prisoners, shut up far longer than he had been, were in a deplorable state, the men all long-haired and bearded, the women wild-looking and dishevelled, and all of them filthy, stinking and barely able to stand.

When the order came to mount the lorry, none of them had the strength to do so. Lance, trying to set an example, felt his arms and legs fail in the effort and he hung precariously half-suspended on the tail of the lorry until a vicious jab in the buttocks from the muzzle of a rifle sent him sprawling. Cursing with pain, he lay on the floor as his fellow-prisoners, men and women, were hurled on top of him in like manner.

A night drive of some thirty miles took them to a new prison, perched high up in the castled hills of Segorbe, on the road to Teruel. This was the Prisión Gubernativa de Segorbe. Remote, lofty and totally enclosed within high walls, it made all who entered its great gates feel at once alone in another world.

On arrival, Lance and most of his fellow-prisoners had to be carried to their new quarters. To his relief, he was not shut up in solitary confinement, as he had been at the St. Ursula prison.

but was taken into a cellar, lit by two small sunken windows below ground level, into which were crowded sixty-eight men, each man being allotted a floor space of six feet by three. It was cold and damp, the floor was covered with dirty straw and the medley of prisoners at the moment lying asleep on it, packed tight like fish in a tin, was almost as dirty. Here at least, thought Lance, was human company of some sort. As they stirred into wakefulness later, he was delighted to find Cockney King among them and there was another Commonwealth citizen in the person of an Indian who gave his name as Dutt, but who carried with him some aura of mystery foreign to that common name.

King greeted his old fellow-prisoner with a grin. "Welcome to the Ritz, mate," he said; "it's a better hotel than the last dump, but, blimey, they've got a queer lot of guests! Reds, blacks, pinks —the lot!"

They certainly were a mixed bag, of violently opposite political and moral faiths, and if only for that reason Lance found them stimulating company down in that dreary cellar. The greater part were ardent Roman Catholics and Fascists, a very brave lot who showed no fear whatever of facing the firing squad, but their political talk bored Lance to tears. Another large contingent were Anarchists (arrested by Communists), who were also not afraid of anybody or anything, very good company, full of good humour and rarely prating of politics. Humanly, there was a good deal in common in these two groups, but the third group, consisting of Communists (arrested by Anarchists), was totally different. These Lance could not stand at any price; they could talk of nothing but their boring "creed", were devoid of humour and appeared to Lance a cowardly lot, frightened of the fate to which they had condemned so many others.

It certainly was a far "better hotel"; indeed the only tolerable one that Lance was to experience. The food was a little more liberal, including even a little meat in the soup, though still no bread. The prisoners went out daily for exercise in a tall walled *patio*; there was a barber's shop, a shower bath and an infirmary. Best of all, however, prisoners were allowed to receive visitors, letters and parcels. Lance received visits from Margery and the lawyer Ballesteros, from Fernanda Jacobson and de Caux of *The*

*Times,* and from the Valencia Consul accompanied by Pearson, the Air Attaché. De Caux thought that he seemed to be taking his imprisonment "very casually, but he was always a mysterious fellow". The Consul, however, wrote home to Jinks that he was "under a severe nervous strain".

Jinks had been sending parcels from a famous London store every week, but it was not until he reached Segorbe that Lance received any and throughout all his long sixteen months of imprisonment he received only one in five. All letters and parcels were opened by the prison authorities and Lance received only the residue of what had been left by his jailers, who stole most of his cigarettes. Some warm clothes that Jinks sent him were a god-send, even when, to the ribald amusement of his fellow-prisoners, one parcel, by a comical mistake on the part of the London store, was found to contain the most intimate sorts of women's underwear.

Back in Madrid, meanwhile, Lance's friends were terribly concerned for his safety when he failed to return from Valencia. Margery Hill, fearing that the next person to be put on the spot would be Pepe, wisely pulled him into her hospital as houseman, where he was relatively safe, and it was as well that she did so, because the secret police were very soon after his blood. As she herself stood so well with Spaniards of all classes, she thought she was safe, but it was a near thing. With an eye to what she hoped to do in the future, she wrote a very "clever" letter to Lance in prison, saying that she knew all true Spaniards were *caballeros* and that if he were unfortunate enough to suffer privation it would be due to "foreign influences" and not to them. She knew, of course, that the letter would be opened by the police, that it would be carefully recorded and that it would count in Lance's favour and her own chances of seeing him.

It was Fernanda Jacobson, however, who appears to have taken the first active step. Through the medium of Jensen, of the National City Bank of New York, she called on the lawyer, Fernando Ballesteros, who willingly offered his professional help to secure Lance's release. There would, he said, be no difficulty. It was merely a matter of the right procedure, but it would be proper for him to see the British Embassy first. He did so accordingly, but was coldly told by some official there to take his fingers out of the Embassy's pie.

The pie, however, grew very cold and as time went by Spaniards were asking: if his own Embassy will not help him, what can one think? To what extent this was due to Lance's own action in declining help before he was actually imprisoned is not clear, but if any steps were taken they fell short of their purpose. It was announced that "efforts were being made to secure his release" and that the Embassy "would make every effort to see that, when brought to trial, Captain Lance would have adequate legal representation". But he never was brought to trial. Did the Embassy really suppose that he ever would be? How many of those who filled the Republican jails were ever "brought to trial"?

The same platitudinous phrase was used to soothe a few people back in England. Angus McDonnell, complaining of diplomatic inertia, wrote "in desperation" to his friend Lord Halifax at the Foreign Office. Ogilvie-Forbes, now at our Embassy in Berlin and obviously unable to take official action there, also wrote to Halifax, and to Jinks he wrote: "I shall never forget his courage and resource". To Jinks and other anxious enquirers on Lance's behalf, the Foreign Office and the diplomatists in Spain wrote soothing and empty letters. "Representations" were being made. It would be a "mistake" to do this or that. Fernanda Jacobson visiting the Embassy at Hendaye, added her urgent pleading, and her animadversions. Jinks, herself, abusively insulted by a woman Socialist M.P. who would have raised Cain if a trade unionist were jailed without trial for five minutes, kept hammering at every door. She actually proposed to go out to Spain herself, first to the Republican side and then to the Nationalist, but in the one case was warned by Leche that she would certainly be arrested by the Republicans and in the other was advised by Sir Ralph Hodgson, our Agent at Burgos, that she would get nowhere by trying to see Franco. But Hodgson added: "Your husband's many friends here remember with gratitude the help he gave them and among those who remember his courage and devotion is Count Jordana, the Foreign Minister." From Burgos she also received a brief letter from General Moreno, thanking Lance for the rescue of his son.

One is left to guess whether this failure of effective action was due to the indifference of the diplomatic people on the spot or to the misguidance of a government at home obsessed with political considerations of neutrality. Whichever was true, Lance's agonized wife and his friends were left feeling that the Foreign Office, both at home and abroad, were completely heartless and indifferent. Spaniards were being helped out of danger, but not Christopher Lance. No one would help the man who had helped so many others.

Christmas 1937 was approaching. In Madrid it was an exceptionally cold winter. News came of the Republican offensive on the Aragon front and of bitter fighting at Teruel in sub-zero temperatures. Margery Hill, saying "how terrible it would be for no one to see Christopher on Christmas Day", asked the British Consul for petrol vouchers and the necessary documents. He refused them point-blank.

But that did not defeat her. She had a word with Jensen, of the American Bank, who had been so staunch a friend to the hospital, and Jensen got Ballesteros to provide them for her. Jensen also lent her his chauffeur, as, to his great chagrin, Margery would not dream of taking Pepe. The astonished Consul atoned somewhat, however, for he then asked Margery to take a diplomatic bag to Valencia, and with it went a certificate that would help her through all the controls as far as Valencia.

Wearing a fur coat, but hatless as usual, she left in the hospital car very early one freezing morning and at Valencia saw one of the British diplomatic officials. We need not mention his name. She told him her intention and he was very much put out, for he was one of the few in that orbit who were not well disposed towards Lance. He said:

"It is quite useless your trying to go to Segorbe now. It is in the war zone, on the main communication route to Teruel, and troops and supplies are going through in large numbers. You haven't a hope of getting through."

"All the same, I intend to try."

"Look here, Miss Hill, I have got six huge parcels here for Lance and I have tried four times to deliver them to him and been turned back each time. If I, in my official position, can't get through, what chance have you?"

"Give me the parcels, Mr——, and I'll deliver them."

She left at nine-thirty next morning, which was Christmas Eve. Far ahead of her, amid the blood, snow and ruins of Teruel, the encircled Nationalist garrison, shelled, bombed and mined, was making its last stand and on all the roads leading forward to it the air was charged with the pressure of desperate and critical times. As she left the coast and climbed up into the hills the icy air bit hard, accentuating the rising diapason of events; undeterred, she won her way through by her quiet sincerity and persuasiveness, negotiating the rough sentries who thrust their rifles through the car window, patiently edging her way through columns of troops and vehicles, jolting over the vile hill roads, crashing through broken culverts, overcoming the fears of the terrified driver as the way led through a more and more forbidding scene under the black snow-clouds. Arrived at Segorbe, she won her way inside the great gates past the sentry who, at first, since she had no permit, told her to "get back into the car and go home". And thus at last she met the Governor.

She found him very courteous and they had a short talk in which he admitted to her that, in spite of the promising operations on the Teruel front, things were getting very bad and that they would soon be in "terrible difficulties". A disreputable and corrupt administration was betraying the cause of republicanism. Hatred and jealousy dominated Government councils. He could not understand, he said, why Lance's Embassy did not get him released. He readily gave Margery permission to see him and even gave them the use of a private room.

The meeting was memorable for both of them. Margery brought with her unimagined luxuries in turkey, tinned chicken, plum pudding, cigarettes and much else, which had been sent to her from England for her own Christmas. What struck her most forcibly in Lance's condition was his cleanliness. She had always known how particular he was, but, having seen a good deal of Spanish prisons and seeing other prisoners on this occasion, it was impressive to see that he was able to appear shaven, hair cut and brushed, hands carefully tended, shirt washed and with an air of being fresh from the bathroom. She remembered what old soldiers had told her of the importance of cleanliness to morale.

In fact, the Governor had given him facilities to get cleaned up for the occasion and had provided him with a clean shirt. But otherwise, she noticed with a quick access of compassion that he was not at all the same Lance. He was blanched and skinny, clearly suffering from malnutrition and lack of air, and there was something peculiar about his eyes that she could not diagnose.

"I shall be jolly glad when I get out," he said; "it is pretty grim here."

Nevertheless he wrote Jinks a jaunty and light-hearted letter, addressed from "The Ritz Hotel", which Margery smuggled out. She spent two hours with him and was allowed by the Governor to come back again on Christmas Day and Boxing Day. But that was the last time.

Like Margery, Lance also found the Governor of the Segorbe prison something out of the ordinary of his kind. He used to send for Lance to deliver his parcels to him personally in his office and there grew up a strange friendship between them, for Lance could not help having a liking for him. He was an educated man, had some sense of humanity quite exceptional among his sort and was, Lance discovered in conversation, still in secret a keen Catholic. It was from him that Lance learned that he was regarded as "Criminal No. 1", a bold and dangerous character enveloped in a veil of mystery.

Lance began to wonder why, in the succeeding months, the Governor used more and more often to send for him merely for a chat; until at last he began to realize that the Governor was far from happy in his post, especially as, like other more realistic Republicans, he realized that the outlook for them, under bad leadership, was getting worse and worse. The Nationalists had mounted a vigorous counter-offensive, had retaken Teruel and were advancing towards the Mediterranean at Tortosa, to cut Republican territory in two. Segorbe itself might soon be in danger of falling into enemy hands.

237

Lance listened intently, wondering what all this might be leading up to. With his strength returning under better conditions, he felt the old itch for adventure, and, with incredible temerity, he asked the Governor:

"Señor, would you like me to help you to escape?"

The Governor, who might have been expected to appear aghast at this suggestion, smiled a slow, elusive smile.

"What! The prisoner help the Governor to escape?"

"Why not, Señor? I don't think you are very happy here."

"You are quite right; I am far from happy. But how is it possible for you, a prisoner under guard, to help me to escape?"

"Oh, that shouldn't be difficult. We only have to think it out. I should come with you, of course. We'd go to England together."

"*Caramba!* Now I know why they call you a bold and dangerous character! Well, let us speak of this another time. I shall send for you again in a day or two."

Lance, grinning with delight, felt "jolly sure" that the Governor's surprise was feigned and that this was what he had been leading up to, knowing that Lance was an expert in escapes. After careful thought, he took King into his confidence and the little cockney grinned with delight, exclaiming:

"Blimey, mate! What a comic turn!"

Lance at once began to think out a plan. Its elements were, like all his other plans, simple, bold and open. Orders were to be received for the release of himself and King and the Governor was to leave next day on official business, meeting them somewhere by arrangement. Time, place and other details had to be worked out with the Governor himself. Before anything could be arranged, however, to the chagrin of all three, orders were received in April for the evacuation of the prison, now threatened with capture as the red-and-yellow standard of the Nationalists drove steadily south-eastward to the sea.

The prisoners were sent off in separate truckloads to different destinations, King and Dutt leaving early. Lance was left to the very last with four other prisoners considered specially "dangerous" and reserved for transfer to Barcelona. It was a bitter blow to his hopes and he had no opportunity of seeing the Governor.

The five prisoners, heavily escorted by nine armed guards, left Segorbe at dusk one day in an open lorry and this time Lance was able to climb up unaided. He was full of new hope that he might be able to make a getaway on this journey, as he knew that the truck would have to pass near the firing-line, where the Nationalists were making their thrust towards Tortosa near the mouth of the Ebro, and the road from Valencia to Barcelona was in danger of being cut.

The guards, Lance noticed, were armed to the teeth with rifles, revolvers and machine-guns, and supplied with several boxes of ammunition, on one of which Lance sat. They were very much on the *qui vive* and it was obvious that they were expecting to have to fight their way past Nationalist posts. That would be Lance's opportunity.

His hopes rose when, as they drove, very fast, along the coast road during the night, he heard the sounds of fighting ahead. He was not anxious to be taken prisoner again by Franco, but the prospect would be as heaven after what he had been through in Republican hands. "Hell's bells," he thought, "after getting Moreno and that lot out, they ought to put out the red carpet for me!"

He sat as relaxed as he could, prepared to take advantage of any opportunity, but hanging on to the sides of the truck, as they were now going very fast and the night shapes were flying past on either hand. By their dark forms all around him, he could see that the guards were sitting very tensed, their weapons ready for instant action. Sounds of fighting came nearer, with spasmodic bursts of rifle and machine-gun fire.

It was as they crossed the Ebro that they were attacked. A burst of fire very close from their left front streamed towards the lorry and whistled about their heads. "For God's sake," Lance was saying to himself, "shoot straight, you blighters! Hit us, hit us!" Never before had he longed for such a fate. His guards were replying vigorously and a tommy-gun was cracking in his ears. Bullets split the woodwork of the truck or ricochetted whining off the metal parts. "Knock us out! Knock us out!" Lance cried inwardly. He was longing for the lorry to be hit in a vital spot and brought to a halt, even overturned. Then he would make a quick dash away into the night.

But he had no luck. The driver crashed his way through, driving at top speed. The firing now was coming from astern and the guards were still replying. Feeling badly let down, Lance thought of jumping over the side while the guards' attention was distracted, but the truck was going so fast that he knew he was bound to break a limb to no purpose.

When, soon after the mid-April daybreak, he was admitted to his new "hotel", which was the Palacio de las Misiones, in the exhibition grounds of Barcelona, and saw the conditions that faced him there, he was filled with disgust. From the bearable conditions of Segorbe he had come to a huge, over-crowded, stinking building, which he very soon found to be ridden with lice and to be not a mere prison but a slave-labour camp. Inevitably he got infested with lice, a particular trial to a man of his habits. Together with other prisoners, he was put to the task of treading sandy clay and straw for bricks, bare-footed. His feet and ankles very quickly became like raw meat, so bad that his jailers were obliged to take him off this work and put him on to the easier employment of carpenter's labourer.

Returning from his work one evening, he found the guards kicking through the dirty straw on the floor of the building where the prisoners were confined, searching for any unauthorized objects. In doing so, one of them disclosed Lance's Prayer Book, which had been such a consolation to him all those dreary months.

The guard burst into furious wrath. Bellowing "Filthy Fascist!" he aimed a violent kick at Lance, but Lance, turning sharply, received it on his thigh. With blasphemous curses against God, the Church, priests, and "Fascists", the guard hurled the Prayer Book on the floor, ground it underfoot, and stuffed the remainder in his pocket.

As a punishment for this illegal possession, Lance was paraded next morning through the streets of Barcelona in an open truck standing at the muzzle of a tripod machine-gun, while the crowds roared threats and insults. He was taken to a beautiful, small chapel that was being perverted to the uses of an army garage and ordered to the hateful task of destroying the altar with pick and crowbar. Here he experienced, however, the only act of mercy he ever received. An army officer who had been to Oxford, seeing his faint and filthy condition, gave him some sandwiches (the only bread he tasted in sixteen months) and a wash-down with a hose. That was to be his last semblance of a bath.

As the summer advanced, the heat waxed fiercer and fiercer, the mosquitoes came in swarms to add their arrows to the barbs of life and Franco's bombs rained down incessantly on the over-crowded city. Lance, beginning to feel the shadows closing, kept his morale alive only by a great effort. He was cheered a little by the arrival of King, whose good humour had still not deserted him, in spite of having been through the horrible Ordeal by Lamp, beaten up by "The Boxer" and had his front teeth knocked out.

Otherwise the company was of the vilest, and the fellow with whom Lance was obliged to share straw for the night a most revolting brute. It was he who had murdered his old mother and he insisted, knowing well how it revolted his bedfellow, in repeating again and again the unspeakable details of how he carried out his foul act. Yet he was not imprisoned for this, but because, in a Communist sphere of influence, he was an Anarchist. To a man of Lance's kind feelings, all these and many other abominations, such as the harrowing incident of the titled girl prisoner shot to pieces in her bridal gown, were an experience even harder to endure than his own physical privations. He began to suffer in soul as in body.

He was now himself, however, to suffer a physical assault which was not of an extreme nature but the humiliation and spontaneous brutality of which he was never to forget.

Anything decent seemed to be Fascist. To reach the latrines Lance had to pass through a *patio*, where, still existing from pre-war conditions, there was a fountain in a pool of water. One night, on passing through, taking advantage of the laziness of the warder who accompanied him, Lance stopped at the pool, and, dipping into it the rag of the red handkerchief still remaining to him, rubbed over his teeth. While he was doing so a uniformed officer of the S.I.M. came into the *patio*, rushed at him furiously, gave him a violent blow in the face that knocked him flat on the ground and roared out with a lewd oath:

"Damned Fascist! Only dirty Fascists wash their teeth."

The brutal incident burnt itself into his memory and was to be recalled with sharpened emphasis when, at the last moment of all, he once more faced the same ruffian in the cold small hours of a Pyreneean night.

After about three months of this treatment and with no parcels or letters, Lance again got into a very low state, extremely weak, fighting dejection and finding no relief except in the prayers that he now knew by heart. He was therefore overjoyed to be unexpectedly told in the middle of June that he was to be ready to leave at once, as he was to be driven to the French frontier and expelled. As usual, the order was given in the middle of the night. Carrying such small possessions as he had in a dispatch case, he walked, faint but as jaunty as he could contrive, to the waiting car, anticipating the long night drive up to the Pyrenees. He found, however, that he was taken instead on the very short drive to the harbour.

"Good," he thought, "one of H.M.'s ships is in and they are putting me on board her instead."

But it was not a warship at which they drew up at the quayside. It was a large liner and he could see her great hull rising high above the quay in the grey night air. She was in complete darkness. His hopes began to waver. What could this ship be?

He was not left long in doubt. At the top of the gangway he was suddenly seized by two men in the blue uniform of the Assault Guards and carried off through faintly lit corridors to an inspection room. With a sinking of the heart, he realized that he had been condemned to the infamous prison-ship *Uruguay*, "most heartbreaking of all the Government's dungeons", as it was to be called by *The Daily Express*, a prison-ship in which one thousand two hundred human beings were herded together in conditions scarcely fit for cattle.

Once more Lance was searched. All the pitifully small possessions that he had, which included one or two odds and ends he had collected in his prisons, were taken from him; except his empty dispatch case, the photographs of Jinks, which were handed back to him with odious remarks, and the signet ring which was between his toes. Feeling outraged, he asked what was the reason for this sudden change in his treatment and was told that, as his health had suffered from the hard labour at the Exhibition ground Palace, he had been sent to this ship "for a rest". "This," he was told, "is a hospital ship."

At home, Jinks also was told by the Foreign Office that he had been sent to a "hospital ship".

He was then escorted by the same two Assault Guards below decks and thrust into some unlighted compartment, black as pitch. "There," said one of the guards, "now you can have a nice, long rest."

The door locked, Lance began to explore the compartment as best he could in the dark. The deck was of iron and as he felt round the walls he grew more and more incredulous and shocked.

He was in the padded cell.

In one corner there was a little loose straw, pulled out from the padding, but no other furniture of any kind. There was a fixed porthole looking directly at a shed on the quay and the only ventilation was by a small grille in the door.

He had not been in this gloomy confinement for long before the sirens of Barcelona began to shriek out the warning of an air raid. Within a few minutes the bombs were crashing at the far end of the harbour. Very quickly the great explosions came nearer and nearer until there was a terrific crash which shook the ship from stem to stern. The bomb had burst on the quay alongside and a large splinter had smashed through Lance's cell and buried itself in the padding. Two other bombs in the same stick had hit the ship directly, but without exploding.

It was a terrifying experience to an ailing man locked up in a madman's cell. In this cell Lance was locked up for a month, without ever going out, even to the latrine, without anyone ever coming in to him, and without any other form of human contact whatever. His latrine was a $1\frac{1}{2}$-inch drain in one corner of the cell and his food, which consisted of a tin of watery soup twice a day, was passed to him through the grille. The whole of this time he never washed, much less shaved, and to add to his distress, his cell was infested, not only with lice, but also with fleas and bedbugs. He grew very foul, his face fat and puffy, his stomach distended and the rest of his body skin and bone.

Every morning, through his porthole that looked on the quay, he watched numbers of corpses, many of them naked, being carried off the ship and thrown into lorries, for down in the overcrowded holds men were dying like flies. At other times parties of prisoners, scarcely strong enough to walk, were marched off to be shot at the old fortress of Montjuich on the hill overlooking the harbour. Every night, with rare exceptions, Franco's bombers came over and added fresh terror to the human cattle on board already terror-struck to distraction. Every morning the deaths, every night the bombings and all day and all night the empty loneliness and the torpor of inaction.

His first, his paramount need, Lance realized after the first night or two, was to keep his reason. Was it, he asked himself, deliberately to send him mad that they had shut him in the madman's cell? Very well, he would set himself with equal deliberateness to defeat that purpose. He occupied himself by every small means he could think of and for which he had the strength, and of all resources found that the most resourceful was the Good Shepherd, in whose company no man is ever lonely.

After twenty-eight days of this nightmare "rest", Lance was allowed to leave the cell for short periods, to regain human contacts, to see a little daylight, and, above all, to wash. Shortly afterwards he was unexpectedly summoned to the Governor's cabin and there, in circumstances of great constraint, was allowed to talk for a while, in Spanish only, to Sefton Delmer, the representative of *The Daily Express*. What struck Delmer most was how clean Lance was, but he did not know that, before Lance was sent up to meet this important Press representative, on the orders of the sharp-eyed Governor, one of the prison staff had entered his padded cell and shaved him, while another rapidly clipped his hair and a third brought him a clean shirt. Nor could Delmer see that beneath the surface Lance was verminous, and in the first stages of scurvy.

Once again, in Delmer's presence, Lance was told that all that was necessary for him to regain his freedom was to reveal who had been his "accomplices"; but he replied steadfastly that he

244

had already told all he knew. After Delmer's visit, however, Lance's treatment improved a little and from then onwards he was allowed to receive Jinks's letters and a few occasional items extracted from the parcels that she sent, and, for the first time, he was allowed to write to her, in Spanish.

From the cigarettes that he received he sent up one a day as long as they lasted to Dr. Gomez Ulla, the distinguished surgeon, who, after enforced service at the Ritz Hotel military hospital in Madrid, had been snared by the S.I.M. into attempting an escape by a bogus agency of their own fabrication and who was now very ill in a cell on the deck above; but the good doctor never received one.

Every night the bombing went on, shattering the nerves of demoralized men shut in close confinement. After some time, however, it became so bad that the Republican authorities decided to abandon the notorious ship. It was October of 1938 and Lance had now been in prison for a year, with absolutely no knowledge of what was going on in the world outside, except for such news as Margery and the governor of the Segorbe prison had given him early in the year. He did not know that, at last, after more than two years, Franco's forces, frustrated in many sectors all the summer, were driving the Republicans into their final corner; nor that, outside Spain, an anxious Europe was being gradually pushed to the precipice of war by the frenzy of Adolf Hitler.

Again Lance's move was only a short one and he found himself back in Barcelona, in another religious establishment turned into a prison and known as Preventorio C (Seminario). As soon as he entered the building, he was at once picked upon by the watching Governor, who said:

"Ah, I've heard all about you! You are the distinguished Criminal No. 1 and we shall treat you with the honours you deserve."

He was taken up into the loft of the building which had been converted in the most extraordinary way. On either side of a central passage were rows of very small wire-netting pens, eight feet by four feet, exactly like chicken runs. Into one of these Lance was thrust. No talking was allowed and the only light was from a few small panes of glass in the roof of the building. Up and down the central gangway four guards patrolled ceaselessly day and night, peering into each pen from time to time and minutely searching each one twice a day. The food was so miserable that Lance wondered how on earth a body could be kept alive on so little. He was visited here by two consular representatives, who informed Jinks, in a letter otherwise full of soothing platitudes, that Lance was "suffering from headaches and dizziness".

In point of fact, an order for his execution had been published by the State Intelligence Service, but the order was suspended when it was found that he had told the truth to their inquisitors about his brief stay in France after expulsion by Franco.

Though he did not know it, the war was nearing its end with rapid acceleration. The Nationalists were now threatening Barcelona itself, so long the hotbed of intrigue, of violence in its harshest forms and of hot-spirited political extremism.

# CHAPTER FIFTEEN

# NUMBER 250

THE last move came. The seventh prison and by far the worst. Again some sort of religious establishment, it was near Gerona, far away on the cold fringes of the Pyrenees, at the extremity of the north-east corner of Spain, which was all that remained under the dominion of the Republicans. The weather was bitterly cold; snow was falling and the mountain wind cut like a knife. Christopher Lance, weak, emaciated, verminous, clothed only in ragged trousers and shirt, yet strangely standing out with some elusive air of distinction from the other prisoners, could not disguise his dismay when he found himself once more in solitary confinement. The prison was one in which all the worst and most dangerous offenders were being concentrated and, together with a few others, he found himself separated from the main body and put into a tiny stone cell, measuring eight feet by six feet, on the third floor, with a small, unglazed, iron-barred window through which the wind whistled with freezing breath. The place was as cold as an ice-box. Vile though his other prisons had been, Lance felt that over this forbidding place, in which the very guards seemed scared, there lay a chill and deadly hand that held every being in an iron grip, final and inexorable. The breath of the grave, earthy and fetid, invaded the stone cells and corridors and stairs.

Lance braced himself as well as his feebleness allowed to face the new conditions. He could not avoid the feeling that the end was near. All his recent experience, beyond and above the mere physical hardships, menaced him with the thought that he had become a pariah, an outcast, physically repulsive to society, repudiated by his own Embassy, forgotten by his friends. Against this mental attack he had to fight as best he could, clinging to the sure knowledge of the love of God and of the faithfulness of his dear Jinks.

In the midst of this mental struggle there came to him an unexpected gleam of hope. For some never-to-be-explained reason, to be set down only as an example of the unpredictable Spanish character, he was sent for by the Governor and kindly received. He found him to be a good-looking young Spaniard, smartly dressed. To Lance's delight, he was given some chocolate and cigarettes from one of Jinks's parcels. Though he knew that these were but a few minor items from an otherwise rifled parcel, he was grateful.

The thing happened a second time, and a third, and on one of these occasions the young Governor even took Lance into his private rooms and introduced him to his charming wife and pretty child, to whom Lance gave some of his chocolate. Did these things, Lance inevitably asked himself, mean that this Governor was of the same way of mind as the Governor of Segorbe? His cold hopes simmered with new life and a tingle of excitement warmed his mind.

But it was the last flicker. Christmas of 1938 passed in icy desolation and the most deadly period of all began towards the end of January. By overhearing the conversation of their guards, the prisoners learnt that Barcelona had fallen, that Franco's troops were moving northwards in their direction and that all the "worst" prisoners in the other jails of Catalonia were to be evacuated to theirs. The truth of this was painfully evident the next night, when into Lance's eight-by-six cell were crowded five other prisoners. The ordeal of solitary confinement was rudely exchanged for a physically worse ordeal, for his fellow-prisoners were cowed, emaciated and stank like stale fish. The six of them had to take turns to lie down, and even to sit, but their weakness was such that they were unable to stand for long hours and simply fell down on top of one another.

In this state of affairs Lance became doubled up with the pains of appendicitis. Clutching his stomach, he prayed for his release by this means, preferring death by the laws of nature, however painful, to the idea of being killed by the hand of his fellow-men. But what he regarded as the worse fate was now staring him plainly in the face, for his fellow-prisoners brought news which intensified the chill that already held the whole prison in its grip and which gave force and substance to Lance's premonition of finality. The Republican Government, said the new arrivals, had given orders that all prisoners were to be slaughtered before they could be released by Franco.

"Could this possibly be true?" Lance asked himself. "Was such inhumanity possible in this age? Was it not more likely to be irresponsible rumour?" He was not left long in doubt.

A day or two later, at an hour when his pains had temporarily subsided, all the prisoners were paraded in a courtyard in the biting cold of an early morning. They assembled in silence, not speaking to one another, shivering in their wretched garments, eyes cast down, dumb with foreboding of what all this might mean. Among them Lance noticed several who had shared with him the tolerable companionship of the vault of Segorbe. Among them also was the little Roman Catholic restaurant-keeper who had given him lunch on the day he and Hall had been captured by Franco. There, too, was the Bishop of Teruel.

The handsome young Governor arrived, looking very smart, very brisk and matter-of-fact. He read out the names of some thirty men, several of whom Lance knew, and ordered them to fall in in front of the rest. No explanation was necessary and none was given. Everyone knew.

An hour later, looking down into the prison yard from the window of his cell Lance saw these same men, drawn up in line, stripped of their footwear and their jackets. Sleet was falling and the cold pierced to the bone. At a word of command, the doomed wretches moved off, filed out of the yard and down an open drive under escort. Behind them strode the smart Governor, tommy-gun under arm.

Two hundred yards down the road, where the spilled earth of a newly dug trench could be clearly seen, the little column was seen to halt and turn about, the sleet driving into their faces. To Lance, who could hear nothing, it seemed as if the poor devils had halted and turned automatically, instinctively, needing no order.

The Governor took up a position twenty-five yards in front of the centre of the line. Without more ado, as casually as if at a shooting gallery, he swung his blazing tommy-gun from one end of the line to the other. Twenty-six out of the thirty fell. Three or four more bursts and they were all down. In a world otherwise deadly silent, that never-to-be-forgotten rattle of the tommy-gun echoed from wall to wall of the stone prison and echoed again faintly against the ramparts of the distant mountains.

Handing his tommy-gun to a guard, the governor then drew his revolver and, walking briskly down the line of dead and wounded, turned over each body and administered the final death-stroke. Calmly he stopped after each sixth body to refill his magazine and as calmly at the end walked home again, stopping only to light a cigarette.

Lance in his silent, crowded cell fell upon his knees and prayed. He prayed for the souls of "those innocent poor chaps", for their wives and children and mothers, for all his fellow-prisoners and for himself. Some of those who had now been butchered he had known in the vault of Segorbe and they had spoken tenderly of their families. One had been from his own cell. Those whom he knew had been guilty of no crime except that of disagreeing politically with the men who had condemned them. The "vivid, ghastly picture" burned itself into his mind and sharpened the knife that was twisting at the pit of his stomach.

That was the beginning. Every morning afterwards about twenty to thirty more were shot down in the same manner. Several of these were prisoners whom Lance knew and one of them was the little restaurant-keeper. The Governor himself personally shot them all. There were no more parades; the victims were merely summoned from their cells and marched straight down to their waiting graves. The guards were surly and morose, not knowing whether there would be a chance for them to get away or whether they would suffer the same fate as their prisoners if they fell into Franco's hands. On the second day, however, Lance was able to have a few words with one of them and learned that there was a nominal roll of prisoners in the order of their execution on the wall of the prison office. He asked the fellow accordingly to find out what his place was on the list and on his next tour of duty the guard told him:

"You are number 250."

That, Lance calculated, gave him approximately eight more

days of life. He began to prepare himself. He wondered whether
the Governor who had been so friendly to him, and to whose
child he had given chocolates, would callously shoot him down
when it came to the point. Was there some faint hope, he wondered, that for that reason, and because he was British, his
name might be put back till the last? But it was a vain hope, for
it soon appeared to him that the end of the death-roll was far out
of sight. Every day, as each batch was slaughtered, fresh prisoners
were brought in from outside. Two more men were sent to their
deaths from Lance's cell, but others took their places. The whole
prison was in the grip of horror, the guards nervous and hot-
tempered, the prisoners shivering in their threadbare clothes as
the icy Pyrenean wind whistled through the bars. Only the
Governor seemed brisk and jaunty as every morning he went
out for his shooting.

Christopher Lance, as he faced his end, hearing daily the
explosive bursts of the tommy-gun and the stabbing shots of the
revolver, grew strangely calmer, notwithstanding the gnawing
pain within him. He prayed for strength to face the tommy-gun
as bravely as he had seen others do so. His mind roved back to
Madrid, where, he thought, it was almost certain that Margery
must have been arrested by now. Those last six refugees of his,
were they still alive? What would they have thought of his
promise, his *palabra inglesa*? What were those fellows at the
British Embassy doing? Were they really going to allow him to
be coldly butchered?

The days and the nights passed, each day heralded by the
crackling bursts of the tommy-gun, each spent in fighting the
onset of black and terrifying thoughts, each ended by the vain
hope of finding in sleep some oblivion from the cruel cold, the
pain, the feral smell of crowded bodies. Each morning Christopher Lance counted the numbers of the condemned as they
paraded in the courtyard below and when their total had reached
240 he knew that the next day would be his last.

It was at midnight that he was unexpectedly roused. A guard
noisily opened the door of his cell, kicking out of his way those
nearest to the door and shouted in a harsh and brutal voice:

"You, Lance. Get out at once and come with me."

Wearily Lance rose. So soon? At night? He should have had a few more hours. He asked:

"Can I take my kit?"

It was the test question. The answer to it told you whether you were for life or for death; whether for the firing squad, or merely for transfer to another jail. Not that Lance's "kit" amounted to any more than an old sandbag containing some dirty straw and his photographs.

"That," answered the guard brusquely, "won't be necessary. Get a move on."

So it was death.

Very well. It had been a long time coming, but he was ready for it. Now that the moment had arrived he felt quite calm and steady. Curiously his weakness and his weariness dropped from him. His mind was clear. But he wished that the night were not so piercingly cold, for it made him shiver.

In the dimly lit corridor he stumbled and clung for a moment to the wall to recover himself. He was hustled forward by his impatient guard, who prodded him in the kidneys with his rifle. He was taken to the prison office, where a clerk filled in a form giving the name and address of next of kin and some other particulars. Why, Lance asked himself again, was all this at dead of night? No doubt because he was a British subject. He must vanish without trace, without witnesses, his fate unknown. The supposition became convincing when he was taken into another room and there saw King, very badly knocked about now and physically dejected, yet still able to force a smile and to say:

"All change 'ere, mate, for Waterloo and Kingdom Come."

Filled with admiration for the little cockney, Lance laughed aloud, to the angry astonishment of the guards, who shouted with oaths to the "dirty Fascists" to be quiet, and threatened them with the butt of a rifle. The guards were in a savage mood that night, black-browed and ready to beat down their prisoners at the slightest excuse. After talking among themselves for a minute in low voices, they suddenly turned and, seizing the prisoners by arms and shoulders, roughly hustled them outside into the night. Instead, however, of marching them down to the shooting ground,

they took them to a large seven-seater car nearby and shouted:
"Get in, you swine!"

Lance, feeling very weak, found it difficult to pull himself up on the running-board in the dark and was brutally kicked. He felt angry and humiliated and very much inclined to attack the guards in one last desperate effort, but knew that it was futile. So he had been right in his surmise; because he and King were British subjects, they were going to be murdered in some remote, undiscoverable place in the Pyrenees. He and King were put into the back seats with two guards facing them armed with rifle and revolver. In front, beside the chauffeur, was the tommy-gunner, but not the Governor this time. As the car moved off, the prisoners were ordered not to talk, but it was comforting to Lance to feel his fellow countryman beside him and he gave his hand a warm and friendly grip, which King returned. It was not likely, Lance thought, to be a long ride; just somewhere out of earshot.

But the car went on and on, up steep and winding mountain roads and then down again on to level stretches, going very fast. These were surely extreme measures, Lance reflected. There must be some more than usual reason why their execution had to be carried out with such caution and obscurity. Perhaps, thought Lance, they were being taken to some special execution ground. In a silence almost as of the grave and in darkness almost as deep, save for the weak lamps that swept the desolate roads ahead, they drove on thus for Lance knew not how long. It might have been for half an hour. It might have been for two hours. He was never to know. Utterly weary, he ceased to speculate. In the car he was warmer and more comfortable than he had been for months and drowsiness began to overcome him.

In spite of himself, he was half-asleep when the car at last slowed down. It came to a halt at an obscure, dark shape that might have been a village school. The lights of the car were switched off and the guards ordered the prisoners to get out.

Lance got out by a last effort. As in a dream, he saw himself as a disembodied figure without substance or feeling. Was he already dead and looking back from the insubstantial world beyond to what had been the body of himself? He was aware only that everything was deathly quiet, utterly dark and piercingly cold. In the same dream he saw himself walking along a dark passage, with the tommy-gunner and some other person ahead and with King and the other two guards behind. At the end of the passage a door opened on squeaking hinges and, with no word spoken, Lance found himself carried onward with a sensation of inevitability into some dim unrecognizable void that might have been a sepulchre or some measureless cavern beyond the grave. Was death then so painless that he had not known it to have occurred?

Awareness slowly returned and at the far end of the room he saw a hurricane lamp on a small table, with the dim moon of a face behind it. He moved forward and recognized the face of the officer who had knocked him down at Barcelona for cleaning his teeth. It was glaring at him now with satanic hate.

So this was the end. Beyond the lamp's dim rays he caught sight also of Dutt, the Indian. He had been right, then. It was to be an all-British shooting party.

He waited for the satanic face to speak, wondering what more there was to be said and what more there was to endure before the shots at last rang out. Was it to be this man's hand that was to press the trigger and was it to be here and now?

As he wondered, bracing himself for the last moment, a dark shadow, cast upon the wall by the extremity of the lamp's rays, moved a little forward somewhere on his right hand, dimly perceived, and out of the darkness came a strong, resonant, English voice, saying:

"Good evening. I am Skrine Stevenson from the British Embassy, and I've come to take you home."

# ENVOI

TODAY, Christopher Lance, who was known to the Spanish Republicans as "Criminal No. 1" and to the rest of the world as the Scarlet Pimpernel of Spain, lives quietly with Jinks on a cliff-top in the Channel Isles, not so sound in health as he was and still suffering from the effects of an experience that he tries vainly to forget. But his laugh is as hearty as ever and in his little house perched on a rocky pinnacle he sits in his sunny "cabin" overlooking one of the most beautiful of bays, enjoying the prospect of the moving waters that first awoke his wonder more than fifty years ago. From time to time he takes the coloured bunting from his signal locker, walks out to his flagstaff and hoists a signal to a friend or a passing ship, remembering without rancour all those who have forgotten him, without malice those who oppressed him so sorely and wishing only that the government whose friends he risked his life to help would take down the barrier which bars him from paying a last visit to the Spain of which he is so fond.

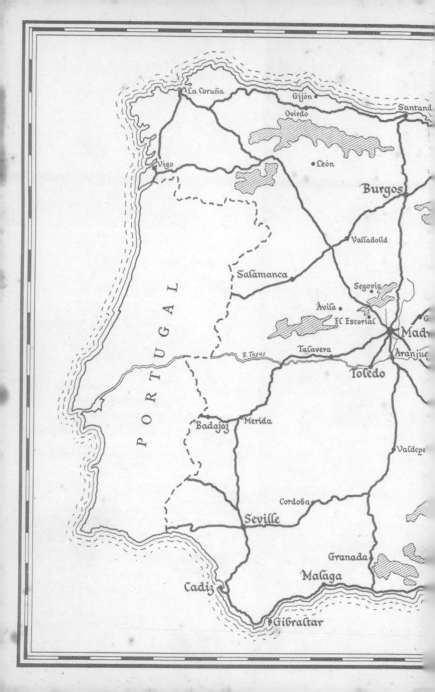